Vol. XCV

No. 4

Bible Expositor and Illuminator

FALL QUARTER September, October, November 2023

Success and Failure

UNIT I: Obedience and Success

UNIT II: Disobedience and Failure

UNIT III: Lessons and Warnings

Editor in Chief: Kenneth Sponsler

Edited and published quarterly by
THE INCORPORATED TRUSTEES OF THE
GOSPEL WORKER SOCIETY
UNION GOSPEL PRESS DIVISION
Rev. W. B. Musselman, Founder
Price: $7.69 per quarter*
**shipping and handling extra*
ISBN 978-1-64495-419-5

 Edited and published quarterly by The Incorporated Trustees of the Gospel Worker Society, Union Gospel Press Division. Mailing address: P.O. Box 301055, Cleveland, Ohio 44130-0915. Phone: 216-749-2100. www.uniongospelpress.com

LOOKING AHEAD

Winston Churchill said success is stumbling from failure to failure with no loss of enthusiasm. He may have been humorously highlighting the need for persistence in muddling through hard tasks. But if this or any other philosophy leaves God out of the picture, it is flawed. True success always comes from a right relationship with God; failure comes from failing to trust Him. The lessons this quarter will remind us of that.

Our first unit shows God's people moving forward in bold faith. We see Joshua leading the Israelite nation in victory over the fierce Canaanite armies (lesson 1), including giants, descendants of Anak that may have been like Goliath of David's day (Josh. 11:21).

The spies who went into Jericho also succeeded when God provided them a surprising ally in Rahab (lesson 2). The Israelites' subsequent defeat of Jericho underscored again the reality that God is truly the source of success (lesson 3).

The next two lessons describe God delivering Israel from cruel oppression. Ehud did not hesitate to strike Israel's enemies (lesson 4), while Gideon needed lots of convincing (lesson 5). In the end, though, both Ehud and Gideon succeeded by trusting firmly in God.

The second unit shows vastly different results due to faithlessness. By ignoring God's direct command, Achan brought humiliation and military defeat to the whole nation (lesson 6). Rather than learning from Achan's ruin, the nation persistently rebelled against God and suffered the painful consequences (lesson 7). Finally, Israel showed the utmost disrespect for God by asking for a king (lesson 8).

The final unit provides stern warnings and real-life examples of what happens when people reject God. Joshua exhorted Israel to obey the Lord; but while they mouthed the words (lesson 9), their history shows a dismal lack of faith and obedience (lesson 10). Even David, their greatest king, transgressed God's commands in a despicable way (lesson 11). Although God sent prophets like Amos to condemn Israel (lesson 12), He ultimately handed down the worst punishment—removal from the Promised Land (lesson 13).

It seems the failures found in this quarter's lessons play out again all around us. The wealth of biblical instruction and examples, however, should inspire us to focus on God, the true source of success.

—*Todd Williams.*

EDITORIALS

Formula for Success?

KENNETH SPONSLER

Success has always been a popular topic. The secular book world is awash in titles that promote success in everything from business to diet and health to raising well-adjusted children. Surefire formulas are offered, often bolstered by compelling statistics and inspiring testimonials. Much of what is out there does offer valuable insights on various topics, and many people benefit in specific ways.

Sometimes even the Bible is cited in the prescriptions for successful living. Often this is done without much understanding of what Scripture actually teaches, but occasionally, valid biblical insights undergird the presentations. Still, the vast majority of books and articles focus on success as the world defines it, meaning the pursuit of happiness or improvement in this present life only. Spiritual realities are rarely even a concern, much less the aim.

The Bible, by contrast, cannot be reduced to a mere success manual, but it does contain principles that, if followed, promote successful living. Unlike the vast array of secular literature, however, Scripture is concerned primarily with living successfully before God—with pleasing Him and growing in His favor and love. In other words, spiritual success is the number one priority, not the ability to amass material wealth or achieve social status.

Moreover, the scriptural prescriptions for success in spiritual matters are far different from, even contrary to, the typical outlook that pervades most secular literature. What the Bible has to say about living successfully in God's sight is rejected as foolish and unworkable by most people today (or in any era), and that is to be expected. Yet God's Word gives the only sure and reliable principles that apply to any and all situations.

What we can glean about success in God's sight from our present quarter of studies comes mainly from the first unit of lessons. What do we find there? The unit begins with God's exhortation to Joshua to be strong and courageous in carrying out his commission to lead Israel in conquering and possessing the Promised Land (Josh. 1:1-6). The second portion of the lesson (11:16-19, 21-23) reports the astonishingly successful result of that endeavor.

From the first portion, 1:1-6, we learn that strength and courage are certainly keys to success in carrying out God's mission. We are, of course, talking about spiritual strength and courage that rests on God's promises (vss. 3-4). And going further in the passage (beyond the lesson text itself), we find that God explicitly links this courage to obeying His Word (vs. 7), in Joshua's case the law given through Moses. Joshua is told to meditate on that law daily in order to do everything in it (vs. 8). Success, or prospering, is directly tied to faithfulness in that spiritual discipline.

A bit farther on in Joshua, we see another amazing success and the equally amazing steps that led up to it. Circling Jericho once each day for six days and then seven times on the seventh day might have exerted a deep psychological effect on the enemy, but there was no actual military reason for it. Yet it was

(Editorials continued on page 186)

SCRIPTURE LESSON TEXT

JOSH. 1:1 Now after the death of Moses the servant of the LORD it came to pass, that the LORD spake unto Joshua the son of Nun, Moses' minister, saying,

2 Moses my servant is dead; now therefore arise, go over this Jordan, thou, and all this people, unto the land which I do give to them, *even* to the children of Israel.

3 Every place that the sole of your foot shall tread upon, that have I given unto you, as I said unto Moses.

4 From the wilderness and this Lebanon even unto the great river, the river Euphrates, all the land of the Hittites, and unto the great sea toward the going down of the sun, shall be your coast.

5 There shall not any man be able to stand before thee all the days of thy life: as I was with Moses, *so* I will be with thee: I will not fail thee, nor forsake thee.

6 Be strong and of a good courage: for unto this people shalt thou divide for an inheritance the land, which I sware unto their fathers to give them.

11:16 So Joshua took all that land, the hills, and all the south country, and all the land of Goshen, and the valley, and the plain, and the mountain of Israel, and the valley of the same;

17 *Even* from the mount Halak, that goeth up to Seir, even unto Baal–gad in the valley of Lebanon under mount Hermon: and all their kings he took, and smote them, and slew them.

18 Joshua made war a long time with all those kings.

19 There was not a city that made peace with the children of Israel, save the Hivites the inhabitants of Gibeon: all *other* they took in battle.

21 And at that time came Joshua, and cut off the Anakims from the mountains, from Hebron, from Debir, from Anab, and from all the mountains of Judah, and from all the mountains of Israel: Joshua destroyed them utterly with their cities.

22 There was none of the Anakims left in the land of the children of Israel: only in Gaza, in Gath, and in Ashdod, there remained.

23 So Joshua took the whole land, according to all that the LORD said unto Moses; and Joshua gave it for an inheritance unto Israel according to their divisions by their tribes. And the land rested from war.

NOTES

Be Strong and Courageous

Lesson Text: Joshua 1:1-6; 11:16-19, 21-23

Related Scriptures: Numbers 27:15-23; Deuteronomy 11:22-25; 31:7-15, 22-23; 34:5-9; Joshua 22:1-9

TIME: 1405 B.C.   PLACES: Shittim; Canaan

GOLDEN TEXT—"Joshua took the whole land, according to all that the Lord said unto Moses" (Joshua 11:23).

Introduction

Some of us grew up singing a little chorus that said, "Every promise in the Book is mine, every chapter, every verse, every line." While the melody is catchy and easy to remember many years later, the message is a bit misleading. As children we did not analyze everything we sang; we just sang for the fun of it. As adults, however, we should pay better attention and realize that many songs and choruses are actually theologically inaccurate. There are promises in the Bible that were for Israel only, for example, and are not for us today.

That does not negate the fact that God's Word is full of promises for His children today. How sad it is that many believers fail to spend quality time in the Bible and as a result do not benefit from those precious promises!

LESSON OUTLINE

I. **THE PROMISE OF THE LAND—Josh. 1:1-6**
II. **THE TAKING OF THE LAND—Josh. 11:16-19**
III. **THE COMPLETION OF THE TASK—Josh. 11:21-23**

Exposition: Verse by Verse

THE PROMISE OF THE LAND

JOSH. 1:1 Now after the death of Moses the servant of the LORD it came to pass, that the LORD spake unto Joshua the son of Nun, Moses' minister, saying,

2 Moses my servant is dead; now therefore arise, go over this Jordan, thou, and all this people, unto the land which I do give to them, even to the children of Israel.

3 Every place that the sole of your

foot shall tread upon, that have I given unto you, as I said unto Moses.

4 From the wilderness and this Lebanon even unto the great river, the river Euphrates, all the land of the Hittites, and unto the great sea toward the going down of the sun, shall be your coast.

5 There shall not any man be able to stand before thee all the days of thy life: as I was with Moses, so I will be with thee: I will not fail thee, nor forsake thee.

6 Be strong and of a good courage: for unto this people shalt thou divide for an inheritance the land, which I sware unto their fathers to give them.

A command (Josh. 1:1-2). Moses was dead. A new era was beginning in the history of Israel. The people were camped on the east side of the Jordan River, having been led there by Moses in their journey toward the land of Canaan. Moses had been told he would not be allowed to lead them into the land (Num. 20:12); so it was time for a new leader. **{**Moses was known as "the servant of the Lord" (Josh. 1:1), a title that is repeatedly used for him throughout this book. Joshua 24:29 shows that the title was also used for Joshua by the time of his death.**}**[Q1]

Since Joshua had previously been appointed as Moses' successor (Num. 27:15-23; Deut. 31:14-23), he no doubt took the leadership role immediately after Moses' death. He had served as Moses' assistant for many years; so he had been well groomed for the position. Nevertheless, a change of leadership always carries certain uncertainties and adjustments. It was important for Joshua to have God reaffirm to him what he was to do. God, who always knows when we need that kind of encouragement, came to Joshua with an important message.

We cannot tell exactly how God gave Joshua this message, but when it came, it was clear. **{**The death of the previous leader did not thwart God's plan for His people. Now it was time for the new leader to move ahead with it.**}**[Q2] Joshua was to lead the people across the Jordan River into the land God was going to give them. This was the land He had promised Abraham (Gen. 12:7). It had been a long time since the promise had been given, but no matter how long it takes, God never goes back on His word to His people.

Perhaps Joshua had been waiting expectantly for this message from God and was listening for it. It is very important that as God's people we listen for God's leading. If we sincerely want to hear from Him, He will never disappoint us.

A promise (Josh. 1:3-4). **{**What an all-inclusive, powerful word this was! Wherever Joshua would lead God's people, God would give them that land.**}**[Q3] We know that much more than simply walking the territory was going to be involved. Times of war and struggle lay ahead for them, but God promised victory. If they would unhesitatingly engage in every conflict with faith in Him, they would gain control of the entire land. The land was already determined to be theirs; all they had to do was take it.

God had given Abraham detailed boundaries: "In the same day the Lord made a covenant with Abram, saying, Unto thy seed have I given this land, from the river of Egypt unto the great river, the river Euphrates: the Kenites, and the Kenizzites, and the Kadmonites, and the Hittites, and the Perizzites, and the Rephaims, and the Amorites, and the Canaanites, and the Girgashites, and the Jebusites" (Gen. 15:18-21).

To Moses He had said, "Turn you, and take your journey, and go to the mount of the Amorites, and unto all the places nigh thereunto, in the plain, in the hills, and in the vale, and in the south, and by the sea side, to the land of the Canaanites, and unto Lebanon, unto the great river, the river Euphrates" (Deut. 1:7). From the great wilderness in the south to the Lebanon mountains in the north and from the Euphrates River on the east to the Mediterranean Sea on the west, all was to be theirs.

The rule over all this territory was realized in the days of David and Solomon (I Kgs. 4:21, 24-25; I Chr. 19:16-19; II Chr. 9:23-26). But this cannot really compare to the extent of the reign of Jesus, who will rule over all (I Cor. 15:24-25).

A reassurance (Josh. 1:5-6). {What more could God say than this? Nobody would be able to successfully resist Joshua's advance and victories. The secret of Moses' success had been the constant presence of God, and now Joshua was being reassured that the Lord would be present with him just as He had been with Moses.}[Q4] God emphatically stated, "I will not fail thee, nor forsake thee." Since Joshua had already observed many times how God had sustained Moses, this reassurance would have given him the added incentive he needed to proceed.

Kenneth Gangel, in the *Holman Old Testament Commentary: Joshua* (Broadman and Holman), likened what Joshua faced at the river to difficulties we sometimes face. He made this observation and analogy: "When we stare at the Jordan River in our lives, what do we see? The swirling muddy water of spiritual failures, sins, fears, and habits? Some persistent physical problem? The steady flow of broken relationships? Like Joshua, we need to take our eyes off the river and fix them on the God of the river." No problem is insurmountable for God.

In this message, God told Joshua four times that he should be strong and courageous (vss. 6-7, 9, 18). The result would be the successful conquering and dividing of the land among Israel's tribes. Joshua would have to exhibit these characteristics because the road ahead was going to be long and difficult. Before everything was done, seven years would pass. The only requirement for him was strength and courage, which he would find in placing his complete trust in the Lord. The battles were going to be God's, not his.

Just as God promised to never fail or forsake Joshua, so He will always be with us. "God is our refuge and strength, a very present help in trouble" (Ps. 46:1). Is anything excluded from that statement? Gangel mentioned spiritual failures, sins, habits, persistent physical problems, and broken relationships. Often when we are in the middle of such circumstances, we are tempted to wonder where God is and whether He cares. The answer is that He is "a very present help." He is not far away but very close by.

THE TAKING OF THE LAND

11:16 So Joshua took all that land, the hills, and all the south country, and all the land of Goshen, and the valley, and the plain, and the mountain of Israel, and the valley of the same;

17 Even from the mount Halak, that goeth up to Seir, even unto Baal–gad in the valley of Lebanon under mount Hermon: and all their kings he took, and smote them, and slew them.

18 Joshua made war a long time with all those kings.

19 There was not a city that made peace with the children of Israel, save the Hivites the inhabitants of Gibeon: all other they took in battle.

The land Joshua took (Josh. 11:16- 17). The conquering of the land of Canaan was accomplished through three major campaigns. The initial one occurred in central Canaan and included the taking of Jericho and Ai, after which the inhabitants of Gibeon through deceit secured a covenant agreement with Israel. When word of this covenant agreement got out, several kings from the southern part of Canaan banded together to punish Gibeon. This obliged Joshua to come to Gibeon's rescue, which was followed by an extended campaign in the south (chap. 10).

When word of all this success reached the northern cities, they formed a huge alliance (11:1-5). But God told Joshua not to be afraid. He was to take the initiative by attacking those allied forces and watch God deliver them all into his hands (vs. 6). **{**Thus, the northern campaign was accomplished quickly, and the city that led the alliance was burned to the ground (vss. 11-13). This completed the fulfillment of everything God had commanded Moses, who in turn had passed the command on to Joshua (vs. 15).**}**[Q5]

Verse 16 summarizes by simply stating, "So Joshua took all that land," and follows this with details. Most of the areas mentioned were in the central and southern regions, but Baal-gad (vs. 17) is specified as being in the valley of Lebanon under Mount Hermon. This was in the far north. The intention of this detailed listing of conquered cities is to confirm that the entire land was taken by Joshua and his army. As God had promised, every place he set his foot he was able to conquer (1:3).

To further emphasize the completeness of Joshua's victory, it is stated that every king was captured, struck down, and slain. **{**Every city was considered to be a separate entity, each with its own king. This explains why there were so many kings in one land.**}**[Q6]

The battles Joshua fought (Josh. 11:18-19). Two facts are given in these verses. First, this war took a long time. Warren Wiersbe, in *The Bible Exposition Commentary: Old Testament* (Victor), explained, **{**"The 'long time' of verse 18 is about seven years.**}**[Q7] Israel's failure at Kadesh Barnea (Deut 2:14), at which time Caleb was forty years old (Josh 14:7), to their crossing of the Jordan was thirty-eight years. He was eighty-five when the conquest was over (v. 10), which means that at least seven years had been devoted to the campaign."

{The second fact is that there was one exception to the conquering of all the cities, namely, Gibeon. In Joshua 9 we read how men from Gibeon came to Joshua pretending to be from a city far away. They carried out an elaborate deception in order to save their lives from destruction. The leaders of Israel, who neglected to seek God's advice about the matter (vs. 14), fell for the ploy and made a costly treaty with them.**}**[Q8]

Because of this treaty, the Israelites could not destroy the Gibeonites: "And the children of Israel smote them not, because the princes of the congregation had sworn unto them by the Lord God of Israel. And all the congregation murmured against the princes. But all the princes said unto all the congregation, We have sworn unto them by the Lord God of Israel: now therefore we may not touch them" (vss. 18-19). When God's people fail to consult and follow Him, they must live with the consequences.

Many readers struggle with the idea that God would command such violence against people. An examination of the evils prevalent in Canaan, which are found in several passages in the Bible, helps us understand that this was a matter of justice on God's part. The sins of the Canaanites included incest, adultery, child sacrifice, homosexuality, and bestiality (Lev. 18:1-25). God's mercy for them had reached its limit, and He used Israel to accomplish His judgment on them.

THE COMPLETION OF THE TASK

21 And at that time came Joshua, and cut off the Anakims from the mountains, from Hebron, from Debir, from Anab, and from all the mountains of Judah, and from all the mountains of Israel: Joshua destroyed them utterly with their cities.

22 There was none of the Anakims left in the land of the children of Israel: only in Gaza, in Gath, and in Ashdod, there remained.

23 So Joshua took the whole land, according to all that the LORD said unto Moses; and Joshua gave it for an inheritance unto Israel according to their divisions by their tribes. And the land rested from war.

Destroying the Anakim (Josh. 11:21-22). When Moses sent the twelve spies into Canaan from Kadesh-barnea, they came back with a mixed review. He had told them to check out the people, the land, and the cities (Num. 13:18-19). They found the land productive, the cities large and fortified, and the people strong (vss. 27-29). But what dominated their thinking was the presence of the descendants of Anak (vss. 28, 33), for they were giants and made the spies feel as small as grasshoppers.

{The Anakim conquered by Joshua were those giants who had once seemed so invincible.}[Q9]

The book of Judges makes it very clear that Israel was unsuccessful in driving all the Canaanites out of the land. While Joshua 14:12-14 says that Caleb asked for the city of Hebron and later drove out the Anakim dwelling there (15:13-14), some of the Anakim remained in other places. The cities of Gaza, Gath, and Ashdod are named as places where they continued to dwell (11:22). These cities would become three of the five major cities of the Philistines. David would eventually face the giant Goliath, who was from the city of Gath (I Sam. 17).

When God's people follow Him obediently, the size of the problem makes no difference!

Fulfilling God's promises (Josh. 11:23). "The last sentence . . . reads almost like a sigh of relief. Finally there was some peace. This had been God's goal for Israel all along" (Gangel).

There was still much to do. {Joshua 13 begins by stating that there was still much land to take. All over the land, however, were established points of control from which the Israelites could work and secure their inheritance. God was indeed fulfilling His promises to them.}[Q10]

—Keith E. Eggert.

QUESTIONS

1. What title used of Moses was later used also of Joshua?
2. What did the death of the previous leader do to God's plan for His people?
3. What promise did God give Joshua prior to his entering Canaan?
4. How did God reassure Joshua that the victories would occur?
5. What was the final phase of warfare for Israel in conquering Canaan?
6. Why were there so many kings for Joshua to conquer?
7. About how long did it take for Israel to capture Canaan, and how do we know that?
8. What one city was not conquered, and why was it left alone?
9. Why was it so important to know that Joshua conquered the Anakim?
10. Since God fulfilled His promises, did Israel fully control the land?

—Keith E. Eggert.

Preparing to Teach the Lesson

People who do not want to do well in life are rare. Few, if any, in this world do not want to lead a comfortable life or at least better themselves. Our first five lessons this quarter teach us that as God's people, we can learn from prosperity. True prosperity comes from listening to God's instructions to us and obeying Him.

TODAY'S AIM

Facts: to show how God kept His promises to His people as Joshua and the people obeyed Him.

Principle: to demonstrate that God is faithful in keeping His promises.

Application: to teach that when we obey God, we will experience His blessings.

INTRODUCING THE LESSON

It is significant that from the early days of Moses and even before, God had been telling His people that one day they would come into their very own land. Years passed, and they were still waiting for those promises to come to pass. It must have been hard for them to keep trusting a God who worked so slowly, and indeed their faith faltered; but God blessed them despite their erring ways. Our lesson this week shows us how God's people learned some lessons about trusting their God. He could be trusted because He would never fail them. He is always true.

DEVELOPING THE LESSON

1. The promise to lead God's people to their land (Josh. 1:1-6). It must be remembered that these promises were given to the people when they were in slavery. Now, forty years later, the promises remained unfulfilled. When we put the promises of God in that context, we understand why it was much easier for them to lose faith than to trust God.

Many people are willing to have faith only after they see that matters are beyond their control. The people of God had little choice except to hold on to His promises, but it was not easy to do in the context in which they found themselves. It was time for them to fight the Anakim giants. They learned, however, that their God is faithful.

Notice how specific God was in His instructions to His people. He promised to give them all the land—to Lebanon in the north, to the Mediterranean Sea in the west, and to the Euphrates River in the east. In order to understand the magnitude of this promise, one must note that this was all enemy territory before they came upon it.

God promised Joshua that He would be with him just as He had been with Moses. He would never leave or abandon Joshua. Lead the class to see that without the presence of God with us, we are going nowhere. Joshua had God on his side, along with all His promises. Stress to your students that God is totally sufficient for any hardship before us. God keeps His word.

2. The fulfilled promise to help Joshua conquer the land (Josh. 11:16-19). We must note that even though God promised to give His people the land that was in enemy hands, they had to conquer the enemies in order to appropriate it. God was going to help them do just that. The area of the "south country," literally, Negev, was not an easy land to conquer. The very name meant "dry" and "parched." Also in the south was an area known as Goshen. Israel also gained control of the Jordan River valley all the way to the valley of Lebanon.

It is interesting that in accordance with God's promises to His people, they defeated the enemies in their path and then moved in. We are told that the only people who made peace with them were the Hivites of Gibeon (vs. 19). The others were defeated. When God assures us of victory, we can move forward in faith. When He does not, it is presumptuous on our part to move ahead.

This passage also shows us that our God can be trusted. He keeps His word to His people. Encourage the class to think through whether they see any clear instruction in God's Word that pertains to some crucial decision they might have to make in the coming days. If there is, they can certainly move forward in faith. If it violates God's Word, they will only encounter trouble by moving forward. We must know His instructions for us.

3. The fulfilled promises to God's people (Josh. 11:21-23). The truth here is that when God says He is coming through for His children, the rest of the world has to make way. On the basis of God's instructions and promises, Joshua moved through enemy territory, wiping out everyone who stood in his way. God had said that the land would belong to Israel, and nothing was going to keep them from receiving what God had promised.

The Anakim, living in the mountains, were destroyed completely and without mercy. This could raise the question of why God destroys other nations, but it would detract from the main point of the lesson. The short answer is that God is always on the side of His people and keeps His word. Verse 22 is significant. It says that none of the Anakim were left in the land of Israel except in three cities. The land was being prepared solely for God's people to inhabit, and God was with them.

Verse 23 is a report of victory. The text records for us that God kept His promises to Joshua just as He had with Moses. God has made promises to our spiritual forefathers that are also for us. But in order for those promises to be fulfilled, we must stay true to God, obediently following Him.

Like our forefathers, we are called to walk in faith so that we can reap the fruits of the promises of God. Get the class to think about how they can make progress in faith, for God still keeps His word.

ILLUSTRATING THE LESSON

We will find God's fullest blessing when we walk by faith, trusting Him to fulfill His promises.

CONCLUDING THE LESSON

Encourage the class to think about God's blessings to them. Remind them that many of those blessings come as a result of trusting His promises.

ANTICIPATING THE NEXT LESSON

Next week we will see that we have nothing to fear if we recognize that God can protect us in any situation.

—*A. Koshy Muthalaly.*

PRACTICAL POINTS

1. The ultimate fulfillment of God's plan is never dependent on any man (Josh. 1:1-2).
2. When God makes a promise for your future, you can consider it already done (vss. 3-4).
3. We can take courage in God's promised presence, provision, and protection (vss. 5-6).
4. God's promises often include our hard work (11:16-17).
5. God fulfills His promises in His time and way (vss. 18-19).
6. Under the authority of God and with His power, no assigned task is too big (vss. 21-22).
7. God always keeps His promises (vs. 23).

—Don Kakavecos.

RESEARCH AND DISCUSSION

1. What are the dangers in exalting any Christian leader? How does doing so diminish our view of God and His work (Josh. 1:1-2; cf. I Cor. 1:10-13; 4:6-7; II Cor. 3:5)?
2. Is all fear wrong (cf. Deut. 6:13; Prov. 1:7)? Explain.
3. Do the promises of God preclude hard work and suffering (Josh. 11:16-19; cf. Neh. 4:6; I Thess. 1:3-7)? Give more examples.
4. Is peace with all men the ultimate aim of the Christian (Josh. 11:19; cf. Rom. 12:18; Heb. 12:14)?
5. On what does the success of the Christian depend (cf. Josh. 1:8)? How do certain of the world's beliefs contradict this?

—Don Kakavecos.

ILLUSTRATED HIGH POINTS

I will not fail thee (Josh. 1:5)

After his three-hundredth mission in the first Iraq War, an air force pilot was surprised to be given permission to fly home on furlough not in a military transport plane but in the same plane he flew in so many assignments.

He and his crew flew across the ocean to Massachusetts and then drove all night by car to western Pennsylvania. When his friends dropped him off at his driveway just after sunup, he was struck by the big banner draped across the driveway: Welcome Home, Dad! When he walked into the house, he found the children getting ready for school.

"Dad!" they screamed. His wife came running.

"How did you know?" he asked.

"We didn't know," she answered through tears of joy. "Once we knew the war was over, we knew you would be coming home. We decided to be ready every day!"

All that the Lord said (11:23)

A special study of the nuclear disaster that happened in Chernobyl in 1968 found glaring falsehoods. According to the U.N. report in 2005, the largest health problem created was the damaging psychological impact due to a lack of accurate information. Thousands were told that they faced a future of cancer, deformity, pain, and decay—and they believed it. It became a self-fulfilling prophecy. There were wild estimates as high as 3.5 million casualties. In actual fact, the deaths were less than 4,000.

Although we should not dismiss the seriousness of dangers, our trust in the Lord should protect us from panic.

—Ted Simonson.

Golden Text Illuminated

"Joshua took the whole land, according to all that the Lord said unto Moses" (Joshua 11:23).

Our golden text stands as the final summarizing statement of this week's lesson, and it serves as the magnificent summary of all that the Lord accomplished through His servant Joshua as recorded in the first eleven chapters of the book of Joshua. It also illumines the shining fulfillment of the promise and command given to Joshua at the beginning of his leadership of the nation of Israel.

In Joshua 1 we read that after the death of the great leader Moses, God commissioned Joshua as the new leader of Israel and commanded him to take possession of the land that had been promised: "Go over this Jordan, thou, and all this people, unto the land which I do give to them, even to the children of Israel. Every place that the sole of your foot shall tread upon, that have I given unto you, as I said unto Moses. From the wilderness and this Lebanon even unto the great river, the river Euphrates, all the land of the Hittites, and unto the great sea toward the going down of the sun, shall be your coast" (vss. 2-4).

In relation to this command and promise, the golden text gives the decisive verdict: Mission Accomplished. "Joshua took the whole land." All that he had set out to do under the Lord's direction he fulfilled. God was obviously pleased with His servant, for Joshua had carried out His orders to a *T*. He fulfilled the divine will, which was not something made up on the spot but rather had been known much earlier: "according to all that the Lord said unto Moses."

It had been a long campaign, spanning several years and encompassing all sorts of battle contingencies and conditions. There had been moments of great triumph as well as crises, but through it all Joshua persevered and saw the faithfulness of the Lord bring about the promised result.

At this point, however, some might be wondering how the text can make the bold claim that "Joshua took the whole land." Just a bit later in the book we read of the Lord telling Joshua himself, "Thou art old and stricken in years, and there remaineth yet very much land to be possessed" (13:1). Judges 1:21-36 gives a long list of cities the Israelites did not take and peoples they did not drive out. Even by the time of David, the Jebusites still controlled the city that would become Jerusalem after he finally conquered it (II Sam. 5:6-10).

Could this possibly be a case of a biblical contradiction, as numerous critics have charged over the years? The short answer is that it is manifestly not. If it were a contradiction, would Joshua not have noticed it himself, as well as all those with him? When the text says that "Joshua took the whole land," it means "he gained control of the whole region even though he did not take every city" (Gaebelein, gen. ed., *The Expositor's Bible Commentary,* Zondervan).

In contrast to the patriarchs, who were sojourners in a land belonging to others, Joshua and his people had control of its length and breadth. There would be battles to fight and trials to endure, but that the land was theirs was not in doubt. The situation could be summarized once again: the mission was accomplished, but the work was just now beginning.

—*Kenneth A. Sponsler.*

Heart of the Lesson

A new era had begun. Moses was dead; after forty years in the wilderness, Israel had a new leader. The task before him and the people remained the same, however. They were to enter the land God had promised to them.

1. A promise given (Josh. 1:1-6). Following Moses' death, the Lord spoke directly to Joshua, telling him to cross the Jordan and enter the land of Canaan. God had long before promised to give this land to His people. They needed only to follow the Lord's instructions. But Joshua was undoubtedly anxious at the prospect.

Joshua had been beside Moses through the wilderness years. He had seen the repeated rebellion of the people against the Lord and the Lord's chosen leader. Years earlier, after Joshua and Caleb had spied in Canaan, the nation rejected their call to enter that bountiful land because they feared the people who lived there (Num. 13—14). Now it was Joshua leading this nation of uncooperative people, numbering perhaps three million.

The Lord answered Joshua's doubts by giving him a wonderful promise. He was assured that he would lead the people in successfully securing the Promised Land. No one would be able to stand before the Lord's people.

The one thing Joshua had to do was be strong and courageous. He was to boldly follow the Lord in the face of opposition, and he needed to continue in obedience. But where would such strength and courage come from? The Lord did not say to be strong and courageous *in order* to take the land but to be strong and courageous *because* of the Lord's promise to give Israel the land (vs. 6). God's promise was sure, and it would give Joshua strength and boldness in the years ahead.

This was a reminder that God, not Joshua, was the real leader of Israel. Joshua did not have to rely on his own abilities or knowledge to successfully lead the people. He needed only to trust God, believing the promise He had given. This is what God calls us to do as well: trust and follow Him regardless of the circumstances. Our success is based on His promises, not our abilities.

2. A promise fulfilled (Josh. 11:16-19, 21-22). It took Joshua and Israel seven years to conquer Canaan. It was not easy, and there were failures along the way. But God was faithful to His word.

Now there were no more military campaigns to be carried out. With the exception of Gibeon, which had secured a peace treaty with Israel, the cities of the land were conquered. They had even defeated the children of Anak, a dreaded race of giants who had struck fear in the hearts of the Israelite spies years before (Num. 13:28). Any doubts that might have lingered for Joshua fell before him as God's promise was fulfilled in the conquest of Canaan.

3. A promise summarized (Josh. 11:23). There was still more to do. The conquered land had to be divided among the tribes of Israel. But the God who had kept His promise to give Israel victory also could be trusted to fulfill His promise to give them this land as an inheritance.

As we trust the Lord and follow Him, we always find Him faithful to His promises. That, in turn, encourages us to continue to trust and follow Him.

—Jarl K. Waggoner.

World Missions

In this week's lesson text, God promised Joshua that he would be successful in his attempts to lead God's people to possess their land inheritance. "There shall not any man be able to stand before thee all the days of thy life: as I was with Moses, so I will be with thee: I will not fail thee, nor forsake thee. Be strong and of a good courage" (Josh. 1:5-6).

Inherent in God's revealed promise to Joshua is the reality of obstacles. Today there are obstacles to the ongoing Christian effort to spread the gospel of Jesus Christ to a lost and dying world. Walt Wilson, founder of Global Media Outreach, identified three obstacles to mass evangelism that uses the model of one-on-one conversations (www.ichristianlife.com).

The first obstacle is economics. "We can play with numbers all day long and the ugly truth is it takes a long time to recruit just one missionary. Then there is training, funding, language school, culture school, and raising support. It takes years. The cost to send a missionary out is somewhere in the range of $100,000 per year" (Wilson).

The second obstacle is politics. The politics of the global environment in which we live dictates that Americans must handle themselves carefully. Many people in various parts of the world distrust and/or dislike Americans. The number of countries that are officially closed to American Christian missionaries constitutes "nearly half the countries on the planet" (Wilson).

The third obstacle is danger. "We have never witnessed the whole-scale hunt for missionaries that we see in the world today. Never have we seen so many revolutions and such political instability in developing countries as we see today" (Wilson).

Mr. Wilson believes that a new model of mass evangelism is required to overcome the obstacles of economics, politics, and danger. The new model of spreading the gospel of Jesus Christ consists of two components: the Internet and the strategy for its use in helping the growth of local churches.

Concerning Internet evangelism, Mr. Wilson claims, "In our ministry at Global Media Outreach, we present the Gospel every 5 seconds, resulting in an indicated decision every 120 seconds from all 191 countries across the world. Currently we see 21 million visitors, and 360,000 decisions for Christ on an annual basis with the numbers growing monthly. We will see hundreds of millions come to Christ through the network in the next several years."

The Internet also can help growth in local churches. Local church pastors can gain important pastoral skills through Internet study materials provided by partnering seminaries. "Individual new believers will grow through the use of easy-to-read-and-understand Bible studies. Internet videos for those who are unable to read can revolutionize the Gospel presentation" (Wilson).

The enemy will continue his battle against the spread of the life-giving message of the gospel. Through the power of the Holy Spirit and the use of new technology, though, the battle can be won. "So Joshua took the whole land, according to all that the Lord said unto Moses; and Joshua gave it for an inheritance unto Israel according to their divisions by their tribes. And the land rested from war" (Josh. 11:23).

—*Thomas R. Chmura.*

The Jewish Aspect

The leadership of Joshua was critical for Israel's success in conquering and dividing the land of Canaan. He holds a special place in the minds and hearts of many Jews. He is viewed as both wise and humble. In rabbinical writings it is claimed that Joshua is the person described in Proverbs 27:18: "He that waiteth on his master shall be honoured."

But as with many prominent persons in Jewish history, a number of unusual myths and traditions have grown up around Joshua. While Moses' face shined like the sun when he came down from meeting with the Lord (Ex. 34:29), Joshua's face is said to have had the radiance of the moon. More than that, rabbinical tradition claims that Joshua married Rahab, the woman who helped the spies in Jericho. Supposedly daughters were born to them, through whom many prophets descended.

Joshua's name was originally Hoshea ("salvation," also spelled as Hosea), but Moses changed it to Joshua (Num. 13:16), which means "*the Lord is* salvation." Some traditions hold that Joshua composed the prayer called *Aleinu* (the second-most-used prayer in Judaism) when he and the Israelites crossed the Jordan. This idea may have arisen because there is an acrostic of his original name in the first four lines of the prayer.

New Testament Scripture gives us more profound and trustworthy points to consider. The inspired teaching in the very Jewish book of Hebrews provides fascinating connections between Joshua and Jesus Christ. The most obvious link between them is that they have the same name: *Jesus* is the Greek form of *Joshua*. But Hebrews emphasizes that while Joshua, as leader of God's people, brought Israel many glorious victories in the conquest of Canaan, the Saviour has brought "many sons unto glory" as the "captain of their salvation" (2:10).

Hebrews also contains an extended section comparing Jesus' work of bringing God's people into their eternal rest to the time when Israel was on the border of Canaan, ready to move into their place of enduring peace and rest (3:7—4:11). The point of this comparison is that Israel at first rebelled against God and refused to trust Him. Because of their unbelief, a whole generation died in the wilderness (3:16-19).

The Jews to whom Hebrews was written are exhorted to not be like those faithless people (3:15; 4:7, 11). They were rather to follow Jesus—as Israel ultimately followed Joshua—to bring them into the heavenly Promised Land. This spiritual land is truly what that Old Testament saints looked for in faith (11:13-16). Even Abraham was not really focused on the physical land of Canaan; he "looked for a city which hath foundations, whose builder and maker is God" (vs. 10).

Through faith, believers are led to the heavenly Jerusalem by Jesus (12:22). By faith we understand that through Him we are allotted an inheritance in our eternal Promised Land (Heb. 1:14; 6:11-12; cf. Matt. 25:34; Col. 3:23-24).

Joshua's work of bringing God's people into the Promise Land is a wonderful illustration of Christ's work of bringing us eternal salvation. Sadly, the Jewish people have largely neglected the new covenant inheritance that comes by faith. Pray that evangelism among them will awaken more and more to trust in the divine Joshua, who is and who gives true salvation!

—Todd Williams.

Guiding the Superintendent

Even when God takes His faithful servants home to heaven, the work of the Lord goes on. He raises up others who will do His will and fulfill the plan of God. This is a reminder that as gifted and talented as some people are, no one is indispensable in the Lord's work—not even Moses.

DEVOTIONAL OUTLINE

1. The promise (Josh. 1:1-6). As important as Moses was in the sight of Israel (despite their frequent complaints), he, along with the generation that perished in the wilderness, was no more. The younger generation had a new and younger leader, and he and they were about to be tested.

The new leader, Joshua, needed to know that he was not alone and that God would be with him as He had been with Joshua's predecessor. The task at hand was to lead God's people across the Jordan into the Land of Promise. This was no small task, and Joshua needed to know that it was achievable. It was achievable—but not apart from the grace of God. Hence, God began His instruction of Joshua with promises: the promise of success (conquer and divide) as well as the promise of His presence.

2. The plunder (Josh. 11:16-19). As the Lord had promised, so it happened—but not without the effort of the Israelites led by Joshua. Here is a grand example of the cooperation of the sovereignty of God with the responsibility of man. Joshua and the people had to do battle with the enemy, even though God had promised to give them the land. It took a long time; so tenacity of purpose and endurance were necessary, even as they are today in the work of the Lord.

The Lord has promised that He will build His church, but He has chosen to use sinful people in the process. It is neither easy nor quick, but we have the promise that it can and will be done.

3. The peace (Josh. 11:21-23). On the other side of the struggle, there was peace. The enemy was defeated, and the land had been conquered and divided according to the number and size of the tribes of Israel. The promise to Abraham (cf. Gen. 12:1; Heb. 11:8-9) was fulfilled.

Abraham, Isaac, and Jacob, among so many others, did not see the fulfillment in their lifetime. They lived by faith that God did not lie. They did not miss out on the fullness of the promise, for there is yet a time to inhabit the land in the coming kingdom of God.

The implications for us are enormous. The church has inherited the promises of Scripture and will also participate in the kingdom and eternity on the new earth. The transition may not happen in our lifetime, but believers live by faith.

AGE-GROUP EMPHASES

Children: Lead the children to develop a trust in the Word of God. They need to know that all of God's Word is true and that the promises of the Lord will come to pass.

Youths: Guide the youths to realize that the Lord will want to use them in some fashion in building His church. It is not just the task of the "older" people in the church.

Adults: Guide the adults to understand that it is always too soon to quit. The battle against evil is a long one, and those who endure to the end are rewarded for their faithfulness.

—Darrell W. McKay.

SCRIPTURE LESSON TEXT

JOSH. 2:3 And the king of Jericho sent unto Rahab, saying, Bring forth the men that are come to thee, which are entered into thine house: for they be come to search out all the country.

4 And the woman took the two men, and hid them, and said thus, There came men unto me, but I wist not whence they *were:*

5 And it came to pass *about the time* of shutting of the gate, when it was dark, that the men went out: whither the men went I wot not: pursue after them quickly; for ye shall overtake them.

6 But she had brought them up to the roof of the house, and hid them with the stalks of flax, which she had laid in order upon the roof.

7 And the men pursued after them the way to Jordan unto the fords: and as soon as they which pursued after them were gone out, they shut the gate.

8 And before they were laid down, she came up unto them upon the roof;

9 And she said unto the men, I know that the LORD hath given you the land, and that your terror is fallen upon us, and that all the inhabitants of the land faint because of you.

15 Then she let them down by a cord through the window: for her house *was* upon the town wall, and she dwelt upon the wall.

16 And she said unto them, Get you to the mountain, lest the pursuers meet you; and hide yourselves there three days, until the pursuers be returned: and afterward may ye go your way.

22 And they went, and came unto the mountain, and abode there three days, until the pursuers were returned: and the pursuers sought *them* throughout all the way, but found *them* not.

23 So the two men returned, and descended from the mountain, and passed over, and came to Joshua the son of Nun, and told him all *things* that befell them:

24 And they said unto Joshua, Truly the LORD hath delivered into our hands all the land; for even all the inhabitants of the country do faint because of us.

NOTES

Rahab and the Spies

Lesson Text: Joshua 2:3-9, 15-16, 22-24

Related Scriptures: Exodus 15:13-18; Joshua 2:10-14; Hebrews 11:31; James 2:25

TIME: 1405 B.C. PLACES: Jericho; mountains of Canaan; Shittim

GOLDEN TEXT—"Truly the Lord hath delivered into our hands all the land; for even all the inhabitants of the country do faint because of us" (Joshua 2:24).

Introduction

God wants His children to rejoice over His love and His blessings, even in the midst of trying times. During those times, we still have the reassurance that He is in complete control and that things do work for the best for those who love Him and are called by Him (Rom. 8:28). Only mature believers, however, are able to find that kind of joy when they are going through great difficulty, for their faith has been tried before.

In spite of the many blessings of life, there is always present with us a sense of uncertainty about the future.

One of the uncertainties we may face is a move from one location to another or from one situation to something else. We usually do what we can to research the possible outcomes before making the change. Joshua and the children of Israel were waiting near the Jordan River for God to lead them across it and into the land of Canaan. There were many unknowns; so Joshua determined to do some research ahead of time.

LESSON OUTLINE

I. **PROTECTION THROUGH RAHAB—Josh. 2:3-9**

II. **PROTECTION THROUGH CAREFUL PLANNING—Josh. 2:15-16, 22-24**

Exposition: Verse by Verse

PROTECTION THROUGH RAHAB

JOSH. 2:3 And the king of Jericho sent unto Rahab, saying, Bring forth the men that are come to thee, which are entered into thine house: for they be come to search out all the country.

4 And the woman took the two men, and hid them, and said thus, There came men unto me, but I wist not whence they were:

5 And it came to pass about the time of shutting of the gate, when it was dark, that the men went out:

whither the men went I wot not: pursue after them quickly; for ye shall overtake them.

6 But she had brought them up to the roof of the house, and hid them with the stalks of flax, which she had laid in order upon the roof.

7 And the men pursued after them the way to Jordan unto the fords: and as soon as they which pursued after them were gone out, they shut the gate.

8 And before they were laid down, she came up unto them upon the roof;

9 And she said unto the men, I know that the LORD hath given you the land, and that your terror is fallen upon us, and that all the inhabitants of the land faint because of you.

The king's order (Josh. 2:3). {In order to prepare for what he faced, Joshua sent two spies to Jericho to see what their initial challenge in Canaan would be like.}[Q1] They arrived, no doubt by divine appointment, at the home of Rahab the harlot, whose home was on the city wall. A report was sent to the king about their presence, and he immediately took action. After all, it was not a secret that just across the Jordan River a huge nation was on the move, with their ultimate destination being the very land that included Jericho.

"So much for undercover work. The presence of the spies was detected immediately. The king of Jericho, suspecting that a local prostitute might be involved in undercover treachery, sent a message to Rahab to turn them over to the authorities" (Gangel, *Holman Old Testament Commentary: Joshua*, Broadman and Holman). {We will soon learn that there was great fear in the city of Jericho over the presence of the Israelites; so it is not surprising that the king hastened to take action when he heard about the two spies.}[Q2]

The king knew that Jericho was just the first phase in the movement of the threatening nation. His observation that the spies had come to survey the whole land indicates this. Perhaps he felt a special sense of obligation—not only to his city but to the entire land. If he could stop this threat, the rest of the land would be safe; if he failed to do so, everyone would be in danger. He had to act swiftly and decisively. He had no other choice.

Hebrews 11 is sometimes called the Hall of Fame of Faith. It is a record of many in the Old Testament who trusted God implicitly, some even to their deaths. Only two women are included in this great record, namely, Sarah and Rahab. What a contrast they present: one the wife of the patriarch Abraham and the other a harlot! Both of them, however, are remembered for their faith in God.

Rahab's lie (Josh. 2:4-5). "By faith the harlot Rahab perished not with them that believed not, when she had received the spies with peace" (Heb. 11:31). "Likewise also was not Rahab the harlot justified by works, when she had received the messengers, and had sent them out another way?" (Jas. 2:25). These verses may indicate that Rahab had some degree of faith even before the spies arrived, and that is probably why God divinely directed them to her instead of anyone else. Her heart had already been prepared for what would happen.

Knowing the men would soon be in danger, Rahab took action to protect them. She hid them so that when she saw and greeted the king's messengers, they were nowhere in sight. {She admitted that they had come to her house, but she then stated that she did not know where they had come from and that they had left when the city gate was being closed because of the approach of darkness. She then added that she did not know where they had gone, but she assured the messengers that they could probably overtake them if they hurried after them.

The only bit of truth in her entire answer was that the spies had come. Everything else was a lie.}[Q3] There has been much written about Rahab's lies in this situation. God is gracious and merciful and does make allowances for new and still immature believers. He is probably more longsuffering toward them than we sometimes are. But Scripture does not encourage us to lie. We must remember that the Bible sometimes records facts without giving a stamp of approval on them. It was her faith that God commends.

We cannot help wondering how this incident would have turned out if Rahab had told the truth. God would have protected those men somehow, and the events might have ended up being even more extraordinary.

The men's pursuit (Josh. 2:6-7). We are finally told in a parenthetic statement how Rahab managed to hide the spies from the king's messengers without being caught. {When flax was harvested, it was apparently soaked in water for a few weeks to separate the fibers, after which it would be spread out in the sun to dry before being used to make linen. One of the convenient places to do this drying was on the flat rooftops of the homes. This was where Rahab had her drying stalks, and they made the perfect cover for hiding the spies.}[Q4]

Rahab's explanation indicated that the Israelite men had hurried out of the city just before the city gates were closed for the night. This satisfied the king's men, who left immediately to pursue the spies in the direction of the Jordan River. For whatever reason, they did not make any attempt to search Rahab's house. The soldiers naturally assumed that the spies must be somewhere outside the city.

Rahab risked her life to do what she did, which is probably evidence of her newfound faith. No doubt she would have been put to death if found out.

"This woman Rahab stood alone in faith against the *total* culture which surrounded her—something none of us today in the western world has ever had to do. For a period of time she stood for the unseen against the seen, standing in acute danger until Jericho fell. If the king had ever found out what she had done, he would have become her chief enemy and would have executed her" (Schaeffer, *Joshua and the Flow of Biblical History,* InterVarsity). Rahab was already willing to suffer great loss for her faith.

Warren Wiersbe has observed, "Ethical problems aside, the main lesson here is that Rahab's faith was conspicuous, and she demonstrated it by receiving the spies and risking her life to protect them. James saw her actions as proof that she was truly a believer (James 2:25). Her faith wasn't hidden; the spies could tell that she was indeed a believer" (*The Bible Exposition Commentary: Old Testament,* Victor).

Rahab's understanding (Josh. 2:8-9). Apparently Rahab had hidden the men on the rooftop very soon after their arrival. We are not told exactly how their presence became known so quickly. Perhaps because Rahab was a harlot, there were men hanging around who spotted the newcomers right away. Somehow Rahab knew early on that the Israelite men were in danger, and she took the steps necessary to protect them.

After the king's messengers left, Rahab went up to the roof to talk with the spies as they were preparing to rest. What she said to them revealed important information about her own beliefs and the general attitude in Jericho about Israel's presence. Her information appears to be exactly what Joshua had sent the spies to find out.

Rahab's statement of personal faith is

quite clear. That she referred to Israel's God as "LORD" (Josh. 2:9-10) indicates this, because this is the Hebrew name "Yahweh." How much she understood about that name we cannot know, but it does indicate she had some knowledge of it and believed in the God the name represented. {Furthermore, she believed fully that Yahweh had already given the land of Canaan to His people. There was no doubt in her mind that this was a certainty. She had already accepted it as truth.}Q5

How much faith did Rahab have? It was no doubt still small and incomplete, but she was acting on what she knew. "Of course, this doesn't mean that the mind must be fully instructed in every aspect of Bible truth before a sinner can be saved. The woman with the hemorrhage only touched the hem of Christ's garment and she was healed, but she acted on the little knowledge that she did possess (Matt. 9:20-22). Rahab's knowledge of the true God was meager, but she acted on what she knew; and the Lord saved her" (Wiersbe).

{Rahab then explained that all the inhabitants were terrorized by the presence of Israel.}Q6 The word translated "faint" (Josh. 2:9) means "to melt"; the hearts of the people had melted in terror, with no trace of strong confidence remaining. They sensed that they were doomed and without power to withstand what was coming, for they had heard of Israel's previous victories (vss. 10-11).

PROTECTION THROUGH CAREFUL PLANNING

15 Then she let them down by a cord through the window: for her house was upon the town wall, and she dwelt upon the wall.

16 And she said unto them, Get you to the mountain, lest the pursuers meet you; and hide yourselves there three days, until the pursuers be returned: and afterward may ye go your way.

22 And they went, and came unto the mountain, and abode there three days, until the pursuers were returned: and the pursuers sought them throughout all the way, but found them not.

23 So the two men returned, and descended from the mountain, and passed over, and came to Joshua the son of Nun, and told him all things that befell them:

24 And they said unto Joshua, Truly the LORD hath delivered into our hands all the land; for even all the inhabitants of the country do faint because of us.

Escape (Josh. 2:15-16). After pleading for her life and the lives of her loved ones to be spared (vss. 12-13) and being assured that they would be (vs. 14), {Rahab let the men down the wall outside her window by means of a rope.}Q7 The location of her home was significant and another reason God took the spies to her. The house, with its location on the city wall, became an avenue of escape for them. Is this not a good reminder to us about God's care for us? He had prepared just the right place for the spies, knowing ahead of time what they would need.

That reminds us of the New Testament promise "There hath no temptation taken you but such as is common to man: but God is faithful, who will not suffer you to be tempted above that ye are able; but will with the temptation also make a way to escape, that ye may be able to bear it" (I Cor. 10:13). God will make ways to escape both temptations and trying situations. Sometimes when situations look impossible, we need to stop frantically searching for answers and look to the Lord for whatever solution He has already determined for us.

{Rahab's advice was that the spies hide in the nearby mountain for three days, allowing plenty of time for the pursuers to do their searching for them and then return to the city.}[Q8] This showed her concern for their safety, because for all she knew they might simply try to sneak back to the Jordan immediately and get caught in the process.

There are times when we have to let God work things out for us in His own timing. To do nothing but wait must have seemed interminable for the spies; yet it was certainly the wisest thing to do in light of the danger connected with trying to quickly cross back over the Jordan.

Return (Josh. 2:22-23). "When the spies left, they went into the hills and stayed there until the pursuers had completed their search and returned to Jericho. The Hebrew is somewhat tricky here. Old Testament scholars note that all that is required in the reckoning of three days is that some part of each day be counted. The point is that the entire adventure from the sending out of the spies to the return may have taken three days" (Gangel). This would fit with the command given in Joshua 1:11.

It is evident that the pursuers did a thorough job of trying to find them, because they searched for them along the entire length of the road. The spies were safe because the mountain about one-half mile west of Jericho had limestone cliffs containing many caves, providing plenty of places in which to hide. After they were certain that the search for them had ended, they returned to Israel's camp, probably under the cover of darkness.

When the spies arrived, they immediately sought out Joshua and gave him a detailed accounting of all that had happened to them. {This would have included their being led to the house of Rahab, their being hidden by her, her lowering them from the window in her home, their promise to her, and their stay on the mountain.}[Q9]

It is good that we can have confidence in the Lord's ability to protect us. However, we see in this account that we should also be wise in doing what we can to protect ourselves and not expect God to have to do extra duty simply because we are foolish.

Report (Josh. 2:24). The confidence of the spies contrasts sharply with the report given to Moses when the twelve spies were sent from Kadesh-barnea (Num. 13). {These two spies told Joshua that the Lord had already prepared the way for Israel to take the land of Canaan. In fact, they said God was giving them "all" the land.}[Q10] They then used almost the same words Rahab had used in describing how terrified the inhabitants of the land were. It was a conclusive assurance from God.

—Keith E. Eggert.

QUESTIONS

1. What did Joshua do to determine what the initial challenge in Canaan would be?
2. Why is it not surprising that the king hurried to find the spies?
3. What did Rahab tell the king's messengers, and how much of it was the truth?
4. What made it possible for Rahab to hide the spies?
5. What did Rahab tell the spies that she personally believed?
6. How did Rahab describe the attitudes present throughout Jericho?
7. How did Rahab help the spies get out of the city?
8. What did Rahab advise them to do?
9. When the spies returned, what did they first tell Joshua?
10. What conclusions about moving ahead did they share with Joshua?

—Keith E. Eggert.

Preparing to Teach the Lesson

Last week we saw that while God wants to give us His blessings, He also has certain expectations of us. This week we explore how He protects us because He loves us.

TODAY'S AIM

Facts: to show how Rahab was used by God to protect the spies Joshua sent to spy out the land.

Principle: to show that God has all kinds of resources to protect His people.

Application: to teach that when we know that God is with us to protect us at all times, we have nothing to fear.

INTRODUCING THE LESSON

We have all felt fear at times in our lives. Fear is something that can cripple us. Satan knows that and uses it to his advantage to put us in a state of paralysis. We see such paralyzing fear in our little children when they have to go to the dentist or get their first haircut. They do not want to move away from the comfort and protection of their parents.

Even as adults, we deal with fear and are often in need of protection. This is exactly what our God offers His children. When God steps in, fear is replaced by courage. God protects His children at all times; we simply need to rely on Him. Our lesson this week shows us how God used a Canaanite woman to protect His own people.

DEVELOPING THE LESSON

1. Providing shelter for the spies (Josh. 2:3-9). Joshua sent out two spies on a special mission to Jericho, the first city the Israelites would encounter in the Promised Land. When the king of Jericho got word of this, he sent people to inquire about the matter. Rahab had hidden the spies on the rooftop and denied that she had knowledge of their whereabouts. The king's men were satisfied with her answer and left immediately.

The focus of our lesson this week is on the way God protects His own people. First, we learn that God is not limited in His resources to help His children. Here we see that He used a local Gentile woman to hide the spies under stalks of flax on the rooftop.

Get your students to see that when we are in trouble, our God already knows about it; in His sovereignty, He has already made arrangements to protect us and to get us out of trouble. The fascinating thing is that God has every resource at His disposal to help His children. Here God used Rahab, a Gentile in the pagan city of Jericho, to help Joshua's spies do His work.

2. Assisting the spies in their escape (Josh. 2:15-16). It is interesting that the Bible tells us that Rahab's house was built upon or into the city wall. It was not without divine design that God picked the person who lived in this house to help the spies.

Aware of every situation His children will encounter, God has key people in place, chosen specifically to provide the exact help they need. God could have chosen anyone in Jericho to help these men, but He chose Rahab. Her house was built upon the city wall. The city gates were shut after dark, but she let the spies down with a rope. They might not have escaped if they had been hiding somewhere else in the city. She was handpicked to protect them. Stress to the students that God has a solution for us even before we ask Him.

Note how God used Rahab here. She knew the area, and the men were new to the place. God put the right person there to protect them and to tell them what to do and where to go. If we are lost, we need someone with answers. God picked Rahab to provide the spies with what they needed. Have your students list the specific instructions that she gave the men. When God speaks, He is very clear. We need to listen. God sometimes uses the most unlikely sources to protect us.

3. Renewing faith in God's protection (Josh. 2:22-24). The spies Joshua had sent out did exactly as they were told by Rahab. They went into the rugged hill country and stayed there three days, until all was clear and safe for them. Their pursuers could not find them and eventually gave up. God can make our pursuers discouraged and cause them to give up. We will encounter trouble, but if our hearts are pure and we seek to follow God, fear will be replaced by courage.

Remind the class that God is on our side when we are in trouble; we can fully trust in His care. The enemy returned home without success in finding Joshua's men. So it will be with us when we are on God's side, for He protects us. We are told here that the spies crossed the Jordan, returned to Joshua, and gave him a detailed report of what they had learned. Note that it was a positive report. When God is with His people, everything will finally turn out right. God never lets us down.

We cannot overlook the exuberance and confidence that the men came back with. They assured Joshua that God would give them the land and that it could certainly be conquered because the enemy was terrified of them. We are reminded that if God is for us, nothing can stand against us (Rom. 8:31).

Ask your students to identify some situations in which they found themselves in need of protection. Get them to share what or whom they relied on for deliverance and how it all worked out. What role did God play in that situation? How was that role discerned?

ILLUSTRATING THE LESSON

We have nothing to fear when we are in God's care. Attacks and even suffering may come, but God ultimately protects His own either from or through such trials.

CONCLUDING THE LESSON

Encourage the class to identify some situations in our world today now that raise fears for many people. Get the class to talk about what they themselves fear most. Some things that might come up are worldwide recession, wars, depletion of the earth's resources, and the dangers of the Internet, especially with regard to our children. Conclude the session by addressing some specific fears. Show how God has promised us His presence and His protection.

ANTICIPATING THE NEXT LESSON

In our lesson next week, we will move from God's protection to seeing how He is truly a victorious and triumphant God.

—A. Koshy Muthalaly.

PRACTICAL POINTS

1. People may have some knowledge, but nothing escapes God's knowledge (Josh. 2:3).
2. Even immature faith, if it is true faith, is willing to take risks for God (vs. 4).
3. God can protect and reward those who put themselves in jeopardy for His sake (vss. 5-6).
4. God is at work, even among our enemies (vss. 7-9).
5. God has placed us exactly where He wants us so that He can use us for His glory (vss. 15-16).
6. God uses people to accomplish His purposes, but our greatest gratitude always belongs to Him (vss. 22-24).

—Don Kakavecos.

RESEARCH AND DISCUSSION

1. Was Rahab right to lie about the spies (cf. Prov. 12:22; Jas. 2:25)? Are the wicked entitled to the truth if they intend to do evil when they learn it?
2. How does God use even the sins of fallen man to accomplish His purpose?
3. Are Christians precluded from listening to the advice of unethical people (Josh. 2:15-16)? What should be the test of any advice one gets from others (cf. Prov. 1:1-7; Acts 17:11; II Tim. 3:16-17)?
4. How can faith in God's promises encourage and energize us for the tasks God gives? What are some of God's specific promises?

—Don Kakavecos.

ILLUSTRATED HIGH POINTS

Hid them (Josh. 2:4)

In May 1995, a thirty-four-year-old construction worker was welding on top of a water tower outside Chicago. He had unhooked his safety gear to reach for some pipes when a metal cage slipped and bumped the scaffold he stood on. He lost his balance and fell 110 feet, landing facedown on a pile of dirt, just missing rocks and construction debris.

As paramedics carried him to an ambulance, he kept his sense of humor. "Please don't drop me," he said. Doctors later said he had only a bruised lung. As He did with Israel's spies, God hid him from harm.

Get you to the mountain (vs. 9)

A youth worker told this story. It was during Communist rule in southern Ethiopia (1974–1991).

"As I waited in prison," he recalled, "my Saviour gave us songs to sing I had never heard before. Seven men had come to Christ in that prison, and we all sang together."

One guard took delight in mocking them. He would put filthy words to the tunes they sang. One night this man patted his revolver and promised, "Death tomorrow!"

Just after midnight that night, a tremendous storm burst over the town and the prison. Huge hailstones fell, wrecking roofs. However, the singing prisoners were kept safe and dry.

The next morning the insulting guard was belt whipped and driven into a cell. Others nearby said, "We told this man to leave the believers alone. God sent terrible punishment upon us all."

The guard explained, "I should have treated you well. Please forgive me." This the prisoners readily did.

—Ted Simonson.

Golden Text Illuminated

"Truly the Lord hath delivered into our hands all the land; for even all the inhabitants of the country do faint because of us" (Joshua 2:24).

This week's golden text confirms the Lord's promise to Joshua, "Arise, go over this Jordan, thou, and all this people, unto the land which I do give to them, even to the children of Israel. Every place that the sole of your foot shall tread upon, that have I given unto you, as I said unto Moses. . . . There shall not any man be able to stand before thee all the days of thy life" (Josh. 1:2-3, 5). In obedience, Joshua had sent two spies to the land of Shittim and the city of Jericho on a scouting mission (2:1). Upon their return, the spies excitedly reported their experiences to Joshua and concluded by proclaiming, "All the inhabitants of the country do faint because of us."

Rahab, the woman who risked her life to hide the spies, had given them this choice piece of insider information. She told them, "I know that the Lord hath given you the land, and that your terror is fallen upon us, and that all the inhabitants of the land faint because of you" (2:9).

Why would the men have been convinced of the truth of these words that came from a woman, and one of questionable character at that? Maybe it was because of their previous experiences with the Lord being faithful to His promises.

These men were from the second generation of liberated Israelites, who had wandered in the wilderness for forty years and had seen God's daily provision for them. They had come to learn that the God of Israel was true to His word.

There had been a similar spy mission almost forty years earlier, with the first generation that had come out of enslavement in Egypt. That mission had ended in tragedy for the nation.

God had told Moses to send twelve men on a mission as a way to give the nation a peek into the good land they were about to enter (Num. 13:1-3). The experience of seeing the land and all that it had for them should have been an opportunity to affirm their faith and experience how God would fulfill His promises through them.

Sadly, only two of the spies, Joshua and Caleb, thought that they would be able to conquer the inhabitants of the land. The negative report of the other ten spies drained the courage from the people (14:1-4). In response to their lack of faith, God had forbidden a whole generation from seeing their inheritance (vss. 20-23).

Despite the catastrophe from the last spy mission, Joshua wanted to send out a covert expedition. He needed updated information about the land and the people so that proper preparations could be made for battle. Even though the undercover mission was discovered by the king of Jericho, God protected the spies through Rahab's ruse.

When the men returned to Joshua, their report was altogether different from the negative one that had been given so many years before. The words from these two spies were full of faith. It was a passionate confirmation of the promises God had made to Joshua and the whole nation. Unlike the generation before them, they would obey God's directives in faith that what God had promised would come to pass.

—Kelly Hawver.

Heart of the Lesson

Even though the Lord had promised Joshua and Israel success in taking possession of the land of Canaan, they still had to carry out the military campaign. And this required some preparation.

The first obstacle in the way was the city of Jericho, just beyond the Jordan River. It was a fortified city ruled by a king, and it stood in central Canaan at the entrance to the Promised Land. Joshua considered it important for military purposes to acquire greater knowledge of Jericho; so he sent two spies secretly into the city.

1. Divine protection (Josh. 2:3-9, 15-16). The two spies entered Jericho and went into the house of Rahab, a harlot (vs. 1). This might seem an odd place to go for men sent on a mission for God's people, but it was one place they would be welcomed and would not raise undue suspicion.

Suspicion arose, nonetheless, as the king heard of their presence (vs. 2). It soon became clear that God had providentially led them to Rahab for their own protection. When the king's men arrived seeking the spies, Rahab told them the men had been there but had left already. The truth was that she had hidden them under stalks of flax she had laid on her roof (vss. 4-6). On the basis of her story, the soldiers left Jericho in pursuit of the spies.

Much has been said about Rahab's lie and whether it was justified. We must remember that having been raised in a pagan culture, she probably did not think twice about lying. It is her faith, not her lie, that is commended in the New Testament (Heb. 11:31; Jas. 2:25).

While Rahab's knowledge of God was limited, it is clear she had some faith. This became even more evident when she later joined herself to the Hebrew people (Josh. 6:25). At this point, she was convinced by what she had seen and heard that the Lord had given the land to Israel (2:9). The terror of Israel had fallen on "all the inhabitants of the land" in fulfillment of God's promise (cf. Deut. 2:25; 11:25).

In light of this, Rahab sent the spies out secretly, telling them where to hide until their pursuers gave up the hunt (Josh. 2:15-16).

2. Divine assurance (Josh. 2:22-24). Had the two spies failed to return, it might have brought great fear upon the Israelites. But God had seen to it, through the providential encounter with Rahab, that they did return to Joshua.

The report of the spies to Joshua makes it clear that God had another reason for leading them to Rahab. Her words had brought them encouragement that they now passed on to Joshua. Her words assured Israel that the Lord had prepared the way by bringing terror into the hearts of the inhabitants of Canaan.

God's promises should be enough for us, but He knows our weaknesses. He often brings us assurances and reassurances that He is working to fulfill His promises. Years before, the Israelites had been terror-stricken when they heard of the might of the Canaanites. Now God had graciously shown them that the Canaanites trembled in fear before them.

The name of the Lord had made them tremble. They had heard about all His mighty works on Israel's behalf.

—*Jarl K. Waggoner.*

World Missions

In this week's lesson text, the Bible reveals an amazing account of how God sovereignly protected His servants when they participated in a plan to accomplish the task revealed to them. Joshua had been commanded to pursue God's will of conquering and parceling out the Promised Land, and he did so with obedient and courageous strength (cf. Josh. 1:7, 9).

As a part of his preparation to enter the Promised Land, Joshua involved two men in a search mission to determine what obstacles he and God's people would encounter. In the course of the mission, God protected the Jewish spies so that they could return and give Joshua an encouraging report. He then proceeded with courageous action.

Today, when individuals accept God's call to participate in the ongoing Christian effort to spread the gospel, God's sovereign protection enables them to minister with bold courage. An anonymous individual once stated, "Unless there is within us that which is above us, we shall soon be consumed by that which is about us" (www.elbourne.org).

As God's missionary servants experience the powerful and protective indwelling presence of the Holy Spirit, they are encouraged and emboldened to proceed in a ministry that results in lost souls receiving eternal life through faith in the Lord Jesus Christ. Lorrie Anderson, missionary to the headhunting Candoshi Shapra Indians of Peru, is an example of this truth.

One morning Lorrie found a quiet place to read Scripture and pray near the edge of a river. She was unaware that witch doctors had pronounced a curse upon her. While she had her eyes closed in prayer, a large anaconda silently glided over to her through the water and buried its fangs in her arm. Several times it struck. She screamed as it began to wrap her tightly in its coils. The serpent reared its head to strike again.

"Then suddenly the giant snake, never known to release its prey, relaxed its grip and slithered off through the water. While Lorrie was being treated, a witch doctor from a nearby village burst into the hut and stared at her. She couldn't believe Lorrie had survived. She said her son-in-law, also a witch doctor, had chanted to the spirit of the anaconda that morning and sent it to kill the young missionary. 'I'm certain,' Lorrie said, 'that except for the protection of God, it would have worked'" (*Our Daily Bread,* August 13, 1990).

God's sovereign protection is an encouraging and hopeful thread that weaves throughout the Scriptures. David witnessed God's sovereign protection when he courageously faced and slew Goliath, the Philistine giant (cf. I Sam. 17:38-54). Nehemiah experienced it as he proceeded with courageous boldness and finished rebuilding Jerusalem's protective wall (cf. Neh. 6:1-16).

Shadrach, Meshach, and Abednego realized God's protection in the midst of the fiery furnace (cf. Dan. 3:19-30). The apostles were intimately acquainted with God's sovereign protection as they obediently pursued God's command to spread His message of redeeming grace (cf. Acts 5:17-42).

When the Jewish spies returned from their mission, they told Joshua, "Truly the Lord hath delivered into our hands all the land" (Josh. 2:24). As we continue to share the gospel, let us do so trusting that God will continue to deliver His protection into our lives to His honor and glory.

—Thomas R. Chmura.

The Jewish Aspect

The account of Rahab illustrates that while God was dealing primarily with Israel throughout the Old Testament, the door was not closed to Gentile salvation. Even among the very wicked Canaanites, some would still respond spiritually to the message they heard. Rahab was even willing to betray her own people on behalf of the people who served the one and only true God, the God of Israel.

The two Israelite spies entered the house of a woman who was a prostitute. There were three good reasons for that. First, two strange men entering the house of a prostitute would not attract unusual attention. Second, her house was located on the wall of the city, and that made for an easy exit. Third, by the providence of God, Rahab was one who had already come to believe in the God of Israel. Both Hebrews 11:31 and James 2:25 note that her actions were motivated by faith and not merely a desire for self-preservation.

Many rabbis had difficulty with a prostitute being an ancestor of both David and the Messiah and so chose to translate the word as "innkeeper," but other rabbis admit the word does mean "prostitute." These rabbis argue that she was also a prostitute to the king and other leaders who would have shared military secrets with her. This, they say, was one reason the Israelite spies targeted her house.

Rabbis also note that Rahab, though from an immoral, sinful nation, nevertheless repented and became an honored member of the holy nation. They maintain she became an ancestress to both prophets and priests. Rahab symbolizes a call to repentance to even the most wicked of people so that they can be accepted by the God of Israel. Rabbinic tradition teaches that she was twelve years old at the time of the Exodus and had now been a harlot for forty years. Also according to rabbinic tradition, Rahab married Joshua. However, Matthew 1:5 states that she actually married an Israelite named Salmon.

Rahab's statement to the spies shows that she and others in the city of Jericho had been hearing about all that the God of Israel had done on behalf of Israel since the time of the Exodus forty years earlier. The difference is that Rahab responded with faith in the message she heard, while her countrymen did not.

Rahab revealed three things to the spies. First, she recognized that God would give Israel the land; second, the Canaanites were fearful and suffering from low morale; and third, she had faith in the God of Israel and even knew God's covenant name (YHWH). In rabbinic teaching, her conversation exempted her from Deuteronomy 20:16, which ordered that not a soul of the Canaanite nation should be left alive.

A key Hebrew word is *hesed,* which is used about 250 times in the Old Testament. It carries the meaning of loyal, steadfast, or faithful love based on a promise, agreement, or covenant. It is a word that is used of God's covenant love for Israel and also of human relationships. Rahab's request was that the spies make a *hesed* agreement (show "kindness") with her and her family, just as she made a *hesed* agreement with the spies by hiding them (Josh. 2:12).

Rahab was rewarded for her conversion to the God of Israel in four ways: she did not perish with those who did not believe (Heb. 11:31); she became part of the commonwealth of Israel (Josh. 6:25); she married into the tribe of Judah (Matt. 1:5); and she became an ancestress of the Messiah.

—Arnold G. Fruchtenbaum.

Guiding the Superintendent

With the days of our lives numbered by a sovereign God, it stands to reason that He protects His own until the appointed time of our departure. The guiding hand of God is clearly seen in the lesson before us this week.

DEVOTIONAL OUTLINE

1. The spies received (Josh. 2:3-9). Joshua had sent two men to spy out the city of Jericho prior to laying siege to it. Upon entering Jericho, they took refuge in the home of a harlot named Rahab. This should not imply that they went there for immoral purposes. More likely, it was a place where they felt they could find lodging without being asked any questions.

Places such as this would also be more conducive to acquiring pertinent information about the city. Also, it was located on the very edge of the city, which afforded them a hasty exit if needed.

God struck the Canaanites with fear just as He promised (Ex. 23:27). The people of Jericho feared the Israelites, but Rahab feared their God. The writer to the Hebrews noted her deed and commended her faith (cf. 11:31).

2. The spies retreated (Josh. 2:15-16). Aided by Rahab, the two men left the city and hid in the mountains for three days before rejoining Joshua and the Israelites. Someone reading the biblical account for the first time would perhaps see more tension involved than those who are acquainted with the outcome.

We are to be reminded, however, that in the Lord's work there is tension at times and sometimes danger as we seek to do His work in a fallen world. Yet we serve an awesome and powerful God who keeps His good hand upon His own until their work is done.

3. The spies reported (Josh. 2:22-24). Upon following the directions given by Rahab, the men descended from their mountain hideaway and rejoined Joshua and the people of Israel. It was time to report, and the report was favorable for attacking the city. They had learned the people were living in fear of them; therefore, the battle was already joined, and success would be easier than otherwise.

It should be noted too that they credited the Lord with victory even before the assault. Faith has a way of trusting God for the outcome, and thanksgiving in advance honors the Lord for what He will do. Faith sees the outcome before it has been accomplished in time. If only God's people today had such a mind to trust Him and thank Him as they pray for needs they face! God loves to have His people trust Him.

AGE-GROUP EMPHASES

Children: Lead the children to see that the Lord works in the hearts of people—both in those who believe in Him and in those who do not.

Youths: Help the teens see that God's plans are often surprising and mysterious. His power is able to bring about success in ways that we could never imagine. Despite the best efforts of the enemy, the spies escaped from Jericho unharmed. Accounts such as this should make us trust Him completely with our futures.

Adults: By God's grace, Rahab became fully accepted into the people of God. No one should be considered far from the grace of God because of his or her sin. This truth is seen elsewhere, as with the woman at the well and the woman caught in the act of adultery, both in John's Gospel.

—Darrell W. McKay.

SCRIPTURE LESSON TEXT

JOSH. 6:2 And the LORD said unto Joshua, See, I have given into thine hand Jericho, and the king thereof, *and* the mighty men of valour.

3 And ye shall compass the city, all *ye* men of war, *and* go round about the city once. Thus shalt thou do six days.

4 And seven priests shall bear before the ark seven trumpets of rams' horns: and the seventh day ye shall compass the city seven times, and the priests shall blow with the trumpets.

12 And Joshua rose early in the morning, and the priests took up the ark of the LORD.

13 And seven priests bearing seven trumpets of rams' horns before the ark of the LORD went on continually, and blew with the trumpets: and the armed men went before them; but the rereward came after the ark of the LORD, *the priests* going on, and blowing with the trumpets.

14 And the second day they compassed the city once, and returned into the camp: so they did six days.

15 And it came to pass on the seventh day, that they rose early about the dawning of the day, and compassed the city after the same manner seven times: only on that day they compassed the city seven times.

16 And it came to pass at the seventh time, when the priests blew with the trumpets, Joshua said unto the people, Shout; for the LORD hath given you the city.

17 And the city shall be accursed, *even* it, and all that *are* therein, to the LORD: only Rahab the harlot shall live, she and all that *are* with her in the house, because she hid the messengers that we sent.

18 And ye, in any wise keep *yourselves* from the accursed thing, lest ye make *yourselves* accursed, when ye take of the accursed thing, and make the camp of Israel a curse, and trouble it.

19 But all the silver, and gold, and vessels of brass and iron, *are* consecrated unto the LORD: they shall come into the treasury of the LORD.

20 So the people shouted when *the priests* blew with the trumpets: and it came to pass, when the people heard the sound of the trumpet, and the people shouted with a great shout, that the wall fell down flat.

NOTES

The Fall of Jericho

Lesson Text: Joshua 6:2-4, 12-20*a*

Related Scriptures: Genesis 15:16-21; Deuteronomy 20:16-18; Joshua 5:13—6:1; Hebrews 11:30

TIME: 1405 B.C. PLACE: Jericho

GOLDEN TEXT—"It came to pass at the seventh time, when the priests blew with the trumpets, Joshua said unto the people, Shout; for the Lord hath given you the city" (Joshua 6:16).

Introduction

The children of Israel were now west of the Jordan River and encamped at Gilgal in the land of Canaan. God had miraculously dried up the river so that the people could cross over into Canaan. Memorials had been set up, manna had ceased coming from heaven, circumcision had been performed, and everybody was waiting for the initial phase of conquering the land. As Joshua waited for further instructions, he decided to go out and look over Jericho and make some observations about their first challenge. How were they going to take Jericho before moving on?

God is always good to give us the directions we need when we are willing to patiently wait upon Him. It might be one of the hardest things we have to do as believers, simply biding our time until He indicates clearly what steps we are to take next. But experience has taught many of us that the only thing harder than waiting on the Lord is wishing we had!

LESSON OUTLINE

I. **WHAT ISRAEL WAS TO DO—Josh. 6:2-4**

II. **WHAT ISRAEL DID—Josh. 6:12-17**

III. **WHAT ISRAEL EXPERIENCED—Josh. 6:18-20*a***

Exposition: Verse by Verse

WHAT ISRAEL WAS TO DO

JOSH. 6:2 And the LORD said unto Joshua, See, I have given into thine hand Jericho, and the king thereof, and the mighty men of valour.

3 And ye shall compass the city, all ye men of war, and go round about the city once. Thus shalt thou do six days.

4 And seven priests shall bear before the ark seven trumpets of rams' horns: and the seventh day ye

shall compass the city seven times, and the priests shall blow with the trumpets.

The promise (Josh. 6:2). Verse 1 tells us that the city of Jericho was securely shut up; nobody could get in or get out. The people inside the city were surely hoping desperately that their walls would provide the safety they needed to avoid being overtaken by the huge nation now camped at Gilgal. On the other hand, the children of Israel could have been looking at the same security and wondering how they could ever possibly overtake such a fortified city. No doubt tensions were running high on both sides!

Jericho was about five miles from the Jordan. It was the most significant city in the Jordan Valley and perhaps the most strongly fortified in all the land. From where Israel entered Canaan, there was no way to proceed without first taking Jericho.

It is possible that Jericho is the oldest city in the world. Old Testament Jericho was built on a hill. Its remains are found in a mound called Tell es-Sultan. Archaeological records indicate that it had a double wall, the outer one six feet thick and the inner one twelve feet thick.

The narrative of verse 2 is a continuation from the last verse of the previous chapter. One might logically conclude that the Commander of the army of the Lord was actually Jesus Christ, here referred to as being the Lord. This name reminds us that Jesus is indeed God; this verse is an Old Testament pointer to the truth of the Trinity.

{The orders now given to Joshua came directly from the heavenly headquarters and the Father Himself. Before specific instructions were given, though, the Lord promised that Jericho had already been given to Joshua.}[Q1] No greater reassurance could have been given than this. There was no reason for Joshua to fear what he was facing, because the outcome had already been determined. All he had to do was be obedient in the time and way in which he moved forward.

The procedure (Josh. 6:3-4). {God's plan was for the armed men and seven priests with rams' horns to march around the city once each day for six days and on the seventh day march around the city seven times.}[Q2] What kind of military strategy was this?

Jericho was on no more than about seven acres of land, with a circumference of about half a mile; so this march would not be all that difficult. The people in front would likely be back at their starting point in less than an hour. What is curious is God's rationale behind such an unusual procedure. No regular weapons of war were going to be involved. What was going on?

Kenneth Gangel made this interesting observation: "We all know God could have spoken the word and Jericho would have vaporized. The real battle with Jericho was not with the Canaanites but with the Israelites, not with the wall of a city but with human hearts" (*Holman Old Testament Commentary: Joshua,* Broadman and Holman). The daily marches would have had a certain psychological effect on the residents of Jericho, but that was probably not the primary result God was seeking through this unusual operation. There was something else.

God was about to reveal Himself once again as a faithful and trustworthy God. Most of the people who had just crossed the Jordan River had not been born when the Israelites departed from Egypt and crossed the Red Sea. They had witnessed the provision of manna throughout the years of desert travel and now the miraculous crossing of the Jordan. But just how deep was their faith? {God would give them the heavily fortified city of Jericho in such a miraculous way that there could be no doubt concerning His power and faithfulness.}[Q3]

We cannot help wondering about the responses of Joshua's leaders when he told them this plan! Perhaps they thought he had been in the sun too long and was suffering from heatstroke!

WHAT ISRAEL DID

12 And Joshua rose early in the morning, and the priests took up the ark of the Lord.

13 And seven priests bearing seven trumpets of rams' horns before the ark of the Lord went on continually, and blew with the trumpets: and the armed men went before them; but the rereward came after the ark of the Lord, the priests going on, and blowing with the trumpets.

14 And the second day they compassed the city once, and returned into the camp: so they did six days.

15 And it came to pass on the seventh day, that they rose early about the dawning of the day, and compassed the city after the same manner seven times: only on that day they compassed the city seven times.

16 And it came to pass at the seventh time, when the priests blew with the trumpets, Joshua said unto the people, Shout; for the Lord hath given you the city.

17 And the city shall be accursed, even it, and all that are therein, to the Lord: only Rahab the harlot shall live, she and all that are with her in the house, because she hid the messengers that we sent.

The order of the march (Josh. 6:12-13). Joshua wasted no time; early the next morning he got everybody in place and began the march. Perhaps the priests are mentioned first to show that this was a spiritual venture rather than a military one. Four priests would have been carrying the ark of the covenant by the two poles that ran through the rings on its corners. God had specifically commanded that the ark was always to be moved in this way (Ex. 25:10-14). When David ignored this command, Uzzah lost his life (II Sam. 6:1-11).

{Seven other priests blew rams' horn trumpets during the entire time of marching. They were in the middle of the marching line, followed by those carrying the ark. Leading the march was the main part of Joshua's army, and behind the priests came the rear guard.}[Q4] There is no reason to believe that the women and children were involved in this. They no doubt stayed in the camp at Gilgal. To involve them would have served only to make everything very complicated. As it was, we can imagine how smoothly and efficiently the process worked.

{The priests were placed in prominent roles, and at the very center of everything was the ark of the covenant, representing the very presence of God Himself.}[Q5] It was before the ark, both in the tabernacle and in the temple built by Solomon, that the high priest stood in the presence of God. When Moses set up the tabernacle the first time, God made His presence known by filling it with His glory (Ex. 40:34). In fact, nobody could enter the tabernacle because of this great glory (vs. 35).

{God was making the entire approach to Jericho an exhibition of His presence with His people.}[Q5] At the climactic moment yet to come, He would receive great honor and glory.

The change in the march (Josh. 6:14-15). Six days in a row an army and a group of priests marched around the city—and nothing happened! The only sounds were the beat of their feet and the blowing of the rams' horns. The absence of vocal sounds (vs. 10) must have been mysterious and perplexing to the people in the city. Perhaps on the first few days they mocked the marchers, but as one day followed another with the same procedure, the mocking very likely was replaced by an eerie sense of dread.

After all, there was no evidence that the marchers had any fear whatsoever regarding Jericho. Each day they approached and circled with absolute confidence. The silent, somber, confident demeanor of the participants might very well have had a psychologically wearing effect on the people of Jericho. Did the tension inside the city become greater each day? What was happening with the Israelites? Was their sense of expectation growing each day, thus increasing their excitement? We are not told whether Joshua explained the final results ahead of time.

The seventh day finally arrived, and everyone was up and ready to go at dawn. Imagine the surprise inside the city as the Israelites began their march earlier than usual and then kept going around and around the city. {God had told them to march around the city seven times, and that was exactly what they did.}[Q6] Surely in the hearts of the Israelites the sense of excitement grew as the end of the march approached.

There are times in our lives when God directs us to do out-of-the-ordinary things. It is important to remember, however, that it is truly not specifically the things we do that bring about spiritual victories. But as we depend on the Lord to fulfill His promises, we experience some soul-thrilling events!

The command of Joshua (Josh. 6:16-17). It would seem logical that Joshua had given these detailed instructions to the people before they began this sevenfold march. They surely needed to know ahead of time what they were to do when they heard the "long blast" of the ram's horn (vs. 5). It would have been impossible for Joshua to explain the details given here (through verse 19) as the horn was actually sounding. However, if they knew what to listen for, they would be expecting it and be ready to respond.

{Joshua told the people that when they heard the blast of the horn, they were to shout because God had already given them the city. It was to be a shout of victory!}[Q7] He then explained that everything in the city was doomed for destruction, including every material thing and all the people. When Joshua said, "The city shall be accursed" (vs. 17), he meant that everything in it was banned from being taken by the people; instead, it was to be devoted to God for destruction. In this case, the judgment of God was going to be immediate and complete.

Rahab, however, was to be allowed to live, along with all her relatives who had come to her house. This was her reward for having protected the spies earlier. She hid them, sent the king's messengers on their way, and then helped the spies escape to the mountain to wait for a safe time to return to Joshua. The spies had made a covenant with Rahab to protect her and her family (2:18-21); so Joshua now gave the instructions for honoring that covenant. It is apparent that she was a believer in Israel's God; so He responded to her.

WHAT ISRAEL EXPERIENCED

18 And ye, in any wise keep yourselves from the accursed thing, lest ye make yourselves accursed, when ye take of the accursed thing, and make the camp of Israel a curse, and trouble it.

19 But all the silver, and gold, and vessels of brass and iron, are consecrated unto the Lord: they shall come into the treasury of the Lord.

20*a* So the people shouted when the priests blew with the trumpets: and it came to pass, when the people heard the sound of the trumpet, and the people shouted with a great shout, that the wall fell down flat.

The detailed instructions (Josh. 6:18-19). These are stern instructions and were meant to be followed without question. {Every material item in the city, with one explicit exception, was under God's ban and doomed for destruction.}[Q8] Therefore, it was not to be taken by anyone in Israel. {In fact, Joshua warned that if anyone took anything that was accursed, that person too would become accursed.}[Q9] Everything in Jericho was doomed and intended for extermination; anyone taking anything from there would be doomed as well.

One would think that no one would dare disobey such a somber warning, but as Joshua 7 reveals, there was one man, named Achan, who chose to ignore the Lord's command. Why is it that we gullible human beings think we can ignore God and escape His chastening? It is significant that the entire camp of Israel would be affected by any disobedience.

A couple of things appear to be behind God's command. First, He was making it very clear that He wanted Israel to have nothing to do with pagan living, including the wicked practices related to their religious activity. God's people need to be separated from worldly activity. We serve the same God who required Israel to be in a pure relationship with Him.

Second, the principle of firstfruits is obvious. This is the broad principle that from our every gain we should give God the first portion. This is behind tithing and is seen in many of the Pentateuch's commands. This first city was to belong entirely to God to do with as He wanted. Later victories would not have such requirements attached to them.

The complete victory (Josh. 6:20*a*). Imagine the moment. {The blast sounded, and an earth-shattering yell arose from the marching crowd, which probably immediately stopped moving and stood in place, ready to charge into the city! The huge wall of Jericho began to crumble to the ground and was soon lying flat.}[Q10] God had just manifested Himself in a way never seen before.

"So when the priests blasted on the trumpets . . . the people gave a loud shout. That shout reverberated through the hills around, startling wild animals and terrorizing the dwellers of Jericho in their homes. At that moment the wall of Jericho, obeying the summons of God, collapsed (lit., 'fell in its place')" (Walvoord and Zuck, eds., *The Bible Knowledge Commentary,* Victor). This great, almighty God of Israel is also our God today.

—*Keith E. Eggert.*

QUESTIONS

1. Where were Joshua's orders from, and of what did they assure him?
2. What was the Lord's unusual military approach to Jericho?
3. What would this battle strategy ultimately teach Israel?
4. What was the order of march the Israelites were to establish?
5. What was significant about the positioning of the priests and the ark in the march?
6. What was different about the marching orders for Israel on the seventh day?
7. What would signal the time to shout?
8. What did God say Israel was to do with the things and people of Jericho?
9. What would happen if God's orders were disobeyed?
10. How does the text describe the final outcome of Israel's action?

—*Keith E. Eggert.*

Preparing to Teach the Lesson

Last week we saw how God protects His people. This week we are given a powerful reminder that our God is a victorious God. God teaches us a lesson through the conquest of Jericho.

TODAY'S AIM

Facts: to show how God helped Joshua and his people overcome Jericho by trusting in Him.

Principle: to show that God is a victorious God who works on the side of those who trust Him.

Application: to teach that when we trust God, He will make us victorious.

INTRODUCING THE LESSON

The word "defeat" brings up sad thoughts of failure, which can be depressing. The opposite of that is "victory," which brings to mind images of jubilation and joy. We face battles every day with the decisions that we have to make, the choices that have to be determined, and the steps that we have to take. The devil does everything he can to make sure we fail. Our lesson this week shows us how Joshua and his men simply followed God's instructions and were victorious.

DEVELOPING THE LESSON

1. Promise of victory (Josh. 6:2-4). Our God is a victorious God. He desires to give us the victory we need in every area of our lives, and He will, as long as we are prepared to follow His instructions. God is sovereign. This means that He is absolutely in control of the whole universe. Nothing can defeat Him or thwart His purposes. Even before Joshua stepped out into battle, God gave him the assurance that he would prevail. The great truth for us is the New Testament promise that the church will ultimately prevail too.

Notice here that God is always victorious. Nothing can defeat Him when He has set His plan in motion. God gave Joshua some simple, almost (in our eyes) ridiculous instructions: victory over Jericho would come through repeatedly walking around the walls of the city. Even if God's instructions seem foolish to us, obedience to them will always bring victory in the end. God assures us of victory just as He did for Joshua that day.

Your class needs to firmly grasp the truth that God assures us of victory even before we go to battle. He already knows our need. He knows our enemy. He has won the battle even before we begin. Our God is a victorious God.

2. Obedience in preparation for victory (Josh. 6:12-14). Here we see that Joshua obeyed God in the most minute details. Sometimes God's instructions may seem frivolous and trivial to us. But if we follow them, we will begin to understand that He has a far bigger purpose in mind. His "foolishness" is far greater than our "wisdom" (cf. I Cor. 1:25). Here we see Joshua rising early in the morning to do what God said. The ark of the Lord went with the people. It was a symbol of the presence of God.

Ask your students how many of them are brave enough to tell others that God is with them in the battles they face. Joshua was not afraid to proclaim that truth. It takes courage to stand up for God. The priests marched ahead of the ark, with armed soldiers preceding them and also following the ark. The priests sounded their horns, announcing the arrival of the beginning of victory. They all marched around the city this way once a day for six days. As foolish as this may have seemed, they did what God said.

Ask the students what they would have done if God had told them to win a battle in that manner. Lead the class to see that God does not work the way we do; yet His way always leads to victory when we comply and obey.

3. The spectacular victory (Josh. 6:15-20*a*). When we are on God's side, we can be sure that we will win in the end. On the seventh day, the people marched around the city seven times. In the Bible "seven" often refers to perfection or completion. As they concluded their march, the people, in obedience to Joshua, shouted. With the unbelievers in Jericho watching, the Israelites were shouting victory for the true God, Yahweh.

Notice the three specific instructions that Joshua gave the people. First, they were to destroy the whole city and take nothing for themselves. Second, they were to keep a promise made to Rahab and her family by saving them. Third, all the gold, silver, bronze, and iron articles were to be sacred to the Lord and brought into the treasury. Ask the students how much of this makes sense to them and how they might have responded if they were there.

Here we learn that Joshua's victory was an offering to God. What we do for God in obedience to Him is our offering to Him. Our daily work should be our offering to our great God, who gave us the opportunity to serve and obey Him.

When the people did what God had told them about marching around the city, the walls came crashing down. We are told by historians that Jericho was surrounded by a wall six feet thick and thirty feet high. Inside this was a second wall; so the bringing down of the walls was no simple feat. But God gave His people the victory. We learn here that although God does not necessarily use traditional methods, He certainly wins in the end. We can trust Him for that outcome every time.

ILLUSTRATING THE LESSON

When we are on God's side, victory is always the outcome. We simply need to claim His promises and act in faith.

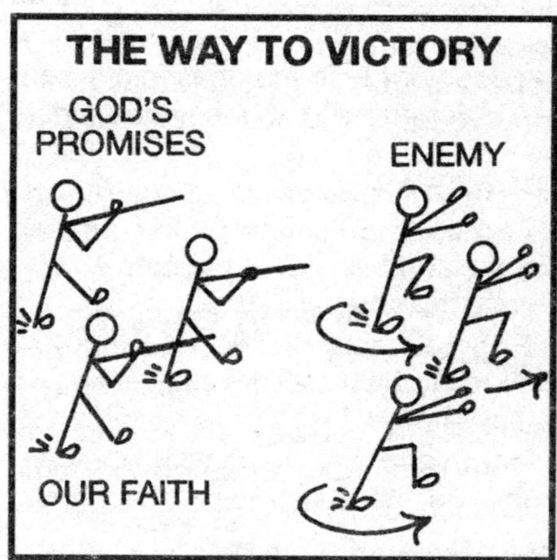

CONCLUDING THE LESSON

Leave the class with the assurance that we have a God who loves us so much that He wants us to have the victory every time. But when we disobey and stray from what He tells us to do, the journey in the wilderness gets longer and longer until we realize that we need to get back to God and obey Him. The sooner we learn to obey His "foolish" instructions, the sooner we will find ourselves on the victorious side. God will always keep instructing His children and waiting for their obedience.

Victory comes from the Lord our God. We dare not forget that every victory in our lives comes from His loving hands as a result of His love for us. Always choose to obey Him.

ANTICIPATING THE NEXT LESSON

Next week we explore how God responded to Israel's pleas for help because of the oppression they were suffering under Moab. God empowered Ehud to lead Israel in victory.

—A. Koshy Muthalaly.

PRACTICAL POINTS

1. You can consider God's promises as good as done (Josh. 6:2; cf. Num. 23:19).
2. Many of God's promises are conditioned on our obedience (Josh. 6:3-4).
3. The best evidence of trust in the Lord is obedience to the Lord (vss. 12-13).
4. Never grow weary in obeying the Lord, even in mundane things (Josh. 6:14; cf. Gal. 6:9).
5. Believe in God's promises, and encourage others to do the same (Josh. 6:15-16).
6. Keep your promises; our Judge is watching (vss. 17-19).
7. God's work done God's way will always be victorious (vs. 20).

—Don Kakavecos.

RESEARCH AND DISCUSSION

1. Why do you think God specifically mentioned the king and the mighty men of valor in His instructions to Joshua (Josh. 6:2-4)?
2. What do the actions of Joshua, the priests, and the armed men tell you about their view of God?
3. What temptations might they have faced as they continued to march around Jericho and then back to the camp for the six days?
4. How did Joshua's "pep talk" on the seventh day serve to encourage the people to obey God? What precautions did Joshua give them? Why were these important?

—Don Kakavecos.

ILLUSTRATED HIGH POINTS

The Lord hath given you (Josh. 6:16)

A Bible college professor pastored a small church in Jerusalem. As a Palestinian living in Israel and a Christian to boot, he faced much persecution. One of the most common forms of harassment came from Israeli soldiers. They often delayed him for hours.

Christ's command to love one's enemies seemed impossible. "Everything contributed to hate—the newspapers, television, neighbors, everything." Again and again, the professor tried to feel love and failed. As he confessed his inability to love others, he came to realize that New Testament love is not a feeling but a decision.

Reluctantly, he began to share the gospel message with the soldiers on the streets. He began to carry copies of a flyer that was written in Hebrew and English with a quotation from Isaiah 53. After several months of this, he became aware that the old feelings of hate and fear were gone.

It came to pass (vs. 20)

A Muslim girl in North Africa read a Christian tract and decided to become a believer. Her father was an emir (Islamic ruler); so she expected to lose her inheritance. But she was completely unprepared for the violence that erupted when she told her family. Her father exploded in rage. They threw her into the street naked. Shaking and tearful, she ran to a friend's house, where she was clothed and given shelter.

The girl could have easily thought she had made a terrible mistake, but God showed His protection and care.

Today this girl is in full-time evangelism.

—Ted Simonson.

Golden Text Illuminated

"It came to pass at the seventh time, when the priests blew with the trumpets, Joshua said unto the people, Shout; for the Lord hath given you the city" (Joshua 6:16).

The conquest of the city of Jericho by Joshua and the Israelites is one of the strangest military engagements on record. Faced with a fortified barrier to their advance into the Promised Land's interior, the Israelites did not bring up instruments of warfare such as battering rams, catapults, or incendiary arrows. They did not lay siege to the city or attempt a subterranean excavation. They did not even try any ruses, such as the Trojan horse the Greeks are said to have used.

What the Israelites did was simply march around the city once a day for six days and then seven times on the seventh day. Priests carried the ark of the covenant as they made each circuit. Seven priests marched in front of the ark and sounded trumpets made of ram's horns. After each march on the first six days was completed, everybody returned to camp.

Where did Joshua get this unorthodox and seemingly pointless strategy? The procedure, of course, had come directly from the Lord, who spelled it out for him in precise detail (Josh. 6:2-5). God did not provide a rationale for the plan or explain how it would work. Making it work was His prerogative; the responsibility of Joshua and the people was simply to take Him at His word and obey.

Thankfully, this is one instance in which the Israelites did obey fully and precisely. Once each day they followed the ark of the covenant one time around the city, the trumpets blowing, and then retired to camp. It was now the seventh day, and they had just completed their last of seven marches around the city, the trumpets sounding again for the final time. It was at this point that Joshua repeated the command of the Lord to raise a mighty shout (cf. vs. 5).

The reason for the shout was an exhilarating one: "The Lord hath given you the city." For a nation of wanderers and animal herders, the conquest of a formidable barrier was certainly cause for exultation. The loud roar of so many voices no doubt also served to melt the resolve of the enemy.

We stop, however, to note that even as Joshua made the bold declaration, the walls of Jericho were still standing firm, and the Israelites were still outside. They had not yet actually taken the city. What was he talking about?

Joshua and Israel were proceeding in faith. And since their confidence was backed by God's promise, their shout was a statement of certainty, to be latched onto in faith by the people and acted upon in exuberant obedience borne of that faith in the word of their all-powerful God. The enemy walls still stood before them, but they could believe Him and conquer or disbelieve and shrink back in defeat.

The Israelites' shout was to be an expression of their crisis-deciding faith. In obeying the order, they gave loud and united affirmation to the promise Joshua had just reiterated. We do not know what they shouted, but it had the impact of a mighty "Amen!" It was in response to that faith that God then moved and brought the walls of Jericho tumbling down.

—Kenneth A. Sponsler.

Heart of the Lesson

Jericho was the first and most formidable city in Canaan. It was the key to Israel's conquest of the land. What happened in this first military encounter would set the stage for that which would follow.

1. The Lord's battle plan (Josh. 6:2-4, 12-16). The Lord Himself presented the battle plan to Joshua. The strategy would not be left to a human military commander. Indeed, it was not one any military leader would endorse!

First, the Lord assured Joshua once again that He had given Jericho into Joshua's hand. The victory was already accomplished as far as God was concerned, but the strategy for the victory was unique.

The Lord's plan called for the armed men of Israel to march around the city once on each of six successive days. They would be accompanied by seven priests, each carrying a trumpet and walking before the ark of the covenant. On the seventh day, this army would march around the city seven times, and the priests would blow the trumpets. Strangely enough, this would bring the victory (vs. 5).

Surely this odd strategy would test Joshua's faith! At other times, he would be counted on to employ sound military strategy, but now he was being asked to do something that had no military significance. He was simply to trust the Lord to give the victory. This battle plan, however, would make it clear to both Israel and the Canaanites that the victory came from the Lord, not from Israel's might.

Sometimes we too need to be reminded that there really is no place for pride or complacency. All our victories come from the Lord. It is He, not us, who deserves the praise for them.

So at the outset of the conquest, Israel was challenged to trust God and follow His plan. At Joshua's instruction, the people followed that plan exactly, encompassing the city of Jericho once a day for six days and then seven times on the seventh day (vss. 12-16).

2. The Lord's final instructions (Josh. 6:17-19). Here we find Joshua relating to the people the Lord's instructions regarding the destruction of Jericho, which was assured (cf. vs. 16). With the exception of Rahab, who was to be protected, all the city was to be "accursed" (vs. 17). This meant that all that was in it belonged to the Lord and was not to be spared or taken for personal use. The gold, silver, bronze, and iron were to be put into the "treasury of the Lord" (vs. 19). Everything else was to be destroyed.

Jericho and its contents would belong solely to the Lord as the firstfruits of the land and a guarantee that He would give the entire land to Israel.

3. The Lord's victory (Josh. 6:20*a*). The city would belong to God just as the victory clearly belonged to God. When the priests blew the trumpets and the people shouted, the massive walls of Jericho collapsed, and the Israelites entered and took the city.

This supernatural victory over the mighty city told the people that indeed the Lord had given them the land. It was up to them to believe God's promise and act on it.

We should view the accomplishments in our lives as victories for the Lord. He has used a pathetic sinner for His glory!

—Jarl K. Waggoner.

World Missions

You may have heard the expression "He was a brick!" Few of us, however, know the origin and significance of it. The term "brick" implies all that is brave and loyal. Plutarch, in writing about the king of Sparta, tells how the phrase was coined.

"An ambassador on a diplomatic mission visited the famous city. Knowing that its strength was acclaimed throughout all of Greece, he had expected to see massive fortresses surrounding the town, but he found nothing of the kind. Surprised, he exclaimed to the ruler, 'Sir, you have no fortifications for defense. Why is this?'

"'Ah, but we are well protected,' he replied. 'Come with me tomorrow and I will show you the walls of Sparta.' The next day he led his guest to the plain where the army was drawn up in full battle array. Pointing proudly to his soldiers who stood fearlessly in place, he said, 'Behold the walls of Sparta—10,000 men and every man 'a brick'!" (www.elbourne.org).

Joshua led an army made up of "men of war" (Josh. 6:3) to overcome and capture the city of Jericho, which thought that it was protected by a wall of bricks and mortar. The real bricks in this historical episode, though, were Joshua, his mighty men of valor, and the accompanying priests, who carried the ark of the covenant and blew trumpets. God used this unique and fearless band of warriors to grant a magnificent victory for His people.

Second Corinthians 2:14-16 reveals the biblical principle that God always causes His evangelistic ministers to "triumph in Christ." This triumph is seen not only when people are being saved but also when the Lord's enemies are defeated. In every instance and among all peoples of the world, Christ is triumphant.

"The history of the efforts of missionaries in Tahiti is a most wonderful one. For fifteen years there was not a convert. The London Missionary Society seriously debated recalling their missionaries and giving their efforts to some other fields. After an earnest debate, it was decided to continue the work and letters were sent to the missionaries telling them of the decision.

"Now, notice a wonderful fact: A vessel sailed from London for Tahiti and at the same time a vessel sailed from Tahiti for London, and they passed each other in mid-ocean, one containing letters to the missionaries telling them to go on notwithstanding the fruitless character of their labors, and the other letters from the missionaries to the Society in London saying that a great revival had spread over Tahiti, that the idol temples were destroyed and that the idol gods were surrendered, and those gods were on that vessel on their way to London where they are now to be seen in the Missionary Society museum" (www.elbourne. org).

Paul Rader (1878–1938) was an evangelist who pastored Moody church in Chicago, Illinois. Mr. Rader also served as president of The Christian and Missionary Alliance. A pioneer in Christian broadcasting, Mr. Rader wrote many gospel hymns, one of which is titled "The Victory."

No more need fear, and no more need doubting,
No more need pride control in my life.
I may be free from all condemnation,
I can have victory now in the strife.
I take the life of victory,
Not I, but Christ Himself in me;
He conquers now, He sets me free;
I take, He gives—the victory.

—*Thomas R. Chmura.*

The Jewish Aspect

Part of the wider context for this week's lesson includes Joshua 5:13-15, which introduces a unique figure who had been playing a role since the early chapters of Genesis. This unique individual is, in fact, God Himself. In virtually every context in which He appears, He is referred to as both the Angel of Jehovah and Jehovah Himself. There are many examples that show this.

In Genesis 16:7-14 there are four references to the Angel of Jehovah (vss. 7, 9, 10, 11), but then in verse 13 the reference is to Jehovah Himself. In 22:9-16 He is called the Angel of Jehovah twice (vss. 11, 15); but in verse 12 He is referred to as God, and in verse 16 He is called Jehovah. In 31:11 the reference is literally to "the angel of God"; but when He speaks in verse 13, He says, "I am the God of Beth-el."

Genesis 32:24-30 is the well-known passage that describes Jacob wrestling with the Angel of Jehovah. Verse 28 can be translated, "You have striven with God." After this, in verse 30, Jacob declares, "I have seen God face to face." The Angel that he wrestled with is recognized to be God Himself. Hosea 12:3-5 also identifies this Angel as God Himself. In Exodus 3:2 it is the Angel of Jehovah who is in the burning bush, but verse 4 says, "God called unto him out of the midst of the bush."

In Judges 2:1 the Angel of Jehovah claims to be responsible for the Exodus and for making the covenant with Israel. A comparison with Exodus 19:4 clearly shows that it was God Himself who was responsible for both these things; the two Persons are synonymous.

Four times in Judges 6:11-24 He is called the Angel of the Lord or Angel of God (vss. 11, 12, 20, 21), and four times He is Jehovah Himself (vss. 14, 16, 22, 23). Nine times in 13:2-24 He is referred to as the Angel of Jehovah (vss. 3, 9, 13, 15, 16, 17, 18, 20, 21), but in verse 22 He is said to be God Himself. Note also in verse 18 that this Angel's name is "secret," or, literally, "Wonderful." In Isaiah 9:6, the same Hebrew word, *pele*, is used. It is used only of God, never of man or an angel. The very fact that He claimed this name for Himself shows that He was not a common angel but God Himself.

In Isaiah 42:8 God says of Himself, "I am the Lord: that is my name: and my glory will I not give to another." When we compare this statement with Exodus 23:21, we are better able to understand the unique nature of the Angel of Jehovah. In Exodus 23:20-23, God is speaking. In verse 20, God says that this Angel will lead the people of Israel throughout the Exodus until they come into the land. This is consistent with Judges 2:1. In Exodus 23:21, several commands are given. Israel is commanded to be obedient to this Angel and not provoke Him to anger. This Angel commands the people's absolute obedience. Why? It is because the Lord says, "My name is in him."

This Angel is very special for several reasons. We are told, "He will not pardon your transgressions" (Ex. 23:21), meaning He has the power to forgive sins—a prerogative only God has. "My name is in him" refers to the name YHWH, a name given only to Members of the Godhead. There are blessings for obeying Him (vs. 22), and He is the Angel of the Exodus (vs. 23).

Isaiah 63:7-14 describes Him as the Angel of God's presence. He is, in fact, the Second Person of the Trinity.

—*Arnold G. Fruchtenbaum.*

Guiding the Superintendent

Too often people unthinkingly refuse to honor God as He deserves. If the admonition of Christ to His disciples to realize they could do nothing without Him is kept in mind, victories along the way will be properly seen as God's work and not man's. This week's lesson examines the victory of God in the fall of the city of Jericho.

DEVOTIONAL OUTLINE

1. The sovereign gift (Josh. 6:2-4). Before the siege of Jericho by the Israelites, it was announced by the Lord that the city would be theirs. The outcome was certain. It was accomplished. It was a gift. God had determined to take it from the current tenants and give it to His people. It was to be the beginning of the fulfillment of the promise made centuries earlier to Abraham, Isaac, and Jacob. The king of Jericho and his once-mighty army would be no match for the army of Israel and its King, the Lord.

What a magnificent truth to hang on to! The child of God does not go through life alone. He goes with the King of kings and the Lord of lords. What God promises, God will deliver.

Joshua was then told what the people needed to do to receive the gift. The gift was theirs, but they needed to take it. Much like the gift of salvation, it needed to be appropriated.

2. The seven days (Josh. 6:12-16). There were precise directions the Israelites needed to follow if they were to receive the gift God had for them. They could not do as they pleased, but as it pleased God. Just as no one can come to the Lord apart from the prescribed way, so Israel had to follow God's guidelines to receive the gift.

Like a modern-day parade, there was a particular order for the priests, the armed men, and the ark of God. They were to circle the city once for six days, but on the seventh day they were to march around the walled city seven times. Then, with trumpets blaring and people shouting, the city would be theirs. It would be a gift from God.

3. A strict word of caution (Josh. 6:17-20*a*). God was to give them the city. The only survivors were to be Rahab and her family because of her kindness to the two spies and hence to Israel. Placed off limits were the spoils of battle. Typically, a conquering army would harvest things of value, but God at first strictly prohibited this. In later instances, Israel would be able to keep what they wanted—but not in this case. Jericho was, in a sense, the firstfruits of war, and the firstfruits belong to God.

Today one might think of the practice of tithing or offering gifts to God. The first to receive of our income should be the Lord.

After receiving instructions from Joshua, the people followed the daily routine. On the seventh day, they received Jericho for their faithfulness.

AGE-GROUP EMPHASES

Children: Lead children to know that the Word of God is given for their well-being and blessing.

Youths: Guide the young people to understand that although God's Word might sometimes seem overly strict and confining, God puts off limits only those things that would be harmful and wrong in His sight.

Adults: Lead your adults to see the hand of God in their everyday lives and that He is the one who brings about victories and success. The glory always belongs to God, for without Him we can do nothing.

—Darrell W. McKay.

Scripture Lesson Text

JUDG. 3:15 But when the children of Israel cried unto the LORD, the LORD raised them up a deliverer, Ehud the son of Gera, a Benjamite, a man lefthanded: and by him the children of Israel sent a present unto Eglon the king of Moab.

16 But Ehud made him a dagger which had two edges, of a cubit length; and he did gird it under his raiment upon his right thigh.

17 And he brought the present unto Eglon king of Moab: and Eglon *was* a very fat man.

18 And when he had made an end to offer the present, he sent away the people that bare the present.

19 But he himself turned again from the quarries that *were* by Gilgal, and said, I have a secret errand unto thee, O king: who said, Keep silence. And all that stood by him went out from him.

20 And Ehud came unto him; and he was sitting in a summer parlour, which he had for himself alone. And Ehud said, I have a message from God unto thee. And he arose out of *his* seat.

21 And Ehud put forth his left hand, and took the dagger from his right thigh, and thrust it into his belly:

22 And the haft also went in after the blade; and the fat closed upon the blade, so that he could not draw the dagger out of his belly; and the dirt came out.

23 Then Ehud went forth through the porch, and shut the doors of the parlour upon him, and locked them.

24 When he was gone out, his servants came; and when they saw that, behold, the doors of the parlour *were* locked, they said, Surely he covereth his feet in his summer chamber.

25 And they tarried till they were ashamed: and, behold, he opened not the doors of the parlour; therefore they took a key, and opened *them:* and, behold, their lord *was* fallen down dead on the earth.

29 And they slew of Moab at that time about ten thousand men, all lusty, and all men of valour; and there escaped not a man.

30 So Moab was subdued that day under the hand of Israel. And the land had rest fourscore years.

NOTES

Ehud Frees Israel

Lesson Text: Judges 3:15-25, 29-30

Related Scriptures: Exodus 2:23-25; 3:7-9; 17:8-15; Deuteronomy 25:17-19

TIME: 1316 B.C. PLACES: near Gilgal; Jordan River Valley and Moab

---

GOLDEN TEXT—"When the children of Israel cried unto the Lord, the Lord raised them up a deliverer, Ehud the son of Gera, a Benjamite" (Judges 3:15).

Introduction

History seems to go in cycles. It is often said that the one thing man learns from history is that he does not learn from history. When we look at the various empires, kingdoms, and powerful nations in world history, it soon becomes clear that each one followed a pattern that eventually led to its destruction. Today we see once strong and prosperous nations following the same course.

The Bible says, "Whatsoever a man soweth, that shall he also reap" (Gal. 6:7). The same is true of nations.

The biblical principle is clear, and history abundantly confirms it. Without repentance and spiritual awakening, countries will fall by the wayside of history—all because they have not learned from history.

The children of Israel did not learn from history, either. Despite glorious victory (see previous lesson) and ignominious defeat due to sin (see next lesson), they continued to fall into sin and idolatry, leading to harsh servitude. But God remained faithful.

LESSON OUTLINE

- I. **GOD'S PROVISION—Judg. 3:15-19**
- II. **EHUD'S ACTIONS—Judg. 3:20-25**
- III. **ISRAEL'S VICTORY—Judg. 3:29-30**

Exposition: Verse by Verse

GOD'S PROVISION

JUDG. 3:15 But when the children of Israel cried unto the LORD, the LORD raised them up a deliverer, Ehud the son of Gera, a Benjamite, a man lefthanded: and by him the children of Israel sent a present unto Eglon the king of Moab.

16 But Ehud made him a dagger which had two edges, of a cubit length; and he did gird it under his raiment upon his right thigh.

17 And he brought the present unto Eglon king of Moab: and Eglon was a very fat man.

18 And when he had made an end to offer the present, he sent away the people that bare the present.

19 But he himself turned again from the quarries that were by Gilgal, and said, I have a secret errand unto thee, O king: who said, Keep silence. And all that stood by him went out from him.

A deliverer (Judg. 3:15). {After forty years of peace, Israel turned again to sinful living, and God gave them over to Eglon, the king of Moab (vss. 11-12).}[Q1] The king allied himself with the nations of Ammon and Amalek, conquered Israel, and took possession of Jericho, "the city of palm trees" (vs. 13), where he could have a stronghold. For eighteen years (probably very long years to the Israelites), Moab remained dominant over Israel (vs. 14). Finally, out of desperation, the children of Israel cried out to God for help.

Is it not strange that so many people have to become desperate before they will cry out to God for help? In the law He gave to Moses, God gave detailed instructions and warnings about being obedient to Him (cf. Lev. 26; Deut. 28). Why is it that people will not take God at His word and stay right with Him? Why does human nature interfere and lead them to sin, even when they know better? The result, of course, is often God's chastening. When this occurs, many of those same people blame God for their circumstances.

{God deliberately raised up just the right person to lead Israel out from under the domination of the Moabites. His name was Ehud, the son of Gera.}[Q2] He was from the tribe of Benjamin, which was located just north of Judah. He was left-handed—an important detail in the development of this deliverance. Ehud, along with the other judges, was no ordinary person but someone God had specially chosen to bring about Israel's deliverance.

Ehud was also respected as a leader of his tribe. It was his task to deliver the annual tribute that Eglon had imposed on Israel. In order to appease the king, it was necessary that someone important in the subdued nation deliver this tribute. This made the king feel more important. His ego was stroked when an official of the other nation had to be so humbled.

A dagger (Judg. 3:16-17). {The tribe of Benjamin was known for having left-handed people, of which Ehud was one (20:16).}[Q3] At a later point in Benjamin's history, we are told there were seven hundred chosen military men who were left-handed (20:16). In David's day, we are told, "These are they that came to David to Ziklag, while he yet kept himself close because of Saul the son of Kish: and they were among the mighty men, helpers of the war. They . . . could use both the right hand and the left in hurling stones and shooting arrows out of a bow, even of Saul's brethren of Benjamin" (I Chr. 12:1-2).

Obviously, Ehud was courageous, like his fellow Benjamite warriors. So when he sensed God's call to deliver Israel from the Moabites, {he immediately began to prepare by making a special dagger. It was double-edged and about eighteen inches long (one cubit).}[Q4] It was short enough, therefore, to be hidden under his clothing.

Ehud strapped the dagger to his right leg, thus making it easy to quickly draw it with the left hand. Since most people were right-handed, such a dagger normally would be strapped to the left leg. The movement of his left hand would not be as suspect, giving him an advantage. What he planned to do would need to be quick and quiet. With this preparation completed, Ehud traveled to Jericho with the annual tribute, which was given to assure Eglon of another year of submissive compliance. {The author added the detail that Eglon was a very fat man.}Q5 This parenthetical thought will be significant in the outcome of the incident, as we are about to see.

A delivery (Judg. 3:18-19). It is possible that the tribute required by Eglon was more than just money. Several men accompanied Ehud in delivering the tribute; so he apparently needed assistance. It might have been silver or gold or perhaps even animals or wool. His companions perhaps carried the tribute for him.

After it had been presented, Ehud and his companions left Eglon's presence and began the journey home. At a certain point, however, Ehud sent his companions on while he turned back. They had already traveled some distance, for it was at the stone quarries at Gilgal that {Ehud sent his companions on their way as he turned back to return to King Eglon.}Q6 There is not complete agreement among Bible scholars as to the identification of this place. The word for "quarries" in verse 19 could refer to graven images and no doubt was a well-known place in Ehud's day. Some have suggested it might be a reference to the pile of stones Joshua made after Israel crossed over the Jordan River (Josh. 4:19-24).

{When Ehud was again in the presence of King Eglon, he stated that he had a secret message for him.}Q7 The Hebrew word is quite ambiguous and could imply a number of different things. Ehud might well have used this word on purpose so as not to give Eglon any clues about what he meant. It had its desired effect, because Eglon immediately commanded him to stay silent and not reveal his message while other people were in the vicinity. If it was secret, he did not want it revealed while others could hear.

Everyone then left the room, evidently at Eglon's command. This left nobody there except the king and Ehud, which was exactly the way Ehud wanted it.

EHUD'S ACTIONS

20 And Ehud came unto him; and he was sitting in a summer parlour, which he had for himself alone. And Ehud said, I have a message from God unto thee. And he arose out of his seat.

21 And Ehud put forth his left hand, and took the dagger from his right thigh, and thrust it into his belly:

22 And the haft also went in after the blade; and the fat closed upon the blade, so that he could not draw the dagger out of his belly; and the dirt came out.

23 Then Ehud went forth through the porch, and shut the doors of the parlour upon him, and locked them.

24 When he was gone out, his servants came; and when they saw that, behold, the doors of the parlour were locked, they said, Surely he covereth his feet in his summer chamber.

25 And they tarried till they were ashamed: and, behold, he opened not the doors of the parlour; therefore they took a key, and opened them: and, behold, their lord was fallen down dead on the earth.

A message from God (Judg. 3:20-21). Eglon is described as "sitting in a summer parlour, which he had for himself alone." It was common in Old Testament days for people to have a special room with latticed windows on the roof of the house. This was the coolest place available during hot weather. We get the impression that this was where Eglon was because the word for "summer," *megerah,* means "a cooling off," and the word for "parlour," *aliyah,* refers to something lofty. Thus, it was a lofty place for cooling off. It was evidently a private chamber exclusively for the king's use.

With nobody else present, Ehud stated that he had a message from God for King Eglon. Upon hearing this, the king rose to his feet. We are not told in the text why he stood up. Perhaps it was out of reverence for the God who was sending him a message, or perhaps he sensed a threatening tone in Ehud's voice. He might have felt more vulnerable while he was seated and rose to have a better opportunity to defend himself if there was indeed a threat.

As Eglon stood up, Ehud quickly reached with his left hand to his right thigh, pulled out the dagger, and thrust it into the king's belly. No doubt it was a lightning-fast movement that left the king without any opportunity to defend himself.

Ehud was obviously a courageous man who was willing to take whatever risk might be involved in such an action. He had it well planned, however, and successfully carried out his plan.

An escape from the king (Judg. 3:22-23). There was no time for the king to cry out in alarm; perhaps the unexpected movement coming from the left hand left him completely unaware of what was happening until it was too late. Ehud plunged the dagger into the king's midsection so far that even the handle disappeared into the fat, which then closed around it. Since time was of the essence and Ehud would not want to be seen with blood on his clothes or body, he simply left the dagger in place and fled. If he had anticipated fighting his way out of the palace, he would now be unable to use his dagger to do so.

In the meantime, Ehud's thrust was so effective that Eglon's bowels eliminated, which appears to be the meaning of the Hebrew words used here. Ehud had thrust with all the force he could muster because he knew he would have only one opportunity to accomplish his mission of deliverance. {He left the upper room and locked the doors behind him.}[Q8]

"The first thought to notice regarding Ehud is . . . he was a courageous man. He often has been criticized for his manner of delivering Israel from Eglon . . . but at least one must see him as highly courageous. He did not know, as he returned alone to Eglon's palace that day, how his plan would work out. He had a plan, and, if all went well, the end would be accomplished without harm to himself. But at so many points things could go wrong" (Wood, *Distressing Days of the Judges,* Zondervan).

We understand, of course, that since Ehud was performing God's work, he was under God's protection. It was God, after all, who had chosen him to bring about deliverance for Israel from the Moabites. Whenever we do God's work in God's ways, we will be both guided and protected as we endeavor to fulfill His will.

Discovery of the master (Judg. 3:24-25). It is possible that the king's servants saw Ehud leave, since they evidently decided the private interview was over and went to attend to the king again. However, they were surprised to find the doors locked. Rather than be disruptive, they retreated to give him time for what they thought he was doing. The phrase "he covereth his feet" is a euphemism for relieving himself. {They decided he was indisposed at the moment and did not pursue getting into the room.}[Q9]

Eglon's servants waited a good while for the king to unlock and open his door. Finally, so much time had passed that they became uneasy to the point of embarrassment. They were, after all, the king's servants who must always be ready to serve their king. It finally dawned on them that there must be something wrong; so they acted.

Since it would certainly be improper to intrude on the king under normal circumstances, we can understand their delay.

They finally got a key to the room and unlocked the door and found their master lying there dead. Three times in verses 24 and 25 we read the word "behold," and each time it is an expression of surprise. First, "Behold, the doors of the parlour were locked." (That was unusual!) Second, "Behold, he opened not the doors of the parlour." (What could possibly be going on this long?) Third, "Behold, their lord was fallen down dead on the earth." (How did this happen, and what should they do now?)

ISRAEL'S VICTORY

29 And they slew of Moab at that time about ten thousand men, all lusty, and all men of valour; and there escaped not a man.

30 So Moab was subdued that day under the hand of Israel. And the land had rest fourscore years.

The delay of Eglon's servants allowed Ehud to escape. He passed the place where he had turned back and went on to Seirath (vs. 26). This place has not been identified, but it was located somewhere in Ephraim. From there he blew a trumpet and rallied troops to join him (vs. 27). He then challenged them to follow him, for the Lord was going to defeat the Moabites and free His people from them (vs. 28).

This was a strong statement of faith on his part, but he could make it because he was confident he was fulfilling God's plan. Everything he had done so far had succeeded in spite of the risks he had taken, and that seemed to give him further confidence that God was behind it all. {The people of Israel sensed his confidence and responded to his challenge immediately. They gathered behind Ehud's leadership, seized the fords of the Jordan River that led back to Moab, and stopped the Moabites from returning home.}[Q10]

Under Ehud's leadership, the Israelites killed ten thousand Moabites. All of them were described as being among the strongest and most elite of Moab's forces. They were all "men of valour" (vs. 29). Israel did not just gain a momentary victory that day; the tables were turned, and the Israelites became dominant over the Moabites. "Moab was subdued that day under the hand of Israel" (vs. 30), and Israel enjoyed eighty years of peace. What an example this is of the way the Lord works on behalf of His children when they sincerely cry out to Him and obey Him by faith!

—Keith E. Eggert.

QUESTIONS

1. Which nation and king did God turn Israel over to when she sinned this time?
2. When Israel cried out to God, what man did He raise up to deliver the people from their enemies?
3. What physical trait did Ehud have that was prevalent in his native tribe?
4. What did Ehud make to assist him in his plot against Eglon?
5. What physical characteristic of Eglon is mentioned?
6. What did Ehud do after presenting the annual tribute to Eglon?
7. How did Ehud get everyone but the king out of the room?
8. How did Ehud escape?
9. Why did it take Eglon's servants so long to discover that he was dead?
10. How did Ehud bring about a great victory over Moab for Israel?

—Keith E. Eggert.

Preparing to Teach the Lesson

Have you ever wondered how you would handle a particularly difficult situation? This week we look at how God's people were given a deliverer who worked in God's strength to deliver them.

TODAY'S AIM

Facts: to show how Ehud delivered the people of Israel from the Moabites using the strength God gave him.

Principle: to show that God cares for His people and delivers them through leaders who act in His strength.

Application: to establish that God provides the leaders we need as well as the strength those leaders need to help us.

INTRODUCING THE LESSON

Life has its ups and downs. For some people it is mostly down, and it stays there for a long time. But what we see in Scripture is a God who loves His people; when we need help, God is always there to provide what we need, showing us His mercy and grace. God is a truly gracious God who arranges for our deliverance even before we come to our crisis point. Thus, He is ready with a solution whenever we need it. He shows His concern for us by waiting patiently and preparing to meet our need.

DEVELOPING THE LESSON

1. Ehud, a new deliverer for Israel (Judg. 3:15-18). After living in subservience to Eglon, the pagan king of Moab, for eighteen long years, the people of Israel were at their breaking point. They cried out to God, and God sent Ehud to them. Ehud became Israel's judge for that time of crisis. We must realize that each of the judges God sent to Israel was sent to deal with a specific crisis. Each one then governed for a time, but none set up a permanent dynasty or rule.

We are not told much about Ehud aside from a few specific details. He was the son of Gera of the tribe of Benjamin. He was also left-handed and secretly hid a dagger under his clothing. Ehud was specifically chosen to deliver the tax money to the overweight Moabite king. Ask the class what they would look for in a person if they had to choose their rescuer. Does what we know of Ehud fit their description? We often find that when God chooses a deliverer, the person does not fit our idea of what a deliverer should be.

2. Swift victory through God's strength (Judg. 3:19-25). If the encounter between Ehud and Eglon almost seems like a setup, that is exactly what it was. When God gets involved, the enemy will be defeated. His methods are sometimes very unconventional. Help the class get the point that when we are on the side of God, we cannot fail, no matter how difficult the endeavor.

Ehud enticed Eglon with the intriguing declaration that he had a secret message from God for him. When he was alone with the king, Ehud pulled out the dagger he had hidden and plunged it into the fat of Eglon's belly. Ehud then made his escape. When the king's servants finally came in after a long delay, they found the king dead. Allow the class to comment on Ehud's bold yet grisly act. They may ask, "How can God allow such cruel killing, even if it is the enemy?"

It is important to help the students understand that God acts decisively on behalf of His oppressed people and against those who torment them. We see this especially in the Old Testament. How He related to Israel is a pattern for how He deals with us. Anyone who came against His people was defeated (except, of course, when God was disciplining His people to teach them a lesson).

The idea of a deliverer, it must be remembered, was familiar to all the Israelites. It was part of their history, and they were always looking for the Messiah, the ultimate Deliverer, to come. This was ingrained in their thinking. So when Ehud came along and delivered them, this should not have been a surprise to them. They had seen God act this way before, providing His strength on behalf of His people.

3. Lasting peace through God's strength (Judg. 3:29-30). The deliverer, Ehud, then called Israel's army together and attacked the Moabites. Ten thousand of the strongest Moabite soldiers were killed at one time. The people of Israel now had peace. The Scripture passage also tells us that this time of peace lasted for eighty years.

Note that the Israelites' time of bondage under Moabite domination was eighteen years (vs. 14). When the deliverer came from God, their peace from God, through the deliverer, lasted eighty long years. Help your students understand that true peace comes when we follow God's leading and do what He wants us to do and when we follow the leaders He has appointed for us.

When we face crises in our own lives, God may raise up special people to help us. They are His agents of deliverance for our particular need at that time, just as Ehud was for Israel during the Moabite oppression.

Encourage the class members to share about times they had particular needs and God sent special people to meet those needs, perhaps in the most unlikely manner. Such people were God's deliverers for them. This scenario is repeated over and over again in the Bible, especially in the life of Israel in the Old Testament. Such events give us assurance of God's continual working on our behalf.

ILLUSTRATING THE LESSON

When there is a need among God's people, God sends a deliverer to match that need with His strength.

CONCLUDING THE LESSON

Leave the class with the assurance that God will always work on behalf of His people, so we should heartily obey Him and follow His rules. He is committed to helping us. Sometimes He sends us deliverers to match our needs at a specific time. Help the students understand that God planned to put these deliverers in place long before we begin encountering the crisis. That is how much He loves us.

ANTICIPATING THE NEXT LESSON

In our lesson next week, we will explore how God empowered Gideon. We must let Him do His work according to His plan. It is very important that we know that He is sovereign in all things.

—A. Koshy Muthalaly.

PRACTICAL POINTS

1. In His mercy, God answers the cries of His children at just the right time (Judg. 3:15).
2. God's empowerment does not preclude our proper preparation (vss. 16-17).
3. It is not wise to let curiosity override sound judgment (vss. 18-19).
4. God's message to man is not always a positive one (vss. 20-22).
5. The wise person plans ahead (Judg. 3:23; cf. Prov. 20:18).
6. God rules over the choices of even unrighteous people (Judg. 3:24- 25; cf. Dan. 4:34-35).
7. With God, nothing is impossible (Judg. 3:29-30).

—Don Kakavecos.

RESEARCH AND DISCUSSION

1. How might God's use of Ehud encourage you to believe that God can use you and your uniqueness to serve Him (cf. Ex. 4:11-12)?
2. What does the example of Ehud suggest about the balance between the empowerment of God and the preparation of man to accomplish God's work (cf. Eph. 6:10-20; II Tim. 3:16-17)? What happens if a person fails to plan (cf. Prov. 20:18)?
3. Is God's message to man always a positive one (cf. Jer. 9:23-25)? Why or why not?
4. How does understanding the sovereignty of God over all people help you to face the difficulties that surround you (cf. Jer. 32:17, 27; II Cor. 10:13; I Pet. 5:10-11)?

—Don Kakavecos.

ILLUSTRATED HIGH POINTS

From God (Judg. 3:20)

The coming of electricity made a big difference—daylight and dark, hot and cold, clean and dirty, work and leisure. But some clung to rug beaters, human-powered sewing machines, cellars, and kerosene lamps out of sheer habit.

There were people then who were suspicious. They ignored the simple arrangements that would have enabled them to enter the kingdom of electricity. They did not want to change. Some thought they could not afford it.

The Israelites had been living in sin and without God's power or blessing. But through God's leading, Ehud tapped into the power of God.

Moab was subdued (vs. 30)

A Chinese Christian leader named Zhang (not his real name) was attending a training course for a house church network when he and the other leaders present were arrested, had their heads shaved, and were interrogated. When they were taken to a prison cell, they faced fifteen other inmates they did not know. The cell leader asked, "Why are you here?"

"Because we are Christians," Zhang replied.

"You do not beat people up?"

"No," Zhang assured him.

The leader then asked to hear the gospel. Later, worship services were scheduled by the prisoners. The Communists were frustrated. Before Zhang and his friends had finished their term in that prison, several of their cellmates had come to the Lord.

Like Zhang, Ehud seemed to be at a terrible disadvantage, but God empowered him to help Israel subdue Moab.

—Ted Simonson.

Golden Text Illuminated

"When the children of Israel cried unto the Lord, the Lord raised them up a deliverer, Ehud the son of Gera, a Benjamite" (Judges 3:15).

In our lesson last week, we saw how God moved mightily on behalf of Israel, giving them success when they obeyed His instructions. This week, we are joining Israel after the time of Joshua and his generation. They were called upon to continue fighting to take the land that God had promised, and they were to uphold His law in their midst (Josh. 23).

However, this new generation faltered. They had not been eyewitnesses to what God had done for Israel (Judg. 2:10), and they deserted the Lord (vs. 11). A cycle of unfaithfulness, foreign oppression, deliverance, and then temporary peace began that was not ever fully overcome in Israel's history. This week's golden text highlights one of the deliverers that God sent to His people, a judge named Ehud.

The Moabites, Ammonites, and Amalekites (3:12-13) were the oppressors in the time of Ehud. Israel had previously defeated the Amalekites in their journey toward the Promised Land (Ex. 17:8-16). God had told Israel to leave the Moabites and Ammonites alone because He had given them their land (Deut. 2:9, 19). Now God was using these nations to discipline Israel (cf. Judg. 2:14-15, 22-23).

The Moabites may have gradually increased the severity of their oppression of Israel, and after eighteen years, Israel had come to the end of themselves (3:14). When Israel could no longer take the oppression, "the children of Israel cried unto the Lord" (vs. 15). They admitted that they had rebelled against their God and called to Him to help them.

As soon as they did, God, being ever faithful, "raised them up a deliverer, Ehud the son of Gera." So who was this deliverer that God had chosen?

The golden text tells us that Ehud was of the tribe of Benjamin. Flip to the map section in your Bible, or grab a book of Bible maps, and you will see that the land allotted to Benjamin would be the first that Moab would encounter if they entered Israel by crossing the Jordan River just above the northern end of the Dead Sea. So the Benjamites may have been feeling the weight of their oppressors more than other tribes.

Beyond the golden text, verse 15 also reveals that Ehud was left-handed. This is somewhat ironic since the name Benjamin means "son of the right hand." Life can be hard for a left-handed person. Tools and equipment tend to be made for those who are right-handed. Even some languages reflect a negative connotation for being left-handed. (Left is *sinister* in Latin.) However, this apparently was a common attribute among the tribe of Benjamin (cf. 20:16). Being left-handed somehow threw the Moabites off their guard and gave Ehud an advantage.

Thus Ehud was selected to take Israel's tribute to King Eglon. This was not a task for someone of little importance. As a means of further humiliation, it was often required that someone of importance from the subjugated people bring the required tribute.

Ehud was God's chosen deliverer, and he was obedient to his call.

—*Kelly Hawver.*

Heart of the Lesson

The first of the judges was Othniel, who delivered Israel from Mesopotamian domination. As a result of his work, Israel enjoyed forty years of tranquillity (Judg. 3:8-11). Soon, however, Israel returned to their wicked ways and "did evil again in the sight of the Lord" (vs. 12). The Lord responded by sending the king of Moab against them.

Moab, which lay east of the Jordan River, was joined by the Ammonites and Amalekites. Together they inflicted defeats upon the Israelites and took possession of Jericho, "the city of palm trees" (vs. 13). The cruel Moabite oppression continued for eighteen years (vs. 14).

1. A God who hears (Judg. 3:15). Finally, the oppressed people of Israel cried out to the Lord for deliverance, and immediately the Lord responded mercifully. He raised up a man of the tribe of Benjamin named Ehud. Like an unusual number of Benjamites, Ehud was left-handed (cf. 20:14-16). Ehud was selected to take to Eglon, the king of Moab, a "present" (3:15), probably Israel's yearly tribute paid to their Moabite overlords.

2. A man to lead (Judg. 3:16-25). Ehud not only was selected by Israel to deliver this gift; he also was selected by God for another task—to deliver His people. Ehud did not lead an army at this time, but he had a plan that God would providentially use.

Ehud "made him a dagger" (vs. 16) and strapped it to his right thigh under his clothing. Both his clothing and the fact that it was on his right side served to conceal the weapon, for a right-handed man would have his weapon on the opposite side.

Ehud delivered the gift to King Eglon but then indicated he wanted to talk to him privately. Once alone with the king, Ehud announced he had "a message from God" (vs. 20) for him. He delivered that message in the form of a dagger thrust into the king's belly (vs. 21)! Ehud then left unnoticed, leaving the dead king behind locked doors. The king's body was not found for some time, allowing Ehud to escape to the territory of Ephraim.

3. A nation to follow (Judg. 3:29-30). Once he was safely away, Ehud "blew a trumpet in the mountain of Ephraim" (vs. 27), calling his people to arms. With the king of Moab dead and with a bold leader to follow, the people rallied to Ehud. The judge led his people in a great victory over the Moabites, striking down some ten thousand of the enemy (vs. 29). As a result, Israel was freed from Moabite domination and enjoyed an eighty-year period of rest (vs. 30).

The account of Ehud's judgment reminds us of the vital importance of bold leadership. As a result of his singular act of bravery, the nation rallied around him and gained their freedom. Often God's people are ready to do what they need to do, but they are waiting for someone to lead them. You may be that leader people are waiting for. Do not hesitate to act boldly when you know the right thing to do.

There is no indication the Israelites heartily repented and changed their ways, however. This reminds us that people need more than a person to follow. The truly godly leader will continually point people to the Lord.

—Jarl K. Waggoner.

World Missions

The biblical account of the killing of Eglon, king of Moab, by Ehud, a judge of Israel, may bring to mind the complex and often volatile relationship between government and the gospel. Does Moab's oppression of Israel correlate with Christian persecution today?

Prior to this week's lesson text, the Bible revealed that God's people "served Eglon the king of Moab eighteen years" (Judg. 3:14). When God's people "cried unto the Lord" (vs. 15), which was a sign of personal and national repentance, God raised up a spiritual deliverer who eliminated the political leader that epitomized and personalized the spiritual oppression that dominated God's people.

When we think about state-sponsored persecution against Christians today, we should remember what the New Testament says about it. First, it is crucial to remember that God's people should submit to civil governing authorities, because those authorities have been appointed by God (cf. Rom. 13:1-7; I Pet. 2:13-14). These scriptural admonitions, however, do not suggest that Christians should sheepishly yield to the ungodly stratagems of persecutors who try to stop the spread of the gospel. Both the apostles Peter and Paul who wrote those admonitions defied the demands of authorities who opposed the gospel (Acts 4:18-20; 17:7). Believers are obligated to actively work against people and policies that contradict God's demands; and yet, in all other things, Christians should honor and obey the authorities God has put in place.

Second, the Bible teaches that God's people should engage in the spiritual discipline of prayer for "kings, and for all that are in authority; that we may lead a quiet and peaceable life in all godliness and honesty" (I Tim. 2:2). God is pleased when His people obey this command, which has a unique evangelistic purpose.

Admittedly, it is not a simple matter to always know how to proceed in seasons when civil governing authorities determine to oppose God's Word and His people who live their lives according to godly principles. Take the situation in India, for instance, where extremist Hindus call for physical violence—even beheading—against any Hindus who convert to Christianity. Open Doors reported an all-too-common incident that happened on October 3, 2021: "More than 10 Christians at a prayer gathering were arrested in Uttarakhand state. Just before the meeting started, a mob of almost 300 people descended on the church in Roorkee, destroying properties and beating up church members" (https://www.opendoorsusa.org/).

Many believers in India are prevented by local authorities from getting even essential food and water. It is important to recognize, therefore, that expecting Jesus' followers to simply obey such authority unquestioningly is implausible.

Such quandaries should lead Christians to ponder what actions would honor God most. Ehud was directed by God to assassinate a king who was oppressing God's people. This does not, however provide a pattern for responding to persecution. Much prayer and faith are essential for any believer to respond to opposition in a godly manner.

As believers continue to submit to and pray for civil authorities, let us also embrace and trust in our sovereign God, knowing that He will one day fully avenge the elect (Luke 18:7).

—*Thomas R. Chmura.*

The Jewish Aspect

Judges 2:20-22 records a divine declaration resulting from Israel's sin. The accused is "this people," or, more literally, "this nation." God calls Israel *ha-goy ha-zeh,* a term that shows His alienation from Israel. The term *goy* (nation, Gentile) is seldom used of Israel; but when it is, it often carries the concept of reprimand for becoming like a Gentile nation.

God accused Israel of violating the law of Moses. So verse 21 notes the cessation of God's preemptive assault on Israel's enemies: "I also will not henceforth drive out any from before them of the nations that Joshua left when he died."

God had now placed a moratorium on His own involvement in the execution of the holy war against the Canaanites. Hence, in none of the wars in the book of Judges is there a conquest of totally new territory. Any overthrow of an oppressor or occupation of territory is only a regaining of an area Joshua had already gained. Any "new territory" taken is only part of a denoted tribal territory that the tribe had failed to capture, like the Jezreel Valley. There is no expansion of Israel's borders described anywhere in this whole book.

God's ceasing to drive out the nations is not a contradiction of Exodus 23:29-30 or Deuteronomy 7:22. Earlier, God said He would not clear the land right away, but step by step, so that the land would not become despoiled. Now He said He would stop driving out the inhabitants of Canaan before Israel as an act of divine discipline.

All this shows the conditional nature of the Mosaic covenant. The reasoning for God's moratorium is articulated in Judges 2:22: "That through them (enemy nations) I may prove Israel, whether they will keep the way of the Lord to walk therein, as their fathers did keep it, or not." Thus, there were two reasons for God to not drive the Canaanites out. The first reason was to punish Israel for their sin. The second was to test Israel: Would they repudiate idolatry and keep the law of Moses?

Verse 23 gives the result of God's judgment of Israel: "Therefore the Lord left those nations, without driving them out hastily." The threat of verse 21 was not the suspension of God's wrath against the Canaanites but the end of any further extermination of them. The implication here is that the Lord would not exterminate any more of these nations in the land as long as Israel persisted in idolatry. But if Israel repented, He would resume the work. Thus, enjoyment of the land was conditioned on obedience.

"Neither delivered he them into the hand of Joshua" shows God's control over the destiny of nations. If Joshua did not finish the task of driving out the enemies, it was because God had not delivered them into his hand. Joshua did not win by his own strength but by the works of God. Success was based on keeping the terms of the Mosaic covenant. The people of Jehovah could fight and conquer only in the power of their God. Disobedience would bring not only defeat but also subjugation to those same Canaanites.

The divine purpose for the continued presence of these opposing people groups is reiterated in Judges 3:4. The test was not for God, who sees all things, but for Israel. It was to give them an objective standard that would measure the level of their obedience or the depth of their disobedience, which deserved the justice of God. The question for the new generation of Israelites: Would they obey the commandments of God?

—Arnold G. Fruchtenbaum.

Guiding the Superintendent

Often the natural response in a crisis is to attempt to overcome the obstacle in one's own strength. It seems to be part and parcel of the sin nature to say, "I can do it myself." Some learn along the way that our own strength is insufficient and that in many cases we make things worse by our feeble efforts to handle our own problems.

DEVOTIONAL OUTLINE

1. God's people admit the need for help (Judg. 3:15*a*). It took years for it to happen, but it happened. After suffering under the strong hand of the enemy, Israel cried out for the strong hand of God. Hopefully, many have the same testimony as I did after struggling under sin's domination for, in my case, some years. I came to the realization that I needed to let go and let God come into my life. It is only when we admit a need beyond our own wisdom and strength that we can be delivered from the clutches of sin.

Israel finally got to the point the Lord wanted. When this happens, He is most willing to respond.

2. God raises up a deliverer (Judg. 3:15*b*). As Israel cried up to the Lord in Egypt and Moses was recruited as a leader, so Ehud was the one recruited in that moment to deliver Israel from the grip of Moab. God always stands ready to hear the cries of His people and respond by His mercy and grace to their need. People still find Him to be the same today.

3. God empowers Ehud (Judg. 3:16-25, 29). Israel was in subjection to Moab and its king. Thus, the occasion of sending tribute to the Moabite king provided an opportunity for God's deliverer to enter the presence of the slavemaster over Israel. Not only did Ehud take the tribute; he also took along a sword, carried in clandestine fashion.

Following the tribute ceremony, Ehud told the king he was on a secret mission. This made the king especially curious. The room cleared of all but Ehud and the Moabite king. Ehud said he had a message from God for him. It was then that he drew the sword and drove it home into the bowels of the king, a man so obese that the fat of his body closed around the sword, handle and all. He fell dead.

Ehud had executed his mission flawlessly and escaped before the king was found. With no king in Moab to lead the Moabites, the Israelites prevailed over their enemy and captor of the previous eighteen years with relative ease. This task was accomplished not in their own strength but in God's.

4. God gives His people rest (Judg. 3:30). The two generations of peace over the next eighty years was the result of the people reaching the point that they admitted their need and cried out to the only one who could save them.

Peace comes only from God and is the portion of the one who turns his life over to Christ. Never before have so many needed the peace Jesus has to offer.

AGE-GROUP EMPHASES

Children: Lead children to know that they can call out to God anytime and He will hear them.

Youths: Guide the young people, who often feel invincible in their teen years, to realize that they need God's strength as much as anybody.

Adults: Lead the adults to know that it is no shame to admit to the Lord that they need His help and wisdom.

—Darrell W. McKay.

SCRIPTURE LESSON TEXT

JUDG. 7:2 And the LORD said
unto Gideon, The people that *are*
with thee *are* too many for me to
give the Midianites into their hands,
lest Israel vaunt themselves against
me, saying, Mine own hand hath
saved me.

**3 Now therefore go to, proclaim
in the ears of the people, saying,
Whosoever *is* fearful and afraid,
let him return and depart early
from mount Gilead. And there returned of the people twenty and
two thousand; and there remained
ten thousand.**

4 And the LORD said unto Gideon,
The people *are* yet *too* many; bring
them down unto the water, and I will
try them for thee there: and it shall
be, *that* of whom I say unto thee,
This shall go with thee, the same
shall go with thee; and of whomsoever I say unto thee, This shall not
go with thee, the same shall not go.

**13 And when Gideon was come,
behold, *there was* a man that told
a dream unto his fellow, and said,
Behold, I dreamed a dream, and,
lo, a cake of barley bread tumbled
into the host of Midian, and came
unto a tent, and smote it that it fell,
and overturned it, that the tent lay
along.**

14 And his fellow answered and
said, This *is* nothing else save the
sword of Gideon the son of Joash, a
man of Israel: *for* into his hand hath
God delivered Midian, and all the
host.

**15 And it was *so,* when Gideon
heard the telling of the dream, and
the interpretation thereof, that he
worshipped, and returned into the
host of Israel, and said, Arise; for
the LORD hath delivered into your
hand the host of Midian.**

8:22 Then the men of Israel said
unto Gideon, Rule thou over us, both
thou, and thy son, and thy son's son
also: for thou hast delivered us from
the hand of Midian.

**23 And Gideon said unto them, I
will not rule over you, neither shall
my son rule over you: the LORD
shall rule over you.**

24 And Gideon said unto them, I
would desire a request of you, that
ye would give me every man the
earrings of his prey. (For they had
golden earrings, because they *were*
Ishmaelites.)

**25 And they answered, We
will willingly give *them.* And they
spread a garment, and did cast
therein every man the earrings of
his prey.**

NOTES

God Confirms Gideon's Mission

Lesson Text: Judges 7:2-4, 13-15; 8:22-25

Related Scriptures: Genesis 41:25-36; Exodus 32:2-4; Deuteronomy 8:11-20; Judges 7:5-12

TIME: 1191 B.C. PLACES: near the hill of Moreh; near Succoth and Penuel

GOLDEN TEXT—"When Gideon heard the telling of the dream, and the interpretation thereof, . . . he worshipped, and returned into the host of Israel, and said, Arise; for the Lord hath delivered into your hand the host of Midian" (Judges 7:15).

Introduction

The biblical account of Gideon begins in a similar way to the other cycles in Judges. A vast horde of Midianite enemies, along with some allies, would appear regularly just at the time of harvest to plunder and destroy the crops (Judg. 6:3-4). Israel was repeatedly left in an impoverished condition as a result. In time the Israelites cried out to God for deliverance, and God responded by calling Gideon to deliver them.

What we remember most about Gideon's call is his reluctance to accept what God was telling him. After all, he was an unknown from an insignificant clan within the tribe of Manasseh and had apparently never been in a leadership position. However, God often chooses unexpected people for important leadership roles and then equips them to accomplish His work. That was His plan for Gideon.

LESSON OUTLINE

I. READINESS—Judg. 7:2-4

II. CONFIRMATION—Judg. 7:13-15

III. CONCLUSION—Judg. 8:22-25

Exposition: Verse by Verse

READINESS

JUDG. 7:2 And the Lord said unto Gideon, The people that are with thee are too many for me to give the Midianites into their hands, lest Israel vaunt themselves against me, saying, Mine own hand hath saved me.

3 Now therefore go to, proclaim in the ears of the people, saying, Whosoever is fearful and afraid, let him return and depart early from mount Gilead. And there returned of the

people twenty and two thousand; and there remained ten thousand.

4 And the LORD said unto Gideon, The people are yet too many; bring them down unto the water, and I will try them for thee there: and it shall be, that of whom I say unto thee, This shall go with thee, the same shall go with thee; and of whomsoever I say unto thee, This shall not go with thee, the same shall not go.

Paring down the troops (Judg. 7:2-3). When "the Spirit of the Lord came upon Gideon, . . . he blew a trumpet; and Abiezer was gathered after him." Then "he sent messengers throughout all Manasseh; who also was gathered after him: and he sent messengers unto Asher, and unto Zebulun, and unto Naphtali; and they came up to meet them" (6:34-35). It was after this gathering of military men that Gideon did his two fleece tests with God (vss. 36-40). God reassured him that He was indeed going to use Gideon for His work.

This time, however, God was not going to accomplish His task in any normal way. **{**He intended to deliver Israel in such a way that it would be obvious it was His doing and not their own.**}**[Q1] For that reason He worked with Gideon to reduce the size of his army. God said, "The people that are with thee are too many for me to give the Midianites into their hands, lest Israel vaunt themselves against me, saying, Mine own hand hath saved me" (7:2). If Gideon's faith was in the size of his army, that faith was about to be tested.

{A simple challenge was thrown out to the gathered men: if any of them were afraid, they could leave and go back home.**}**[Q2] Probably because of the length of time they had been dominated and because of the strength of the enemy, there was much fear among them. Can you imagine the look in Gideon's face as he watched 22,000 men leave and only 10,000 remain? While it might have been shocking to him, perhaps he reasoned that 10,000 could still win, especially since they were being commissioned by God for the task.

Warren Wiersbe has noted, "God tests our faith for at least two reasons: first, to show us whether our faith is real or counterfeit, and second, to strengthen our faith for the tasks He's set before us. I've noticed in my own life and ministry that God has often put us through the valley of testing before allowing us to reach the mountain peak of victory" (*The Bible Exposition Commentary: Old Testament,* Victor).

Further paring needed (Judg. 7:4). If Gideon was shocked that he was going to have to proceed with just 10,000 men, imagine his thoughts after God's next instruction! The Lord said there were still too many men! We discover later that the Midianite force numbered 135,000 (8:10); so it was a formidable foe that Gideon faced. To have God reduce his little army from 32,000 to 10,000 was quite a test! But now God said it needed to be reduced even more. There would be no glory for Israel from this battle!

God's instruction was for Gideon to take the men to the water and have them drink. He would then tell Gideon which ones should stay with him and which ones should leave for home. He did not explain what the criterion was going to be in His decision; so Gideon had to obey with simple faith. We cannot help wondering what his thoughts were. God had already reduced his army to a pitiful number; now He said He would reduce it even more. Perhaps Gideon was confident because of the assurances he had received earlier.

{The test, unknown to the men, was an observation of how they drank (vss. 5-6). **}**[Q3] It appears that those who knelt down and put their faces right down to the water were separated from those who reached for water with their hands, drawing it up to their mouths to drink.

Only this latter group was kept, perhaps for the logical reason that in drinking this way they remained more alert to their surroundings than did the others. Gideon was left with 300 men to face an enemy army of 135,000. Clearly, it would be God's battle, not Israel's!

CONFIRMATION

13 And when Gideon was come, behold, there was a man that told a dream unto his fellow, and said, Behold, I dreamed a dream, and, lo, a cake of barley bread tumbled into the host of Midian, and came unto a tent, and smote it that it fell, and overturned it, that the tent lay along.

14 And his fellow answered and said, This is nothing else save the sword of Gideon the son of Joash, a man of Israel: for into his hand hath God delivered Midian, and all the host.

15 And it was so, when Gideon heard the telling of the dream, and the interpretation thereof, that he worshipped, and returned into the host of Israel, and said, Arise; for the Lord hath delivered into your hand the host of Midian.

Dream (Judg. 7:13). God assured Gideon, "By the three hundred men . . . will I save you, and deliver the Midianites into thine hand" (vs. 7). As Gideon and his men were camped on a hillside above the Midianites, {God gave him more instruction to help encourage him and erase any fear he might have in his heart. He told Gideon to go down to the Midianite camp with his servant and listen to what was being said there (vss. 9-11).}[Q4] Gideon and his servant Phurah quietly slipped down into the valley to the outskirts of the Midianite camp. {While there they overheard a man telling his companion a dream he had just had.}[Q5] It was surely the hand of God that directed them to this place at this moment, because the Midianite camp was huge: "For they came up with their cattle and their tents, and they came as grasshoppers for multitude; for both they and their camels were without number: and they entered into the land to destroy it" (6:5).

{The dream was that a loaf of barley bread had come tumbling into the Midianite camp. When it reached one of the tents, it knocked it over and completely collapsed it.}[Q5] In Old Testament days, dreams often had messages for those who dreamed them. A good example of this is Joseph, who had two dreams when he was young that indicated he would someday rule over his family. So when this man had a dream, he took it as carrying some kind of message. He might have been repeating it to his companion because he wondered what it meant.

We know God was in this entire scenario. He had commissioned His servant Gideon to lead the Israelites out from under the bondage of the Midianites. In the flow of events, He had even given the dream!

Interpretation (Judg. 7:14). The dream itself might have been somewhat encouraging to Gideon without any further explanation, since it described a mishap within the Midianite camp. And yet God chose to provide the dream as well as a powerful and very specific interpretation to give Gideon extra assurance about what He was going to do. We read what the companion of the dreamer said concerning the dream, but we cannot know for certain what his attitude was. Was he trying to jest, or was he somewhat fearful?

It seems possible that the Midianite camp was aware that Gideon had gathered some forces to come against them, but how much was known about Gideon's army is impossible to conjecture. Maybe this man was making fun of the fact that Gideon was preparing to come against them with a small force of men, or maybe he sensed that God's people were a force to be reckoned with and not taken lightly. {His statement was that the dream indicated the sword of Gideon was about to defeat the Midianites and turn them over to his hand. The dream spelled defeat!}[Q6]

"Catch the humor here. What destroys the tent? Not a hurricane, a cyclone, an earthquake, a tornado, a brush fire, a plague, a rockslide, a bolt of lightning, a tidal wave, or an avalanche. No, it was a barley bun. Not a big, oversized bun, either. If you want to get the idea here, think of a bagel. . . . From Gideon's perspective, God showed him (again) that a small, insignificant, almost silly object can attack and overcome the most prodigious of foes" (Phillips, *Holman Old Testament Commentary: Judges, Ruth,* Broadman and Holman).

{Once again we see that the sovereign God was in control of this situation. His timing was perfect in that Gideon arrived just as the Midianite was telling his dream.}[Q7] This was all Gideon needed to confirm his assignment from God. The meaning of the dream was clear to him.

"A principal thought to notice is that God knows and understands the human needs of His children. He knew Gideon's perplexity and He took occasion to remove it. God did not need to do this, for Gideon really should not have been perplexed. God had told him from the beginning that He would deliver Midian into his hand. Later, He graciously told him this again, through the unusual 'fleece' test.

"Gideon should have simply believed God, no matter what developed, recognizing that God had known all about these developments when He had given the earlier assurances. Gideon should not have let the circumstances influence him to doubt" (Wood, *Distressing Days of the Judges,* Zondervan). While this quote might very well be true, most of us are not so strong in our faith that we could accept such unusual instructions without wondering about them and experiencing some doubts as Gideon did.

Worship (Judg. 7:15). In hearing the dream and its interpretation, God gave Gideon exactly what he needed at that moment. He immediately recognized the dream and its interpretation as a message from God. {His first response was to worship, after which he returned to camp with confidence and announced that the time had come for Israel to advance, because God was going to deliver the Midianites into their hands.}[Q8]

Often God graciously confirms for us the direction in which He is leading us. If we are sensitive to such confirmations and observant of their presence, we can know much joy in following Him.

CONCLUSION

8:22 Then the men of Israel said unto Gideon, Rule thou over us, both thou, and thy son, and thy son's son also: for thou hast delivered us from the hand of Midian.

23 And Gideon said unto them, I will not rule over you, neither shall my son rule over you: the LORD shall rule over you.

24 And Gideon said unto them, I would desire a request of you, that ye would give me every man the earrings of his prey. (For they had golden earrings, because they were Ishmaelites.)

25 And they answered, We will willingly give them. And they spread a garment, and did cast therein every man the earrings of his prey.

A request refused (Judg. 8:22-23). Using very unusual tactics, Gideon led his men against the Midianites. Having stationed three hundred men around the camp, Gideon had them break pitchers, blow trumpets, and yell. God used this unorthodox means to cause panic among the Midianites. "And they stood every man in his place round about the camp: and all the host ran, and cried, and fled. And . . . the Lord set every man's sword against his fellow, even throughout all the host: and the host fled" (7:21-22).

Once the Midianites had taken flight, a large army gathered around Gideon and pursued the enemy, completing the victory. After a number of details were taken care of following the victory, the men of Israel came to Gideon with a proposal. Their request was that Gideon rule over them and establish a dynasty that would continue after his death. They were so grateful for the way he had led them in victory over the Midianites and so confident of his leadership abilities that they wanted him to give them this added security.

Gideon, however, realized that it was not really his ability that had given them their victory. He knew it was God, who had given him explicit instructions and a series of confirmations. {He knew that their desire for him to be king indicated their lack of understanding about God's role in what had happened. He refused their offer and declared, "The Lord shall rule over you" (8:23).}[Q9]

A request accepted (Judg. 8:24-25). These verses set the scene for a very sad ending regarding Gideon. After refusing the people's request for him to rule over them, Gideon presented a request of his own. He asked that everyone bring to him all the earrings that had been taken in the plunder following their victory over the Midianites. The text explains that they were made of gold. The Midianites wore gold rings on their ears or noses, and these had been taken by the Israelite soldiers as part of their plunder.

The soldiers had no idea why this request was given, but their gratitude for what Gideon had done for their nation caused them to cooperate immediately. They said they were glad to do that for him; so they spread out a garment onto which everyone could place the earrings.

It would be nice if the account of Gideon's life ended with his declaration that God should rule. That ought to be the desire in each of our hearts—that He be in charge of our lives. Gideon's life, however, serves not only as an example but also as a warning. He grew in faith and accomplished a great work for God, but he also did something that was extremely harmful to both himself and the people of Israel whom he had delivered. {He took the gold and made an ephod, which later was used in idol worship (vs. 27).}[Q10]

—Keith E. Eggert.

QUESTIONS

1. Why did God decide to accomplish the delivery under Gideon in such an unusual way?
2. What was the first test God used to reduce the number of Gideon's army?
3. What follow-up test did God have Gideon do to further reduce the size of his army?
4. What did God tell Gideon to do in order to give him one more word of assurance?
5. What did Gideon hear when he went to the Midianite camp?
6. What did Gideon understand the dream and interpretation to mean?
7. How do we see the sovereignty of God in this situation?
8. What was Gideon's initial response after getting this message of reassurance from God?
9. What request from the Israelites did Gideon refuse?
10. What did Gideon do that brought harm to himself and Israel?

—Keith E. Eggert.

Preparing to Teach the Lesson

Our lesson this week is about Gideon and his people learning that God's strength is fully sufficient in every situation. We too need to learn to trust God at all times—even when we do not understand what He is doing.

TODAY'S AIM

Facts: to show that God helped Gideon and his people understand that the Lord was still in charge in dealing with the Midianites.

Principle: to grasp the truth that God is in control of every situation we face.

Application: to teach that because God is in total control of our situation, we must learn to let God rule.

INTRODUCING THE LESSON

Have you ever had to ride with an unsafe driver? In such situations, it might be difficult not to grab the steering wheel and take control. Sadly, we often act the same way with God, who has control of our lives. We seem to think He is inept and we must take the wheel. As a result, we steer the wrong way, often in the opposite direction. We tend to think that we know better than He does. Our lesson this week shows us that we need to get out of the way and let God rule so that He can steer us to victory.

DEVELOPING THE LESSON

1. Demonstration of the true source of strength (Judg. 7:2-4). As Christians we often underestimate the power of our almighty God. As a result, we do not trust Him enough, especially when we face seemingly overwhelming obstacles. We think that we know better than He does. Gideon learned in a unique way that he had to trust God to direct his steps. In fact, God told Gideon (whose other name was "Jerubbaal") that He wanted him to reduce his army, weeding out those who were afraid to go into battle.

After that, God told Gideon to take his men down to the water, where the Lord would disclose how He would weed out even more men before they went to war with the Midianites. Through all this, God was making it very clear that when the battle was over, the Israelites would know that it was by His strength that they had won and not by their human strength or wisdom. Twenty-two thousand fearful men went home at first, leaving only ten thousand to go into war. Then at the water, Gideon's army was reduced to a mere three hundred!

There is a lesson here for us. God can bring victory in any situation, with many or few people. The number does not matter to Him, but He does graciously choose to work with us to accomplish His goals. Ask class members to relate an experience when they thought God did not do something they thought He should be doing to straighten out a difficult situation. What do they now think about that same situation in hindsight?

2. Unusual assurance of victory (Judg. 7:13-15). God is not limited by any circumstance. He is always in control. Here God used an enemy soldier's dream to let Gideon know that the Lord was still in charge and that His people would be victorious if they would trust Him. The dream was about a barley loaf that came rolling down the mountain and demolished a Midianite tent. The other man in the conversation saw this dream as a sure sign that Gideon would defeat the Midianites. This was exactly the assurance needed by Gideon, who was eavesdropping.

Point out that God works in various ways. Sometimes it is by destroying an army; at other times He provides encouragement to go forward, as in this passage. Either way, when we trust God and let Him rule, we will be winners because He is on our side. Ask students to share some of their experiences with trusting God in difficult situations and any good words of blessing or encouragement God gave them through someone else.

We cannot forget here that even before the victory was won, God assured Gideon of victory; this gave him the courage to go forward. God does this for us all the time—if we would only get past our own doubts and discouragement long enough to listen to Him. We can listen to God in such times by reading His Word regularly. The very words we need for the day often show up in our regular reading of the Bible.

3. Affirmation of God's rule (Judg. 8:22-25). Victory often goes to our heads and makes us proud. It was not so with Gideon. The people wanted to make him their ruler, but he refused the offer. Humility marked this great man of God, and this is something that we can truly follow. Gideon pointed the people back to the God who gave them every victory. His emphasis to them was that it was God, not him, who had brought them the victory.

Help the class to see that very often when we are going through a crisis, we cry out to God and God steps in and helps us. However, when the crisis is over, we forget to thank Him; worse still, we sometimes forget Him altogether.

Here it is clear that Gideon wanted the Israelites to know that their victory came from God. Gideon told the men of Israel that the Lord alone would be their Ruler. All he asked for were the earrings taken from the enemy soldiers, perhaps to remind him of the victory from God. This may be a good place to point out that their enemies were Ishmaelites, descendants of Ishmael, son of Abraham and Hagar. The term "Midianites" was another name for the same people.

If asked, most of your students would probably say that they acknowledge God as the Ruler of their lives. A fruitful discussion might center around what circumstances and temptations keep them from making this a practical reality in their day-to-day living. Gideon certainly acknowledged his God for the great victory he experienced and turned down the opportunity to rule the people, because he knew God was the rightful ruler.

ILLUSTRATING THE LESSON

Whether in good times or difficult situations, we have to trust that God is still on the throne and still rules.

CONCLUDING THE LESSON

Leave the class with the truth that if we are to let God rule, we truly have to exercise faith in the fact that He is in charge and is the Victor. He will win in the end.

ANTICIPATING THE NEXT LESSON

Next week we will ponder the far-reaching consequences when we disobey God.

—A. Koshy Muthalaly.

PRACTICAL POINTS

1. God's plans are designed to bring Him, not His servants, glory (Judg. 7:2).
2. Obeying God is always best, even when we do not fully understand His ways or plans (Judg. 7:3-4; cf. Isa. 55:8-9).
3. God's sovereign work is universal, and His timing is always perfect (Judg. 7:13-14).
4. True faith sees that God is at work and responds in worship and obedience (Judg. 7:15; cf. Heb. 11:6).
5. Wise is the person who knows when to say no (Judg. 8:22-23).
6. True gratitude finds a way to say thank you (vss. 24-25).

—Don Kakavecos.

RESEARCH AND DISCUSSION

1. How do you think Gideon and his army felt when God reduced their number to three hundred? How do you think you would have felt if you had been one of them?
2. What does God's allowing Gideon to hear the Midianite soldier's dream and its interpretation tell you about His care for us? What does Gideon's response to it tell you about him?
3. In Judges 7:15, Gideon said to his troops, "The Lord hath delivered into your hand the host of Midian." How did his view of God's promises (6:16; 7:7) demonstrate his faith and embolden his troops?
4. How does one decide what is right to accept from others?

—Don Kakavecos.

ILLUSTRATED HIGH POINTS

Delivered into your hand (Judg. 7:15)

I once had a friend named John who would take me to lunch every week. Each time he would insist on paying the bill. I appreciated his generosity, and after many times, I said to him, "John, let me pay today. You always pick up the tab." He answered, "No, no, no!"

One week I got to the restaurant early and said to the waitress, "When the bill comes, would you bring it to me?"

She said, "John told me you might do this. I promised not to give it to you."

I said, "You must be kidding!" But she replied that that was exactly what he had told her.

Think about this: Jesus has "picked up the tab" for us not once but many times. Because of that relationship, a person will come to the point of wanting to do the same. We love because He loves us.

A request of you (8:24)

Charles sat in the living room signing and sealing birthday cards for several of his second-grade classmates. Dad saw a card with an unusual message. It read "I am thankful for you," but two thick, black lines were scrawled over the word "thankful."

When Dad lifted this card from the stack, Charles burst into tears. "Every day that girl calls me names!" he sobbed. "Do you think I should just forgive her?"

"Yes," said his father. "Jesus does not want you to hurt her."

The boy considered the choice that was before him. Then he picked another card and addressed it neatly to the girl who had hurt him so badly. He would offer forgiveness.

—Ted Simonson.

Golden Text Illuminated

"When Gideon heard the telling of the dream, and the interpretation thereof, . . . he worshipped, and returned into the host of Israel, and said, Arise; for the Lord hath delivered into your hand the host of Midian" (Judges 7:15).

Of all the judges whom God used to bring deliverance to His people, Gideon was one of the least likely candidates. He himself certainly thought so, vehemently citing his inadequacy for the task (Judg. 6:15). God had to put Gideon through a lengthy process to get his courage up, starting with a risky assignment to root out idolatry on his own father's property (vss. 25-32) and then giving him a doubled assurance through the sign of the fleece (vss. 36-40).

Now that the moment of deliverance was at hand, Gideon's courage apparently needed one more boost to get him going. So during the night the Lord told him to sneak down to the enemy camp, where he would hear something that would cement his resolve (7:9-11). The mere act of creeping up to the Midianite encampment had to take some courage itself, for their numbers were such that they covered the valley. But Gideon's effort was rewarded immediately when he overheard a Midianite soldier recount a vivid dream to a companion, who then declared it portended certain victory for Gideon and the Israelites (vss. 13-14).

Gideon's first response when he heard the dream and its interpretation was entirely appropriate: "he worshipped." He knew without a doubt that God was assuring him of complete victory. It was the boost to his faith that he needed, and he was grateful to God for granting it.

Gideon's second response was also exactly what was called for. He returned to his people and passed on to them the assurance that he had received. When God gives us encouragement, we are not to keep it to ourselves. He expects us to bolster the faith of others with the strengthening we have received.

"Arise; for the Lord hath delivered into your hand the host of Midian." Again, as Joshua had at Jericho, Gideon declared the promised victory as an accomplished fact before it actually happened. As with Joshua, it was a statement of faith. But since the object of faith was the Lord and His promise, it was also a certainty. There was no possibility of the Midianites' gaining the upper hand, despite their vast superiority in numbers and armaments. Gideon now knew that none of that mattered.

Gideon had come a long way in a remarkably short time. Earlier this man was found threshing grain in a winepress—a location decidedly unsuited to the task—for fear of being noticed by enemy occupiers. Now he was boldly exhorting a token force of three hundred men to take on an army numbering well over 100,000! True faith, however, does not look at the supposed odds stacked against it; true faith looks at the power of God and sees everything else in that light.

In the task that God has called us to—that of bringing His message of salvation to all the earth and making disciples of all nations—it would be easy to look at the daunting obstacles and despair of making headway in the endeavor. The world is hostile to the gospel.

But if we look instead at God's power, we can be emboldened to do our part in the task that cannot fail.

—Kenneth A. Sponsler.

Heart of the Lesson

The Israelites had again turned away from the Lord, and in the time of Gideon they were suffering under the cruel hand of the Midianites. These nomadic people from the south raided Israel, destroying their crops and leaving them impoverished (Judg. 6:1-6).

When the people cried out to God, the Lord once again answered by raising up a judge named Gideon. Gideon considered himself ill-prepared to deliver God's people, and his faith was weak. But God assured him of success and eventually brought to him an army of Israelites prepared to battle their enemy. The account of Gideon, however, is really the account of God, who through it all shows Himself to be the true Leader and Ruler of Israel.

1. God directed the selection (Judg. 7:2-4). Gideon had with him an army of 32,000, which was still a mere fraction of the 135,000 Midianites encamped nearby (8:10). Yet God knew that if He gave this army victory, the people would only take pride in themselves rather than give God the glory (7:2). So the Lord instructed Gideon to reduce the size of his army by allowing those who were fearful to return home. This left Gideon with only 10,000 men.

The Lord then told Gideon there were still too many men for the job (vs. 4)! He instructed Gideon to select only those soldiers who drank from their hands when they went to the water for refreshment. This reduced Gideon's army to only three hundred men (vss. 5-6).

God's purpose was clear. He and He alone was to be acknowledged as Israel's Deliverer. Neither Gideon nor his army could possibly claim credit if they defeated the vast Midianite army with a force of only three hundred.

2. God encouraged Gideon (Judg. 7:13-15). Even with God's clear direction, the task before Gideon must have seemed daunting. Earlier, Gideon in his weakness had sought supernatural assurance from God that He would save Israel through him. Now God graciously gave Gideon further assurance even though He had not requested it.

The Lord told Gideon to go down to the Midianite camp, where he would be strengthened to go into battle (vss. 9-11). When Gideon did so, he overheard a Midianite recounting a dream, which another Midianite interpreted as meaning that the Midianites would fall before Gideon. This news greatly encouraged Gideon, and he returned to prepare his troops for battle (vss. 13-15).

The Lord knows our weaknesses and concerns even before we voice them, and He graciously and repeatedly encourages us to walk in faith, trusting Him. Such encouragement was just what Gideon needed. He went forth and saw God give Israel a great victory (vss. 16-25).

3. God rules His people (Judg. 8:22-25). Following the amazing victory over the Midianites, the people of Israel called upon Gideon to rule over them as king. Even if the people had not learned the lesson, Gideon had. How could he rule as king when God had not decreed it and when God had shown that He alone was their King? It was to God that they owed their deliverance, not Gideon. Like Gideon, we must never claim glory for ourselves for those things God alone has done.

—Jarl K. Waggoner.

World Missions

The biblical account of Gideon's victory over the oppressive Midianites includes an emphasis on God's preparation of Gideon to engage the enemy. The Lord prepared Gideon by first revealing to him that "the people that are with thee are too many for me to give the Midianites into their hands" (Judg. 7:2). He also used a dream and its interpretation to cause Gideon to confidently say, "Arise; for the Lord hath delivered into your hand the host of Midian" (vs. 15).

When we consider the account of Gideon and his victory as one of Israel's great judges, we realize that he faced a daunting task. Similarly, it can be rather daunting when we consider what a missionary is up against. The missionary often faces not only overwhelming cultural differences but also people groups who have been captured and enslaved by Satan for generations. In light of these obstacles, what are some typical ways God might prepare a person for missionary work?

The core preparation must involve the missionary's spiritual life. Unless the Lord, through the work of His Spirit, produces within the missionary a life of spiritual vitality, nothing of any substance will occur. One of the best ways this preparation can be accomplished is for the missionary to first become involved in a mentoring relationship with a spiritually mature person. This relationship will help the missionary think through specific growth steps that will glorify the Lord.

The spiritually prepared missionary will embrace the principle that God does not call him alone into ministry. The missionary is usually called to minister within a team framework; so he must acquire an ability to develop partnering and networking skills. This ability begins with the missionary's immediate and extended family. If relationship conflicts exist, the missionary should seek to resolve them and replace them with spiritually healthy relationships.

The missionary should also seek to build relationships with friends who are committed to the ongoing Christian effort of spreading the gospel. Moreover, the missionary must make certain that he not only attends church faithfully but also gets involved in group ministries such as Sunday school and, if available, small-group Bible studies.

When a person is called to missionary service, it is evident that God has already gifted that person for ministry. However, God expects the missionary to sharpen his ministry skills. This sharpening can best take place in the context of the local church. The missionary should become involved in numerous ministries of the local church, giving the Lord the opportunity to confirm spiritual gifts and reveal spiritual gifts that the missionary may be unaware of.

Finally, the missionary should trust the Lord to develop his knowledge base. If at all possible, the missionary should complete a college degree. Bible studies and cross-cultural studies are both areas to consider. Other areas of emphasis might be education and business. During his educational preparation, the missionary must be aware of and stay away from the trap of extensive financial debt. Minimizing debt allows the freedom to faithfully pursue God's chosen ministry.

As God prepares His chosen individual for evangelistic activity, it is vital for the missionary to let God rule his life.

—Thomas R. Chmura.

The Jewish Aspect

A biblical principle that permeates Scripture is that since man rebelled against God, God is the one who determines how someone approaches Him. God never had "many ways to heaven" but always one specific way. It has always been true that man was saved by grace through faith, even though the exact content of faith was determined by what God had revealed up to that point.

The same principle applies to worship. God determines how a person comes to Him in worship. Under the Mosaic Law, worship first was centered in the tabernacle, which in the time of the judges was located in Shiloh. There was to be no competition to the Shiloh tabernacle; yet Gideon himself set up a system, perhaps inadvertently, that put his own town and center in competition with the tabernacle.

Judges 8:22-23 records Gideon's rejection of the offer of kingship. After Gideon had delivered Israel from the Midianites, the men of Israel offered to make Gideon their king. It was both a personal offer ("Rule thou over us") and a dynastic offer ("both thou, and thy son, and thy son's son also"). The reason for the offer was that he had saved them "from the hand of Midian." The people were now beginning to see the advantages of a king who could provide strong central leadership and save them from their enemies.

While Gideon rejected the offer (vs. 23), he nevertheless began to act like a king. His ephod is described in verses 24-27. In spite of his claims, Gideon increasingly took on the trappings of royalty. By requesting that each man give him a gold earring from his share of the spoils of the war, he was, in effect, calling for symbolic gesture of submission. The quantity of gold taken amounted to a royal treasury.

Verse 27 informs us, "And Gideon made an ephod thereof." For the first time in the book of Judges, it was a judge who began to foster idolatry. Furthermore, Gideon "put it in his city, even in Ophrah." There were two disastrous results. First, the text states, "All Israel went thither a whoring after it." Ophrah became the center of idolatrous worship. Second, the ephod "became a snare unto Gideon, and to his house." It became a snare because his sin consisted of two hings: he took upon himself the role of a priest, and he established a worship center away from the tabernacle, which was in Shiloh.

Gideon's sin consisted of his encroaching on the prerogatives of the Aaronic priesthood and drawing people away from the one chosen sanctuary. Gideon thereby undermined the theocratic unity of Israel and provided occasion for the people to relapse into the worship of Baal after his death. The ephod became a trap to Gideon because it would ultimately result in the slaughter of all but two of his sons, and one of them died in battle later.

At least four lessons can be deduced from the Gideon cycle. First, if anything positive happens in the lives of the people of God, it is because of God's grace. Second, with God on Israel's side, no enemy is invincible; thus, an army of 300 could defeat 135,000. Third, the greatest obstacle to the work of God is the faithlessness of His own people. Fourth, those called to leadership in the divine program will face the temptation to exchange the divine agenda for personal ambition.

—Arnold G. Fruchtenbaum.

Guiding the Superintendent

The glory of God and the humility of man are to be found in this week's lesson as we continue our journey in this unit about obedience and success in God's sight. Considering the rapidly changing times in which we live, today's believer would do well to listen carefully for God's guidance.

DEVOTIONAL OUTLINE

1. God protected His glory (Judg. 7:2-4). During the time of domination by the Midianites, Israel suffered greatly. They had no one to blame but themselves for the situation they were in, for it was a result of departing from the Lord. Once again finding themselves in untoward circumstances, they cried out to God to save them. In His mercy, He chose to work through a man named Gideon.

When Gideon was about to do battle with the Midianites, the Lord determined that the army of Israel was too large for His purposes and instructed Gideon to pare down its size. He did this not once but twice, until there was just a small contingent left, comparatively speaking, to go to battle.

Surely the motivating factor behind God's instructions was protecting His own glory. If a large army won the battle, the people would take credit, not seeing the hand of the Lord in it. If just a few went to war under God's dictate, the victory would clearly be seen as His. One thinks here of the apostle Paul much later being told by the Lord that he had to endure his physical limitations, for in his weakness God's strength would be seen (cf. II Cor. 12:9).

2. God prepared His servant (Judg. 7:13-15). Just before the battle, the Lord emboldened His servant Gideon by means of a dream given to one Midianite and interpreted by another. Gideon overheard the interpretation, in which was prophesied an Israelite victory with God's help, and that was enough to impart further bravery to Gideon. He worshipped and then told his men that God would bring about a favorable outcome.

It was a matter of faith, to be sure. Is that not what is required of God's people today? What God has promised, He will deliver. We can trust our very lives to Him.

3. The servant pointed the people to God (Judg. 8:22-25). After a resounding victory over their enemies with Gideon at the helm, Israel wanted him to become their ruler. Gideon, knowing full well that the victory was by the hand of God, humbly refused the office and instead told them to let God be their Ruler.

In lieu of an office in Israel, Gideon asked for a gift—the golden jewelry the men of Israel had taken from those they conquered. As the account continues, one finds that the item he made from the gold in time became a snare both to him and to the people, regardless of his primary intentions. Nevertheless, Gideon, in spite of his faults, was a man used by God to deliver His people.

AGE-GROUP EMPHASES

Children: Lead children to know that God stands ready to help those who look to Him for help.

Youths: Lead youths to have faith in a sovereign God and to trust Him to fulfill His Word.

Adults: Guide adults to develop the practice of pointing others to the Lord. When we give God the glory that belongs to Him, it exalts the Lord and, in turn, tends to keep us humble.

—Darrell W. McKay.

SCRIPTURE LESSON TEXT

JOSH. 7:1 But the children of Israel committed a trespass in the accursed thing: for Achan, the son of Carmi, the son of Zabdi, the son of Zerah, of the tribe of Judah, took of the accursed thing: and the anger of the LORD was kindled against the children of Israel.

10 And the LORD said unto Joshua, Get thee up; wherefore liest thou thus upon thy face?

11 Israel hath sinned, and they have also transgressed my covenant which I commanded them: for they have even taken of the accursed thing, and have also stolen, and dissembled also, and they have put *it* even among their own stuff.

12 Therefore the children of Israel could not stand before their enemies, *but* turned *their* backs before their enemies, because they were accursed: neither will I be with you any more, except ye destroy the accursed from among you.

20 And Achan answered Joshua, and said, Indeed I have sinned against the LORD God of Israel, and thus and thus have I done:

21 When I saw among the spoils a goodly Babylonish garment, and two hundred shekels of silver, and a wedge of gold of fifty shekels weight, then I coveted them, and took them; and, behold, they *are* hid in the earth in the midst of my tent, and the silver under it.

22 So Joshua sent messengers, and they ran unto the tent; and, behold, *it was* hid in his tent, and the silver under it.

23 And they took them out of the midst of the tent, and brought them unto Joshua, and unto all the children of Israel, and laid them out before the LORD.

24 And Joshua, and all Israel with him, took Achan the son of Zerah, and the silver, and the garment, and the wedge of gold, and his sons, and his daughters, and his oxen, and his asses, and his sheep, and his tent, and all that he had: and they brought them unto the valley of Achor.

25 And Joshua said, Why hast thou troubled us? the LORD shall trouble thee this day. And all Israel stoned him with stones, and burned them with fire, after they had stoned them with stones.

26 And they raised over him a great heap of stones unto this day. So the LORD turned from the fierceness of his anger. Wherefore the name of that place was called, The valley of Achor, unto this day.

NOTES

The Sin of Achan

Lesson Text: Joshua 7:1, 10-12, 20-26

Related Scriptures: Deuteronomy 7:23-26; Joshua 7:13-19; I Samuel 15:1-31; I Timothy 6:6-10

TIME: 1405 B.C. PLACES: Jericho; Valley of Achor

GOLDEN TEXT—"Achan answered Joshua, and said, Indeed I have sinned against the Lord God of Israel, and thus and thus have I done" (Joshua 7:20).

Introduction

Douglas McArthur once wrote: "Rules are mostly made to be broken and are too often for the lazy to hide behind." There is truth in that, but God's rules are always meant to be obeyed.

God had given specific instructions about the destruction of Jericho, and Joshua passed them on: "And ye, in any wise keep yourselves from the accursed thing, lest ye make yourselves accursed, when ye take of the accursed thing, and make the camp of Israel a curse, and trouble it" (Josh. 6:18). All but Rahab and her family were to be slain and everything destroyed, except for certain valuables that were to be placed in the treasury of the Lord's house (vss. 17, 19). Jericho was the firstfruits of the land of Canaan.

Could any instruction have been clearer than that? Surely there was a clear understanding of it in everyone's mind, and there should be no problem with adhering to it. But human nature is tricky, and our hearts cannot always be trusted. "The heart is deceitful above all things, and desperately wicked: who can know it?" (Jer. 17:9).

LESSON OUTLINE

I. SIN COMMITTED—Josh. 7:1, 10-12

II. SIN DEALT WITH—Josh. 7:20-26

Exposition: Verse by Verse

SIN COMMITTED

JOSH. 7:1 But the children of Israel committed a trespass in the accursed thing: for Achan, the son of Carmi, the son of Zabdi, the son of Zerah, of the tribe of Judah, took of the accursed thing: and the anger of the LORD was kindled against the children of Israel.

10 And the LORD said unto Joshua, Get thee up; wherefore liest thou thus upon thy face?

11 Israel hath sinned, and they have also transgressed my covenant

which I commanded them: for they have even taken of the accursed thing, and have also stolen, and dissembled also, and they have put it even among their own stuff.

12 Therefore the children of Israel could not stand before their enemies, but turned their backs before their enemies, because they were accursed: neither will I be with you any more, except ye destroy the accursed from among you.

A trespass (Josh. 7:1). For the moment, everything looked good! "It started when the walls of Jericho fell. What a victory. And everything happened just the way God said it would. Israel was on a spiritual, emotional, and military high. Taking the promised land was going to be a piece of cake. A little marching, blowing trumpets, some shouting—and every city in Canaan would be theirs. They knew it wouldn't always be easy, but they were full of confidence" (Gangel, *Holman Old Testament Commentary: Joshua,* Broadman and Holman).

If that sounds too good to be true, it was. {Joshua was unaware of something that had taken place during the conquering of Jericho, and what he did not know was going to result in disaster for the Israelites. Joshua 7:1 serves as a transitional statement between the great victory over Jericho and the tragic defeat at Ai. What follows is a reminder to us of the devastating effects of disobedience to God. Here we are told that Achan committed a trespass relative to those things that were to be dedicated to God (cf. 6:17-18).}[Q1]

{The thing that catches our attention, however, is the fact that God was angry. That statement indicates that there would no doubt be some follow-up activity on His part, for His anger would have to be pacified.}[Q2] It is clear that even though only one man out of the entire army was at fault, God took notice. And in this case, the entire nation was going to suffer because of it.

This reminds us of these words after David's adultery with Bath-sheba and murder of Uriah: "When the wife of Uriah heard that Uriah her husband was dead, she mourned for her husband. And when the mourning was past, David sent and fetched her to his house, and she became his wife, and bare him a son. But the thing that David had done displeased the Lord" (II Sam. 11:26-27).

A revelation (Josh. 7:10-11). After the victory over Jericho, Joshua immediately made plans to take the next city, Ai. As he had done with Jericho, he sent spies to learn about Ai (vs. 2). They reported that this should be an easy task and that a small number of men could handle it (vs. 3). Three thousand were dispatched, but they were soundly defeated, and thirty-six of them were killed (vss. 4-5). Joshua tore his clothes and fell on his face before God, seeking understanding (vss. 6-7). The thrill of victory had just been followed by the agony of defeat.

"This distance between a great victory and a terrible defeat is one step, and often only a short one at that. A fact of reality is that in a fallen world we can be riding high on the cloud of some great spiritual success, and the very next moment find ourselves in the valley of spiritual failure and despair. One moment we can be like Elijah standing victoriously on Mt. Carmel, and the next hiding out in a cave, fearing for his life, . . . (I Kings 19:10)" ("The Agony of Defeat," Bible.org).

{God responded to Joshua by telling him that lying there on his face would not solve the problem. Action on his part was required. The reason? There was sin in the camp of Israel, and it had to be dealt with.}[Q3] The Lord left no doubt about what He was referring to: "Israel hath sinned, and they have also transgressed my covenant which

I commanded them: for they have even taken of the accursed thing, and have also stolen, and dissembled also, and they have put it even among their own stuff" (vs. 11).

This was a brusque response from God that reveals how seriously He viewed the transgression. It was not His fault that Israel had been defeated; it was the fault of Israel herself. Sin was present and had to be dealt with immediately.

A consequence (Josh. 7:12). **{**Israel was now seen by God as being under the ban spelled out in 6:18: "And ye, in any wise keep yourselves from the accursed thing, lest ye make yourselves accursed, when ye take of the accursed thing, and make the camp of Israel a curse, and trouble it." They were now accursed, that is, doomed to destruction just as Jericho had been.**}**[Q4] No wonder they had been unable to stand against the army of Ai! God had not gone with them, and He would not do so until their sin was judged.

In Joshua 6:27 we are told that the Lord was with Joshua, but now he was given the foreboding word that the Lord would not be with him until the accursed thing that was now in the midst of Israel was destroyed. Otherwise, they would be endeavoring to conquer Canaan in their own strength. Most of us have learned the hard way that we cannot fulfill God's purposes in life by relying on our own strength. Without the power of the Holy Spirit working in and through us, we struggle and fail spiritually.

{God's standards were consistent. He had told Israel to destroy the Canaanite nations because of their wickedness. It would not be right for him to overlook and excuse the same kind of evil among His own people that had provoked Him to destroy the Canaanites.**}**[Q5] How disappointing it must have been to Him to see that His own children were disobedient to Him, just like those heathen nations! How disappointing it must be to Him today when He sees professing believers living more like the world than like children of God!

Israel suffered consequences after their sin. God freely forgives sin but often allows us to suffer the consequences brought on by it. Thank God that He is merciful, or we would suffer much more than we do.

SIN DEALT WITH

20 And Achan answered Joshua, and said, Indeed I have sinned against the Lord God of Israel, and thus and thus have I done:

21 When I saw among the spoils a goodly Babylonish garment, and two hundred shekels of silver, and a wedge of gold of fifty shekels weight, then I coveted them, and took them; and, behold, they are hid in the earth in the midst of my tent, and the silver under it.

22 So Joshua sent messengers, and they ran unto the tent; and, behold, it was hid in his tent, and the silver under it.

23 And they took them out of the midst of the tent, and brought them unto Joshua, and unto all the children of Israel, and laid them out before the Lord.

24 And Joshua, and all Israel with him, took Achan the son of Zerah, and the silver, and the garment, and the wedge of gold, and his sons, and his daughters, and his oxen, and his asses, and his sheep, and his tent, and all that he had: and they brought them unto the valley of Achor.

25 And Joshua said, Why hast thou troubled us? the Lord shall trouble thee this day. And all Israel stoned him with stones, and burned them with fire, after they had stoned them with stones.

26 And they raised over him a great heap of stones unto this day.

So the Lord turned from the fierceness of his anger. Wherefore the name of that place was called, The valley of Achor, unto this day.

A confession (Josh. 7:20-21). God instructed Joshua to sift through the tribes and people of Israel to find out who the culprit was who had taken the accursed thing (vss. 13-14). The penalty was destruction by fire (vs. 15). Joshua was immediately obedient, beginning early the next morning (vs. 16). After Achan was revealed as the perpetrator, Joshua asked for a confession of what he had done so that God would receive glory (vs. 19).

{Achan confessed immediately, acknowledging that what he had done was sin against God. He explained that he had seen a beautiful Babylonian garment, some silver, and some gold. When he saw them, he coveted them and took them. He had hidden all the items in his tent.}[Q6] While Achan answered honestly, we have no way of knowing his heart attitude about the trouble he had brought upon Israel. This might have been a case in which he was sorry he had been caught but did not feel sincere repentance over his actions.

{It is important to notice the three critical steps of Achan's sin. He saw; he coveted; he took.}[Q7] It is the same downward path Eve took in the Garden of Eden. She saw the fruit of the forbidden tree; it was desirable to her; and she took of it and gave some to Adam (Gen. 3:6). Likewise, David saw Bath-sheba, desired to have her, and took her. The "lust of the flesh, and the lust of the eyes, and the pride of life" (I John 2:16) will cause spiritual defeat when not resisted. Achan now faced the consequences of his disobedience.

A discovery (Josh. 7:22-23). After Achan told him where to find the coveted articles, {Joshua sent people to retrieve them. It was immediately confirmed that what Achan had said was true: "Behold, it was hid in his tent." They proceeded to gather up all the items they found and took them to Joshua.}[Q8] Since the entire nation was affected, they were taken also "unto all the children of Israel." In this case, what Achan had done had affected the entire nation; so he was accountable to all of them. The true facts of Achan's confession and his sin also needed to be understood by and proven to all Israel. Most important, however, was his confession to the Lord. All the things he had taken were "laid . . . out before the Lord" (vs. 23). The Hebrew word that has been translated "laid" means "to pour out." This is probably descriptive of the pouring out of the silver. The idea in this is that everything was spread out before the Lord because these were things that were supposed to have been dedicated to Him.

God expected Joshua to be thorough in his dealing with this matter of disobedience, and indeed he was. Strong leaders should follow his example instead of trying to take an easier way out or to minimize the seriousness of the matter.

Joshua's way of handling Achan's sin is instructive. We would do well to learn from his actions. First, just as Israel took time to narrow down who was at fault, we should carefully evaluate ourselves and specifically identify our guilt. Second, we should clearly express before God what we have done wrong, just as Joshua had Achan do. Third, we should get everything out in the open, as Israel did—never holding back any part of the truth. It is spiritually dangerous to make a half-hearted confession.

A stoning (Josh. 7:24-25). As the process continued, everyone remained involved. {Joshua moved ahead with what God had told him to do, and "all Israel with him" participated.}[Q9] This probably means the heads of each tribe. They took Achan, his family, his herds and flocks, his tent—everything he possessed, and everything he had stolen—out to a valley that would become known as Achor, meaning "trouble." There Joshua asked Achan why he had troubled Israel and said that God would now trouble him.

{The people then proceeded to stone Achan to death. The implication is that his family and every living thing among his possessions were included. After that they burned everything with fire.}Q9

These actions may strike us as very harsh when we consider the mercy we see emphasized in the New Testament. It is true that Jesus beautifully presented the mercy of God, but He sacrificed Himself to satisfy God's holiness.In this incident with Achan, however, we see the justice and holiness of God emphasized. He had a specific purpose and plan for Israel and refused to let His people become corrupt and unable to fulfill it.

The Bible instructs churches to maintain purity within their congregations by disciplining their members when they fall into sin. Thankfully, this does not involve the same kind of punishment as Joshua used! The main purpose of New Testament church discipline should always be restoration, and this will often occur when the discipline is done in a biblical way.

A reminder (Josh. 7:26). After everybody and everything belonging to Achan had been stoned and burned, a great heap of stones was raised over Achan's body. This was intended to be a visible warning to everyone who saw it in the future.

{There were two results of this incident. The first thing is that the Lord turned from His anger against Israel.}Q10 The removal of the one who had committed the sin satisfied Him. This reminds us of the New Testament teaching that Jesus Christ is the propitiation for our sins (Rom. 3:25; I John 2:2; 4:10). Jesus satisfied God's righteous demand of payment for sin when He died on the cross.

{The second thing is that the valley received its permanent name, the Valley of Achor.}Q10 "The Hebrew words for Achan and Achor are probably related. Thus Achan, which possibly means 'troubler,' was buried in the valley of Achor, the Valley of 'Trouble.' But because Israel was willing to deal with the sin problem in their midst, God's burning anger (7:1) was turned away and He was ready to lead them again to victory" (Walvoord and Zuck, eds., *The Bible Knowledge Commentary,* Victor).

—Keith E. Eggert.

QUESTIONS

1. What had happened following the fall of Jericho that Joshua was not aware of?
2. What was God's reaction to this?
3. How did God respond to Joshua's plea as he was lying on his face before the Lord?
4. What was tragically different about Israel because of what occurred during Jericho's fall?
5. How was God using a consistent standard in punishing Israel's sins?
6. What did Achan tell Joshua after he was revealed as the cause of the problem?
7. What were the three steps Achan took in committing his sin?
8. How did Joshua confirm that what Achan told him was true?
9. What punishment did God prescribe for Achan, and who was involved in carrying it out?
10. What were the two results of Israel's punishment of Achan?

—Keith E. Eggert.

Preparing to Teach the Lesson

This week we learn how easy it is to move away from God in times of prosperity. We have to be on guard against the sin of disobedience. The way God dealt with Achan's disobedience shows us how repugnant sin really is to Him.

TODAY'S AIM

Facts: to show how God led Joshua to deal with Achan's sin of disobedience.

Principle: to show that our God deals sternly with disobedience in the lives of His children.

Application: to illustrate that when we disobey God, there are consequences; the removal of sin is the path to restoration.

INTRODUCING THE LESSON

My memories of growing up in a godly home include the stern way my parents dealt with disobedience. It was not easy to endure. But I very quickly learned that the pathway to restoration is confession. When sin was not confessed, it weighed heavily on my heart. The sooner I confessed my sin, the sooner I found peace. One only has to read Psalms 32 and 51 to find how disobedience took its toll on David. Our lesson this week shows us how Joshua dealt with the sin of disobedience.

DEVELOPING THE LESSON

1. Achan's sin of disobedience (Josh. 7:1). Our lives of Christian discipleship are marked by both failures and victories. Here we see that despite the wonderful works of God on behalf of His people, it is easy to fall back into sin and forget the One who has blessed us. Achan is described as being unfaithful to God by disobeying His command.

You will remember from our lesson last week that certain items from Jericho from Jericho were to be consecrated to God (cf. 6:17-19). Achan disobeyed God by taking some of those things for himself. In the Old Testament in particular, what is set apart for God is holy and must not be contaminated or defiled. God teaches us that what is holy cannot be tampered with, for our God is a holy God. Notice that details about Achan's family and tribe are given here. He had disgraced his family as well.

Remind the class that whatever God says in His Word is to be taken seriously, for we cannot take God's holiness lightly without serious consequences. Discuss possible ways in which we make mistakes in this area, and show how we can avoid them.

2. The short slide from disobedience to defeat (Josh. 7:10-12). It was immediately after Achan's disobedience that Israel was defeated at Ai (vss. 2-5). Here is something we can learn from the way God deals with His people in the Bible. When we sin, we step away from God. Consequently, His blessing is removed from us. So it was with Israel at this time. One man's sin caused the blessing of God to leave His people and brought defeat by their enemies.

Joshua was utterly humiliated and cried out to God (vss. 6-9). God revealed to him that someone had stolen that which was to be set apart for God alone. God could not bring victory when His commands were not obeyed. That which was to be destroyed had to be destroyed, and that which was to be set apart for God had to be kept holy.

In this case, defeat did not come because Israel was not well prepared but because she did not have God's blessing on her. Emphasize to your class that without God's blessing on us, we can never go forward. Sin brings defeat. Have your students relate some of their own experiences when they succeeded in seemingly impossible situations only because God was with them.

3. Punishment and national restoration (Josh. 7:20-26). Punishment in Old Testament times sometimes seems very harsh when we look at these accounts through today's eyes. But there is a message here. What is holy is to be kept holy. Here we see Achan confessing to Joshua his sin of covetousness. He also revealed where he had hidden the stolen items. Joshua had them brought to him and displayed before everybody as an object lesson.

The Israelites took Achan to the Valley of Achor (which means "the Valley of Trouble") along with his family, who possibly participated in his sin. There the people stoned them to death and burned them and all that they had. Then they piled a heap of stones (a common practice in that day when people wanted to remember something) over the remains to mark the place where this happened.

Point out to the class that such punishment was meted out because Achan violated the holiness of God and disobeyed Him. This served as a lesson for future generations as well. God was still God, and one could not get away with disobedience. Achan had knowingly and willingly disobeyed the clear command of God, and there were national consequences as well as personal ones. Only when the sin was punished was restoration for the nation accomplished.

ILLUSTRATING THE LESSON

Whether we obey or disobey God's commands is our choice. Obedience brings His blessing; disobedience assures His discipline.

CONCLUDING THE LESSON

Stress to the class the utter importance of obeying what God tells us in His Word. When Achan disobeyed God and took those things that were set apart to be holy, the people stoned him to death, along with his family. The sin had to be purged from the camp. Achan acknowledged his sin once he was caught (Josh. 7:20), but punishment was necessary.

The cross of Christ assures us forgiveness if we sincerely confess our sins and repent of them. We may suffer certain consequences for disobeying the Lord, but God is always willing to forgive us when we turn to Him. Achan suffered severe consequences for his disobedience; in his case severe temporal punishment was necessary. Obeying God is an important part of following our Lord Jesus, and we dare not take that lightly.

ANTICIPATING THE NEXT LESSON

Next week we will explore more failures of the Israelites, showing their truly rebellious nature. But we will start by seeing how God graciously raised up judges to lead His people during a distinct period in their history.

—A. Koshy Muthalaly.

PRACTICAL POINTS

1. True victory can be had only when God is obeyed fully (Josh. 7:1).
2. Too often we blame God for our failures rather than recognize the consequences of our own and others' sin (vss. 10-12).
3. Beware lest your looking turn into coveting and your sinful coveting turn into action (vss. 20-21).
4. Public acts of judgment should always be based on demonstrable facts (vss. 22-23).
5. Our sin always impacts us and those around us (vss. 24-25).
6. God's anger burns until His people fully turn from their sin (Josh. 7:26; cf. John 3:36; Rom. 5:9).

—Don Kakavecos.

RESEARCH AND DISCUSSION

1. Was it just for God to punish all Israel for Achan's sin (Josh. 7:1, 10-12)?
2. Is Achan's answer to Joshua in Joshua 7:20 merely an admission of guilt rather than a confession to God? If so, how important is that difference (cf. II Cor. 7:5-12)?
3. How does Joshua's demonstration of the evidence of Achan's sin serve to guide the church in discipline cases (cf. Matt. 18:15-20)?
4. How did God's judgment on Achan and his family portray His holiness? What objections might people have concerning this punishment? How would you answer these objections biblically?

—Don Kakavecos.

ILLUSTRATED HIGH POINTS

Committed a trespass (Josh. 7:1)

A little girl was discovered making mud pies in her backyard. She called her creations "warm chocolate."

Her grandmother cleaned up the mess and forbade any more messes. Undeterred, the two-year-old continued manufacturing "warm chocolate." Three times she said, "Don't look at me, Grandma. OK?"

When we choose to disobey God, it is silly to think we can hide our sin from Him.

Israel hath sinned (vs. 11)

A school-crossing guard in Florida tried everything to get drivers to slow down as they drove through a school zone. Nothing worked until he took a blow-dryer, wrapped it in electrical tape, and pointed it at passing cars. It looked like it might be a radar gun. It was amazing how quickly drivers hit the brakes! This is a small example of how fear can change behavior.

Why hast thou troubled us?

Here is a story about the crime of vandalism on a college campus. It had come to the attention of the college president, and he called the culprits to his office. In the midst of the scolding, one boy reached into his pocket and said, "Just tell us the cost of the damages, and I will pay the bill!"

The president was furious. "Put away your checkbook! This week in assembly, all of you will make public acknowledgment of your offense, or you will be expelled. Do not think a few miserable dollars can ever repay your debt to the founders of this university and the sacrifices they made to build this place and endow it at great cost and care!"

—Ted Simonson.

Golden Text Illuminated

"Achan answered Joshua, and said, Indeed I have sinned against the Lord God of Israel, and thus and thus have I done" (Joshua 7:20).

This week begins a new unit of study that focuses on how disobedience to the Lord is a sure-fire way to bring failure. In lesson 3, we learned that when Israel followed the Lord's instructions precisely and completely, they met with great success in defeating their enemy at Jericho. Unfortunately, that was not the end of the story.

God's instructions for taking Jericho also included how the plunder was to be handled. Nothing was to be taken for personal gain. All the people and property were to be utterly destroyed, or if the property was valuable, it was to be given to God as a sacrifice to Him (Josh. 6:17-19).

All seemed to be going well, and Joshua moved on to take the next city, Ai. In this battle, however, Israel received a thorough pummeling from the Canaanites (7:4-5). In response to Joshua's lament to the Lord about not only the loss in battle but also the loss of advantage over the enemy, the Lord revealed the reason for the defeat and His anger—disobedience.

Joshua had warned the people that disobedience would bring trouble (6:18), and the warning came true. God required the "accursed" thing to be removed before He would again go before them in battle (7:12-13).

After Joshua and the people followed all of God's instructions to find the offender, Achan stood before all of Israel and confessed his sin.

What happened next may cause some to bristle. Instead of being forgiven, Achan and his family were immediately taken to their execution by stoning. After that, their bodies were burned.

What we see here may seem extreme, but when an offense toward God happens for the first time, it is not unprecedented for the punishment to be especially harsh to express the great seriousness of the evil. Take, for example, Adam and Eve's rebellion. They did not confess their disobedience to God until He came looking for them (Gen. 3:7-12). Their punishment of spiritual death, and eventually physical death, was the first expression of God's punishment for sin.

One may also think of Israel's first king, Saul. His disobedience led to the kingdom being taken from him and given to another (I Sam. 13:8-14). Turning to the New Testament, God's response to the deception of Ananias and Sapphira was one that brought fear among the people (Acts 5:1-11).

God has not judged every sin with such measures, for if He did who of us could stand? Yet each of these examples, as well as others, showed a defiant heart. Each knew the right thing to do and elected to test God and not do it. The heart attitude can only be judged by God (I Sam. 16:7).

Those who have placed their trust in Christ's atonement for sin have received a new heart, one that desires to please the Lord. We still sin, yes, but we do not *want* to sin. May we be quick to confess our sins and seek a restored relationship with God (I John 1:9) so that He might "renew a right spirit within" us (Ps. 51:10).

—*Kelly Hawver.*

Heart of the Lesson

Israel witnessed a great victory at Jericho, but they soon would learn that past victories do not guarantee future success. It is a lesson we need to learn as well. Victory in our spiritual battles is dependent on our continuing obedience to God.

1. The sin committed (Josh. 7:1). Joshua had told the people of Israel not to take anything from the city of Jericho, for everything there belonged to God (6:17-19). However, that warning was not heeded by one man of the tribe of Judah, a man named Achan. While Achan was able to keep his sin hidden from others, the Lord was well aware of it.

2. The sin revealed (Josh. 7:10-12). The sin came to light only because Joshua went to the Lord in despair over what happened at the city of Ai. After the glorious victory at Jericho, Israel had suffered an inglorious defeat at Ai, a city that was far less formidable than Jericho (vss. 2-5). Joshua could not understand this demoralizing defeat in light of God's promise.

The Lord revealed to Joshua that success at Ai could not be given because Israel had violated the command of God regarding the taking of things from Jericho that were under the Lord's ban. This sin had to be dealt with if Israel was to be successful in the days ahead.

3. The sin judged (Josh. 7:20-26). The Lord instructed Joshua on the procedure to be followed to reveal the guilty one (vss. 13-15). The people first sanctified themselves, thus recommitting themselves to their covenant with God. Then the sinner was revealed as God selected by lot the tribe, the family, the household, and finally the individual who had committed the sin. That individual was Achan.

Once Achan was chosen, Joshua urged him to confess his sin and give glory and praise to God (vs. 19). Achan willingly complied, confirming his guilt and thus making the way for divine forgiveness. He did not excuse his sin but described the temptation that led him to take some of the silver and gold and a fine garment.

This was confirmed by messengers who were sent to Achan's tent and found the stolen items. Whether Achan's confession was heartfelt or not, he at least had the opportunity to seek God's forgiveness. Punishment, however, could not be averted.

Our "secret" sin affects other people, and in Achan's case it affected an entire nation. While we can be thankful to a merciful God who always offers forgiveness when we confess our sins and repent, in this life we may still have to suffer consequences for those sins. Such was the case for Achan.

The items Achan had taken were brought before all Israel, as was Achan himself. Acting on orders from God, the people stoned to death Achan and his family. His family died along with him, perhaps indicating that they were aware of what he had done and thus were participants in his sin.

Achan probably had every intention of following the instructions regarding Jericho, but his downfall was materialism. He put material possessions ahead of spiritual concerns. In our materialistic culture, we would do well to remember Achan and take warning.

—Jarl K. Waggoner.

World Missions

In this week's lesson text, it is revealed that Achan, who was of the tribe of Judah, sinned against the Lord by keeping for himself a few of the items that had been set apart for the Lord as a result of the Israelite victory over the city of Jericho and its inhabitants. Achan's disobedience had consequences not only for him and his family but also for the entire nation of Israel (cf. Josh. 7:12).

This week's lesson text's stark yet honest revelation of personal defeat invites the question of how the body of Christ deals with personal failure and defeat in the lives of Christian leaders, especially those who are entrusted with the responsibility of spreading the gospel. The rest of this article will present biblical principles related to this question.

First, it is imperative that all believers, but especially Christian leaders (including missionaries), recognize the reality of the possibility of personal defeat. The Bible is replete with examples of leaders who miserably failed the Lord through personal acts of disobedience. Moses, for example, disobeyed the Lord by striking a rock in anger rather than speaking to it, thus detracting from the Lord's glory and causing his own exclusion from entering the Promised Land (Num. 20:1-14).

David, whom God described as "a man after mine own heart" (Acts 13:22), was guilty of committing adultery with Uriah's wife, Bath-sheba, who became pregnant with David's child. David then tried to cover up the affair by arranging to have Uriah killed (cf. II Sam. 11:1-27). The reality is that God's servants often face the unrelenting pressures of ministry and do not always choose the path of personal victory.

Second, it is also imperative that Christian leaders embrace the hope that, no matter how deep the humiliation and guilt of personal defeat, God does not abandon His servants. There are several things a missionary can do to experience forgiveness and ministry recovery. The Christian servant must believe that God still deeply loves him and that His promise "I will never leave thee, nor forsake thee" (Heb. 13:5) is absolutely true.

The missionary must also realize that even though God may set him aside for a time as a consequence of his sin, He probably still has a future place of ministry prepared for him. Until that time comes, the missionary should be patient and not give up on God. He should focus instead on faithful relationships in the body of Christ that foster hope and healing.

Finally, it is imperative for believers to embrace the part they can play in ministering to a Christian leader who has experienced personal defeat. Even though the calling of a missionary is extraordinary, the needs of a missionary are common to man (cf. Acts 14:15). The most powerful and vitally important spiritual discipline believers can engage in on behalf of God's servant, fallen or otherwise, is prayer.

Believers should pray that the struggling missionary would experience the joy and freedom of personal confession (cf. I John 1:5-9). Moreover, believers should pray that the missionary would gain wisdom to understand and embrace God's purpose and plan for his life (cf. Col. 1:9). Our prayer concern should be that the missionary's heart would remain sensitive to the spiritual needs of lost people.

—Thomas R. Chmura.

The Jewish Aspect

Joshua 7:1 reads, "But the children of Israel committed a trespass in the accursed thing." Actually, only one man committed the sin; but God deals with Israel corporately, and therefore the sin of one was the sin of the nation. In verse 15 the sin is called a "folly in Israel." In verse 11 God declared, "Israel hath sinned." He then added, "They have also transgressed my covenant which I commanded them," showing that the violation of the commandment was also viewed as a violation of a covenantal obligation. Again, only one man was guilty; yet God used the plural pronoun to show the principle of collective responsibility, since Israel was viewed as being a covenantal community.

God instructed Joshua to find the guilty party and render judgment against him. Obviously, God could easily have identified Achan by name; instead, He used a very slow process that would make a necessary impression upon Israel as a whole concerning the seriousness of this one sin, a covenantal violation.

Although the process is not specifically named, the description suggests it may have involved the use of the urim and thummim. The Hebrew words mean "lights" and "perfections," respectively, and refer to objects kept in the breastplate of the high priest that enabled God to communicate directly with His covenantal people. Apparently, they could indicate by some means God's answers to questions that required simple positive or negative responses. Perhaps, if the answer was yes, the objects would indicate this in some way.

If Joshua employed these, the whole procedure had to be a process of elimination (vss. 16-18). Thus, individual tribes had to parade before Joshua until the tribe of Judah was selected. Then the different clans of Judah came before him, and one clan was chosen. Then the families of that clan would pass by until one was chosen. Finally, one specific member of the family was chosen—Achan.

The execution in verses 24-25 was also a collective obligation, since corporate guilt required corporate removal of the guilt. Because Achan violated a covenantal curse, the execution included his sons and daughters so that his name was blotted out of Israel; he no longer had a family line. Furthermore, the family may have known of the crime, since the stolen items were buried inside their tent. Corporate punishment does not violate Deuteronomy 24:16, which deals with crimes not specifically covenantal in nature.

The wider context this week includes Joshua 8:30-35, where there was a renewal of the Mosaic covenant. After hearing the reading of the Mosaic Law at Mount Ebal, the people assented to it and submitted to it and affirmed a commitment to keep it. Sadly, that commitment lasted only one generation beyond the time of Joshua.

As we look back on the events contained in the book of Joshua, we can make certain observations concerning Joshua's spiritual leadership. While not perfect, he was certainly consistent. First, the book opens with three admonitions to meditate on and observe he Mosaic Law, which Moses had just recently committed to writing. Clearly Joshua sought to obey these commands. Second, he stood by the promise to Rahab (although he had no role in making it), again recognizing Israel's corporate responsibility. Third, he did not use his position for any personal gain whatsoever.

—Arnold G. Fruchtenbaum.

Guiding the Superintendent

Sometimes people think that the Lord does not see them, or perhaps that He will not know if they transgress. They may feel He does not really mean what He says; hence, they feel they can disobey without repercussions. For some, the inner strength—or lack thereof—is no match for the temptation at hand; they disobey in order to please themselves.

DEVOTIONAL OUTLINE

1. The committing of sin (Josh. 7:1, 10-12). God gave Israel the gift He had promised—Jericho. But in the process of taking the gift, one man took that which had been placed off limits by the Lord. It is not surprising that out of the entire army of Israel there was one man who sinned. The surprise might be that there were not more who disobeyed.

The first ramification of Achan's sin was a stunning defeat for Israel on their next attempt to conquer the land. The Lord then explained to the astonished Joshua the reason He had allowed Israel to be humiliated before their enemies. It was because someone had sinned. God refused to bless His people until they dealt with sin in the camp.

This should serve as a strong reminder that one person's sin is sufficient to affect the entire congregation. The blessing God has for the whole may be withheld because of just one. Note also that though only one sinned, God considered the entire group to have sinned. We all are members of the same body.

2. The confession of sin (Josh. 7:20- 21). Upon following the directions of the Lord, Joshua was led to the culprit. Achan, in turn, confessed. He admitted he had failed morally when his eyes spied items of value. This led him to covet and take them. Achan then told Joshua where he had hidden them.

Worthy of note is the pattern of Achan's sin. The pattern was established by Eve in the Garden of Eden— she saw, coveted, and took of the forbidden fruit (Gen. 3:6). King David would later follow the same path to sinning with Bath-sheba when he saw, coveted, and took (II Sam. 11:2-4). Perhaps we notice the same pattern in our own lives when we sin.

Like so many people, Achan did not confess until he was discovered. His conscience had not led him to come clean, but being found out did. Certainly God would rather have His people be stricken by an uneasy conscience and confess.

3. The consequences of sin (Josh. 7:22-26). With the uncovering of the stolen items stashed in the tent of Achan, the stage was set for discipline. The entire house of Israel participated in the execution of the culprit, which satisfied the anger of the Lord against the nation.

The incident had to be a powerful lesson for God's people that sin has its consequences. Another lesson is that one's sin affects the whole. The reality is that we cannot control the effects of our sins. We do not sin in isolation. Our family could be affected, or maybe our friends, our business, or our church.

AGE-GROUP EMPHASES

Children: Lead the children to know it is very important to believe God means what He says.

Youths: Guide the teens to understand that they must be vigilant with their feelings and desires because it is so easy to sin to satisfy self.

Adults: Lead adults to see that one's life should include self-examination as a routine practice so that the Lord will not need to discipline His own.

—Darrell W. McKay.

SCRIPTURE LESSON TEXT

JUDG. 2:16 Nevertheless the LORD raised up judges, which delivered them out of the hand of those that spoiled them.

17 And yet they would not hearken unto their judges, but they went a whoring after other gods, and bowed themselves unto them: they turned quickly out of the way which their fathers walked in, obeying the commandments of the LORD; *but* they did not so.

18 And when the LORD raised them up judges, then the LORD was with the judge, and delivered them out of the hand of their enemies all the days of the judge: for it repented the LORD because of their groanings by reason of them that oppressed them and vexed them.

19 And it came to pass, when the judge was dead, *that* they returned, and corrupted *themselves* more than their fathers, in following other gods to serve them, and to bow down unto them; they ceased not from their own doings, nor from their stubborn way.

20 And the anger of the LORD was hot against Israel; and he said, Because that this people hath transgressed my covenant which I commanded their fathers, and have not hearkened unto my voice;

21 I also will not henceforth drive out any from before them of the nations which Joshua left when he died:

22 That through them I may prove Israel, whether they will keep the way of the LORD to walk therein, as their fathers did keep *it,* or not.

23 Therefore the LORD left those nations, without driving them out hastily; neither delivered he them into the hand of Joshua.

NOTES

A Backsliding People

Lesson Text: Judges 2:16-23

Related Scriptures: Deuteronomy 9:1-8; Judges 3:1-7; Psalm 106:34-48

TIME: from about 1380 to 1050 B.C. PLACE: Canaan

GOLDEN TEXT—"The Lord raised up judges, which delivered them out of the hand of those that spoiled them" (Judges 2:16).

Introduction

During the three centuries following the death of Joshua, Israel's history followed a cycle repeated over and over again. The people fell into apostasy and came under the domination of a pagan nation until the people cried to God and He sent deliverers, or judges, to free them. They then served the Lord for a time before again apostatizing, starting the cycle again.

Among Israel's judges were an array of men and one woman. These included Othniel, Ehud, Shamgar, Deborah, Barak, Gideon, Abimelech (though many would not include him), Tola, Jair, Jephthah, Ibzan, Elon, Abdon, and Samson. Samuel could also be considered one of the judges of Israel.

These individuals were not so much judges charged with settling disputes as they were deliverers, or saviors, appointed by God to deal with oppression by Israel's enemies.

Joshua died when he was 110 years old. After he and his generation passed off the scene, another generation rose up that was not in close communion with the Lord and what He had done for Israel.

Our text for this lesson deals with the institution of the judges. It is a general description of how God used them to help Israel.

LESSON OUTLINE

I. GOD'S PLAN—Judg. 2:16-17

II. GOD'S PATIENCE—Judg. 2:18-19

III. GOD'S ANGER—Judg. 2:20-23

Exposition: Verse by Verse

GOD'S PLAN

JUDG. 2:16 Nevertheless the LORD raised up judges, which delivered them out of the hand of those that spoiled them.

17 And yet they would not hearken unto their judges, but they went a whoring after other gods, and bowed themselves unto them: they turned quickly out of the way which

their fathers walked in, obeying the commandments of the LORD; but they did not so.

Deliverance (Judg. 2:16). {The Lord used pagan people to chastise the Israelites for their sins.}[Q1] It was His sovereign prerogative to do this as part of His stated intention of making them His special people (Ex. 19:5-6). They forsook Him on a regular basis, but He did not forsake them. If it appears that He did, this has to be seen in the light of His plan to discipline them and drive them back to Himself for forgiveness and restoration.

{That is why God raised up judges from time to time to lead the Israelites in their opposition to oppression and grant them the deliverance they needed.}[Q2] Israel operated under a theocratic monarchy; God served as King and He appointed the judges. {They were in leadership positions for a limited time, and they had no royal family line to succeed them as earthly kings did. Some were also limited to certain sections of Canaan rather than the whole land.}[Q3]

Disappointment (Judg. 2:17). The Lord and all who sought to serve Him were bitterly disappointed at what happened during the time of the judges. Verse 17 indicates that the people's waywardness took place even while their respective leaders were still alive. Verses 18-19, as we shall see, show that the people became even more wayward after their judges died.

The sinfulness of the Israelites was displayed in two primary ways. {First, they chased after gods worshipped by by pagans in the land of Canaan.}[Q4] They bowed down to them, thus violating the first two of the Ten Commandments—"Thou shalt have no other gods before me" and "Thou shalt not make unto thee any graven image, . . . Thou shalt not bow down thyself to them, nor serve them" (Ex. 20:3-5; cf. Deut. 5:7-9).

The second way the Israelites displayed their sinfulness was by turning quickly out of the way followed by their fathers (ancestors). Those worthy predecessors had obeyed the commandments of the Lord. These new sons and daughters of Abraham, Isaac, Jacob, and Moses deliberately took detours from the path marked out for them and wandered off into heathen territory controlled by Satan and his host of demons.

Believers today can take a lesson from the ancient Israelites. Despite the advantages we might have today, the threat of backsliding and apostasy is always present. Allowing anything or anybody to displace our devotion to God the Father, the Son, and the Holy Spirit can develop into spiritual idolatry. Even the apostle John, writing in the latter part of the first century of the Christian era, closed his first epistle with this admonition: "Little children, keep yourselves from idols" (5:21).

Scripture indicates that idolatry is closely connected with demonic activity (Deut. 32:16-17; Lev. 17:7; I Cor. 10:20). One of the disturbing developments in our world today is the growth of pagan religions, occult organizations, and New Age teachings. These all have the potential to draw true believers away from the truth and into whole systems of error, leading to apostasy and its consequences.

GOD'S PATIENCE

18 And when the LORD raised them up judges, then the LORD was with the judge, and delivered them out of the hand of their enemies all the days of the judge: for it repented the LORD because of their groanings by reason of them that oppressed them and vexed them.

19 And it came to pass, when

the judge was dead, that they returned, and corrupted themselves more than their fathers, in following other gods to serve them, and to bow down unto them; they ceased not from their own doings, nor from their stubborn way.

Sympathy (Judg. 2:18). The first part of this verse repeats what was stated in verse 16, but it adds that the Lord raised up the judges to deliver the Israelites out of the hands of their enemies "all the days of the judge." Keep that in mind while looking forward to verse 19, for that will tell us what happened after the judges died.

It is the latter half of verse 18 that concerns us here. We are faced with a problem with the meaning of the word "repented." If God is omniscient (all-knowing), why would He decide something and then later repent of it? If He is immutable (unmovable, unchanging), is it actually possible for Him to change His mind and do something different?

To assert that the groaning and vexation of the Israelites due to pagan oppression caused God to abandon the plan He had determined to follow would be to say that people can manipulate God. Since we know that cannot be done, we must seek another explanation for why God is said to have "repented." The theological answer can be summed up in the following way. **{**The Hebrew word in Judges 2:18 translated "repenting" can carry the idea of relenting or taking pity. This may include the thought of becoming softer or less severe and harsh. In other words, God's plan never changed. What changed was that He was now ready to rescue them because their suffering had finally caused them to earnestly ask for His help.**}**[Q5]

Although God knows the end from the beginning regarding His dealings with us, we are required to walk by faith and not by sight. His ear is always open to our cry, and His love is ready to be poured out upon us. We are responsible to obey God faithfully and should never blame Him if our waywardness brings His chastisement upon us.

Stubbornness (Judg. 2:19). As mentioned before, verse 17 seems to indicate that the Israelites were wayward while their judges were alive. Verse 19 speaks of the people's waywardness after their judges died. **{**Even after deliverance, the apostasy seems to have continued, with or without judges being on hand—and this went on for about three centuries.**}**[Q6] This fits with Moses' scorching description of their rebelliousness (Deut. 32:15-21, 28-33). Satan does not easily loosen his grip on people once he has them in his power.

GOD'S ANGER

20 And the anger of the LORD was hot against Israel; and he said, Because that this people hath transgressed my covenant which I commanded their fathers, and have not hearkened unto my voice;

21 I also will not henceforth drive out any from before them of the nations which Joshua left when he died:

22 That through them I may prove Israel, whether they will keep the way of the LORD to walk therein, as their fathers did keep it, or not.

23 Therefore the LORD left those nations, without driving them out hastily; neither delivered he them into the hand of Joshua.

Decision (Judg. 2:20-21). Many today want to portray God only as loving and kind, regardless of how they treat Him. They use frivolous terms such as "the man upstairs" or "somebody up there" to refer to Him and cast Him in the role of a glorified Santa Claus ready to shower them with blessings but no responsibilities. They certainly do not want to see Him as the Judge of the universe or as being angry enough to show His displeasure by punishing anyone.

{Verse 20 declares that "the anger of the Lord was hot against Israel." This is a blunt statement that cannot be reduced to something less severe.}[Q7] Since God does not change, we can be sure that He is just as angry with sinners today as He was then. That is a most sobering thought.

God made a decision regarding the Israelites who had broken His covenant. He said that He would not drive out all the heathen left in the land of Canaan by Joshua when he died. Let us back up and look at three Scripture passages that show that the Israelites had been adequately warned about what God would do if they were unfaithful to Him.

Moses had said, "If ye will not drive out the inhabitants of the land from before you; then it shall come to pass, that those which ye let remain of them shall be pricks in your eyes, and thorns in your sides, and shall vex you in the land wherein ye dwell" (Num. 33:55).

Joshua had said, "Know for a certainty that the Lord your God will no more drive out any of these nations from before you; but they shall be snares and traps unto you, and scourges in your sides, and thorns in your eyes, until ye perish from off this good land which the Lord your God hath given you" (Josh. 23:13).

The Angel of the Lord had said just prior to the beginning of the period of the judges, "Ye shall make no league with the inhabitants of this land; ye shall throw down their altars: but ye have not obeyed my voice: why have ye done this? {Wherefore I also said, I will not drive them out from before you; but they shall be as thorns in your sides, and their gods shall be a snare unto you" (Judg. 2:2-3).}[Q8]

Display (Judg. 2:22). This is an interesting verse to analyze. {God said that He used the pagan people of Canaan to "prove," or test, Israel. He allowed these heathen people to remain there, alive and functioning in the midst of His chosen people, in order to display, or reveal, Israel's spiritual character or lack of it.}[Q9] They served as a thermometer to show whether the Israelites were spiritually warm, tepid, or cold.

If the Israelites sternly resisted pagan beliefs and practices and refrained from intermarrying with the heathen, and if they tried to turn these wicked people toward the Lord, these would be signs that all was well. If the Israelites held themselves aloof and tolerated pagan activities, this would indicate spiritual apathy. If they forsook the way of the Lord and moved over the line into pagan worship and practices, their apostasy would be evident. It was the latter that all too often happened.

In our own time, we sometimes find that God tests the sincerity of our faith by placing us in spiritually hostile environments. That does not make God guilty of tempting us. "Let no man say when he is tempted [tested], I am tempted of God [to do evil]: for God cannot be tempted with evil, neither tempteth he any man: but every man is tempted, when he is drawn away of his own lust [passion], and enticed" (Jas. 1:13-14).

If we endure the testing with faith and patience, God uses these situations to develop our spiritual muscles and make us mature. If we fail the tests, God is grieved, we ourselves are weakened, and our testimony is diminished. As a result, unbelievers are not attracted to our Saviour, and Satan and the forces of evil are pleased.

Distress (Judg. 2:23). Canaan, the Land of Promise, became a spiritual battleground after Israel had subdued it and settled it. God took away many of the great blessings He could have bestowed upon it because the Israelites did not live up to their part of the agreement.

Joshua had failed to drive out all the pagans as God had commanded. Joshua's successors also failed to do so. Therefore, the Lord withdrew His full support, which seriously distressed the Israelites for a long time.

{It was not until the ascension to power of King David and his son Solomon that full control was established over Canaan and the boundaries were extended through military prowess, political alliances, and wise administration.**}**[Q10]

Looking on to Judges 3, we read these sad words: "The children of Israel dwelt among the Canaanites, Hittites, and Amorites, and Perizzites, and Hivites, and Jebusites: and they took their daughters to be their wives, and gave their daughters to their sons, and served their gods. And the children of Israel did evil in the sight of the Lord, and forgat the Lord their God, and served Baalim and the groves. Therefore the anger of the Lord was hot against Israel, and he sold them into the hand of Chushan–rishathaim king of Mesopotamia: and the children of Israel served Chushan–rishathaim eight years" (vss. 5-8). Unfaithfulness early on resulted in even more sin later on.

It was at that time that the Lord raised up Othniel, the first judge, to deliver Israel from foreign oppression. He was "the son of Kenaz, Caleb's younger brother. And the Spirit of the Lord came upon him, and he judged Israel, and went out to war: and the Lord delivered Chushan–rishathaim king of Mesopotamia into his hand; and his hand prevailed against Chushan–rishathaim. And the land had rest forty years" (vss. 9-11).

It has been said that those who forget the lessons of history are doomed to repeat its mistakes. The book of Judges makes that very clear with its record of the repeated cycle of apostasy, oppression, and deliverance.

If we are wise, we will learn to stay true to God, doing our part and trusting Him to do what He has promised. This is victorious living!

—Gordon Talbot.

QUESTIONS

1. In what surprising way did God use the pagan nations in Canaan?
2. Why did the Lord occasionally raise up judges in Israel?
3. How did judges differ from kings?
4. What sins characterized Israel during the period of the judges?
5. Since God is unchanging, what does Judges 2:18 mean when it says that God repented?
6. How did the Israelites react to the various deliverances from their enemies?
7. What emotion did the waywardness of the Israelites create in the Lord?
8. What did Israel suffer as a result of not driving all the pagan people out of Canaan?
9. How did God display the true state of Israel's character?
10. Under whose leadership did Israel eventually gain full control of its borders and expand them?

—Gordon Talbot.

Preparing to Teach the Lesson

This week we will consider another aspect of God's covenant with His people. We now look at how it applied to judges and kings. They played an important role in the history of the nation of Israel and were very influential in turning the people to or from God.

TODAY'S AIM

Facts: to examine how God raised up leaders to meet the need of His people at every crucial moment in their history.

Principle: to show that God raises up the right people at the right times to do His work in this world.

Application: to demonstrate that when we turn away from God, He often sends the right people before us to turn us back to Him.

INTRODUCING THE LESSON

Just before Joshua passed off the scene, the people of Israel enthusiastically declared that they would follow their God. This lesson covers how they forgot their promise and how God dealt with an erring people. It may be that we can learn how God deals with us when we choose to turn away from Him.

DEVELOPING THE LESSON

1. God raised up judges (Judg. 2:16). Even though we see that the people of Israel had turned away from God and their promises to Him and back to the ways of the world, we find a merciful God working on their behalf. He raised up judges to instruct them and to lead them back into the ways of God.

This raises a big question for us. How long can we run away from God before He stops helping us? The truth is that our God is a very merciful God who works to turn us back to Him. And we read that when Israel was in trouble with their enemies, God raised up capable, godly leaders to meet the people's specific needs and drive those enemies away.

2. Israel turned away from God (Judg. 2:17). We read that after God made provision to take care of Israel's needs as a nation, the people turned away from Him. They forgot the promises that they had made to Him along with Joshua and his household. They forgot to follow in the path of those who had been faithful to God before them. They forgot the heritage of godliness that preceded them.

It is fitting here to discuss with the class whether we as Christian believers have forgotten our promises to God and our godly heritage. How do we compare with the erring people of Israel at this juncture of their history? It is important to realize that turning away from a holy and almighty God makes us candidates for His inevitable chastening.

One would think that after God had done something wonderful in their lives, such as delivering them from their enemies, the people of Israel would wholeheartedly turn back to Him. Discuss with the class what makes God's people prone to turning away from God even after He has helped them in amazing ways. Consider Romans 2:4, which reminds us that the goodness of God should turn us back to repentance.

3. God's mercy seen through the judges (Judg. 2:18). God reminds us in His Word that He is merciful. When God saw His people suffering at the hands of their enemies, He sent judges to deliver them. He had pity on them. In the same way, God's heart softens in pity when He sees us suffering, and He works (despite our wayward ways) to set us free from our trying circumstances. He gave the Israelites judges who would lead them. God is a merciful God who does everything to turn us back to Him. He sends us godly people to instruct us and lead us.

4. Israel again turned away from God (Judg. 2:19). The people followed God for a time, but when that judge died, they forgot to follow Him and went back to the gods of the nations around them. Here we can raise the question: Does following God get wearisome after a time? What are the reasons we give up following God? What can we learn from the people of Israel?

The lesson for us is that when God sends us godly leaders, we ought to follow them and their instruction. Doing so will pull us out of our suffering. We see that as long as there was godly leadership, the people of Israel were motivated to follow the ways of God.

5. God removed His blessing (Judg. 2:20-23). The people had to learn a bitter lesson, one that is certainly appropriate for us today as well. When they disobeyed Him, God removed His blessing.

The covenant with God was broken. He burned with anger against His people. His mercy changed to wrath. He vowed that He would no longer drive out the enemies of His people. The truth for us is that without God's protection, we are totally vulnerable.

Notice also that God sometimes puts us in situations in order to test our faithfulness to Him. Difficulties have a way of trying our faith. When God withdrew His hand of blessing upon His people, they had to fend for themselves. The truth for us is that when we disobey, God may take away His blessing from us. That is too much of a risk to take for the ardent believer. We are open to Satan's attack without God's protection.

In turbulent times of our lives, God sends us His leaders to lead us. We must follow them to find victory.

ILLUSTRATING THE LESSON

When we are going the wrong way, God sends us godly leaders to turn us to the right.

CONCLUDING THE LESSON

In this week's lesson we have seen not only that God is merciful to us in the times we turn away from Him but also that He provides us a way to get back to Him. In the lesson we saw how God provided godly leaders for the people of Israel at their times of crisis. As long as they followed their godly leadership and instruction, they were safe from their enemies and God kept His hand of blessing on them. When they disobeyed, God removed His blessing. As disciples of Christ, we are called to return to Him. Christian leaders can help us do this.

ANTICIPATING THE NEXT LESSON

In our lesson next week we see how Israel rejected God's kingship over them and how He dealt with this sad situation.

—A. Koshy Muthalaly.

PRACTICAL POINTS

1. We too easily forget what the Lord has saved us from and get caught up in the wrong things (Judg. 2:16-17).
2. God does not enjoy having to chasten His people and will deliver them as soon as possible (vs. 18).
3. Without someone to hold us accountable, it is easy to lapse into sin (vs. 19).
4. We should not expect God's help in overcoming difficulties when we are living in disobedience to Him (vss. 20-21).
5. Trials and obstacles are often what we need to help us stay faithful (vss. 22-23).

—Kenneth A. Sponsler.

RESEARCH AND DISCUSSION

1. Why did God keep raising up judges to deliver His people when they kept proving faithless to Him (Judg. 2:16-17)?
2. Since the people would turn to idolatry as soon as a judge died (vs. 19), why did God not simply institute permanent leadership, that is, a king?
3. How did the continued presence of idolatrous enemies in the land serve God's purposes (vss. 21-23)? How might He use the enemies of the faith in the world today?
4. What purpose might God have had in allowing the recurring cycle of deliverance, apostasy, affliction, repentance, and renewed deliverance in the period of the judges? What are the lessons for us today?

—Kenneth A. Sponsler.

ILLUSTRATED HIGH POINTS

Because of their groanings (Judg. 2:18)

During the Battle of Gettysburg, a touching incident took place after Union soldiers retook Culp's Hill. According to *On the Bloodstained Field* by Gregory A. Coco (Thomas Publications), the opposing soldiers reclined behind breastworks less than seventy-five yards apart. Between them lay a number of dead and wounded.

One of the wounded, in addition to his injury, was suffering from acute thirst and called out for water.

Unexpectedly, a soldier named Webb leaped over the bulwarks and ran to the afflicted man amid a shower of enemy bullets. After resting briefly on the ground beside the man, he left the canteen and ran back to the safety of the Union lines—completely unharmed! His actions remind us of the Lord's compassion for Israel, which moved Him to bring about their deliverance.

Keep the way of the Lord (vs. 22)

The Ivory Coast in West Africa was torn by violence and unrest. Very few missionaries remained by the end of 2004.

The Protestant population of about 870,000 was now deprived of much leadership. Foreign Christian missionaries feared that the fledgling churches there might not survive without their help. ("A Church Largely on Its Own," *Christianity Today,* February 2005).

The subsequent years severely tested the faithfulness of the Christians there as never before. True believers, however, had their faith purified in their trials and gained patience, experience, and hope (Rom. 5:3-4). The Ivorian church survived under God's protecting hand.

—Todd Williams.

Golden Text Illuminated

"The Lord raised up judges, which delivered them out of the hand of those that spoiled them" (Judges 2:16).

Following the leadership of Moses and Joshua, God raised up others to take their place. Those who were called by God into leadership positions over a four-hundred-year period were collectively known as the judges.

Leadership in Israel in the judges' day was different from leadership prior to the entry into and the settling of the land. Moses was a unique man for a unique mission—the Exodus from Egypt. Joshua followed this man of God, took the people across the Jordan into the Land of Promise, and governed them during the time of conquest and settlement. Once they had settled in the land and Joshua had died, there was no single leader to give guidance and direction. There was no stable government or head of state.

Joshua had no successor; consequently, the people began to do what they wanted to do, and the flesh, being what it is, took over. To put it bluntly, they became a shameless, wicked nation. The people recklessly and eagerly forsook God to go after other gods and get involved with all manner of sinful practices.

This is a caution we had better be aware of. When we get away from God and have no mentor to check up on us and warn us if we begin to drift, we too can easily forsake the living God for idols of our own making. It has happened to God's people so many times down through the years, and it is still happening today. But thankfully, God often sends someone along to confront us and lead us in the right direction. In the days after Joshua, God sent those known as judges.

Our golden text is actually a commentary on an event that repeated itself regularly over hundreds of years. Israel fell headlong into apostasy; then God sent other nations to oppress them; finally they cried out to God and He sent a judge to bring them back to Himself. In the process He used various persons, both men and women, to deliver Israel from those who overcame them during times of apostasy.

The history of Israel shows that God will allow His people to live in rebellion against Him just so long, and then He will use various means to humble them. Once conquered or in great distress, the Israelites would come to their senses and cry out to God. It was in such times that a judge would be raised up by God to be the leader of His people for a period of time. History also shows that Israel never learned from history. She repeatedly made the same mistakes, and God repeatedly showed Himself to be merciful and forgiving.

God remained true to His covenant people then, and He does the same today as well. Christians are in a covenantal relationship with the Lord, and we experience the same care and love that God showed Israel. Sadly, we too may stray from the Lord. "Prone to wander, Lord I feel it," wrote Robert Robinson some years ago in his hymn "Come, Thou Fount"—apparently as a statement of the human condition. It is a failing that occurs all too frequently.

Thankfully, the God who entered into covenant with His people allows them only so much leash to sin and then eventually draws them back with the cords of love (cf. Hos. 11:4). Praise God for His great mercy!

—Darrell W. McKay.

Heart of the Lesson

Imagine trying to drive on a busy road without any traffic laws. You might encounter a truck coming head-on and refusing to stop or a car going ninety miles an hour. Traffic signals would be nonexistent, since no one would obey them anyway. There would be accidents all over the place! Another word for this kind of situation might be "anarchy." "Anarchy" means a state of lawlessness.

"Anarchy" would be a good term to describe the time after Joshua died. Too often the people of Israel lived as they wanted instead of following God's laws. The result was oppression from their enemies. God chose to raise up judges to lead His people.

1. Israel rejected the judges (Judg. 2:16-19). God appointed judges to lead Israel. These were people led by God's Spirit. They were usually military leaders, rescuers who used God-given wisdom to save the people from their enemies, who were constantly trying to defeat them.

Often the people would not follow the judges. They would continue forsaking the Lord, therefore causing pain and suffering for themselves. The people had such short memories! They had already forgotten God's work in their ancestors' lives. Of course, they had not experienced firsthand the parting of the Red Sea or the manna, but they also did not seek to know God in a personal, vital way.

The Israelites lived a type of roller-coaster pattern. God would raise up a judge, who would save them from their enemies. As soon as that judge died, though, the people would return to their corrupt ways. Things would get even worse, causing a downward spiral of behavior.

Our God-given conscience becomes dulled by repeated sin. The first time we commit a particular sin, we know it is wrong and ask God for forgiveness. When we commit the same sin again, however, it can become an ingrained behavior.

God knows our hearts. He knows when we are truly repentant. He knew the Israelites had turned their backs on Him.

2. Israel's painful consequences When the people turned away from God, they turned to idols. They tried to replace he Almighty God with mere clay and stone figurines.

God is extremely patient with His children when they sin and stands ready to forgive. During the time of the judges, though, the people had sinned so many times that their supposed repentance rang hollow.

God was angry. The people had broken their covenant with Him.

Because the people had disobeyed Him, God declared that He would not protect them against their enemies anymore. In the past He had gone before them and driven out their enemies. Without Him, success was not possible.

God used unbelievers, pagan people who did not even know Him, to test His people. His plan was that Israel's suffering would eventually cause them to call on Him for help.

God will use painful circumstances to help us see our need for Him. When we trust to our own devices, we find that we will fail and court further misery. By His grace, God uses various ways to bring change into our lives. Too often when our lives are going well, we forget all about God, thinking we do not need Him. The truth is that we need Him all the time. We need Him for every breath we take!

—Judy Carlsen.

World Missions

Where there is no order or direction, people get lost. At this time in Israel's history, judges were God's instruments for order and deliverance. Today the Lord sends missionaries. Missionaries endeavor to reach lost people, who often are in circumstances of squalor, ignorance, and idolatry. Many places in need of missionaries are out of reach for the time due to prohibitive laws and oppression.

Scotland largely does not have these common external problems for missionary work. Once the home of great Christians like John Knox and David Livingstone, it now is adrift instead in loose living and the shadow world of demons and superstition. American missionary couples have worked hard on the Scottish field with little to show for it.

Romania, a poor country once in the grip of godless communism, is a fertile field for the gospel. Christian workers from the United States and European fields have gone into the country for short terms to teach and mentor national believers. The program https://www.carrubbers.org/ministries/romania/ mentions the Golgota Bible School and Mission in Talmaciu, which it has aided in sustaining their work, including helping with the salaries for the Romanian faculty and national pastors.

At one point, a team of missionaries from Scotland took over thirty hours of teaching each week and augmented the dining room staff.

Is this unusual arrangement worthwhile? The Golgota students have planted many churches in and around the institute, and many missionaries welcomed the temporary change in the field of service.

For decades, most of the missionaries on foreign fields were Americans or Western Europeans. That is no longer the case. Korean believers, for example, are working all over the Muslim world. Christians from Mexico, Guatemala, Venezuela, and Argentina are sending missionaries to East Asia, North Africa, and the Middle East.

Brazil was once a priority mission field. Today, Brazilian evangelicals number over twenty-one million, and their numbers are growing rapidly. They have sent out hundreds of missionaries to other countries. At the same time, Chinese Christians from Hong Kong and California have been reaching the large Chinese population in Brazil.

One of the most astounding movements involves mainland Chinese believers. At great risk, they are investigating Middle Eastern fields. They are studying Arabic, English, and other languages!

The plight of the millions under the tyranny of Islam is a major prayer burden for believers the world over. There is some light in that darkened world. A West African Muslim believer gained his liberty after a prison sentence for converting from Islam, but many of his Christian friends remained in custody. A Muslim told the young man, "I want to be a Christian." "Did you see what they did to me in prison?" the young man asked. "Yes, I did. No one would go through that unless he was telling the truth," the Muslim replied.

In an unusual testimony, a Muslim Hausa of Nigeria kept having repeated dreams of Jesus. He could not get away from the reality of his nighttime impressions. He went to a mission station to inquire about the matter and was won to Christ. He is now a missionary to his own people.

—*Lyle P. Murphy.*

The Jewish Aspect

In the opening chapter of Judges, Israel asked the Lord which tribe should lead them into battle. The Lord told them Judah should lead them in the campaign. This divine command shows the importance of Genesis 49:10, which contains Jacob's prophecy about Judah. In this unique verse, we find the wonderful messianic title "Shiloh."

Jewish tradition says "Shiloh" is a title for the Messiah. Targum Onkelos, an Aramaic version of the Pentateuch, translated "Shiloh" as "Messiah" (Kac, *The Messianic Hope,* Baker). Furthermore, the Palestinian Targum, another ancient Jewish source, translated Genesis 49:10 as "Kings shall not cease from the house of Judah, nor scribes teaching the law from his children's children, until the time King Messiah shall come, whose is the kingdom, and to whom all the kingdoms of the earth shall be obedient."

The root meaning of "Shiloh" could be "tranquility." Isaiah enlarged this idea with his title for the Messiah: "The Prince of Peace" (Isa. 9:6). Even Jews who do not believe in a personal messiah associate the term "messiah" with a future age of peace for Israel and the nations. In the *tekkun olam* (repairing the world) movement, Jews believe that enlightened human effort can bring about a golden age of peace and justice.

The Stone Tanach, the modern Jewish Orthodox Bible, tells its reader that Shiloh is King Messiah (Scherman, ed., *The Tanach: The Stone Edition,* Mesorah Publications). The majority of Orthodox Jews believe the Messiah will come to earth, establish God's kingdom, and build the third temple described in Ezekiel 40 through 43. Orthodox Jews, however, do not believe the Messiah will be God incarnate, even though in Isaiah 7:14 the Messiah is named "Immanuel," meaning "God with us." They think the Messiah will be a great man and a true descendant of David, but they emphasize the Messiah will not be as great as Moses (Kolatch, *The Second Jewish Book of Why,* Jonathan David Publishers).

Understanding the biblical doctrine of the Messiah is important in our witness to Jews. Essential elements of this truth are the appearances of Messiah Jesus in the Old Testament. Judges 2:1-6 reveals one of these Christophanies. John MacArthur wrote that this is "one of 3 preincarnate theophanies by the Lord Jesus Christ in Judges (cf. 6:11-18, 13:3-23). This same Divine Messenger had earlier led Israel out of Egypt (cf. Ex. 14:19). . . . God would be faithful until the end, but the people would forfeit blessing for trouble, due to disobedience (cf. [Judg. 2:] 3)" (*The MacArthur Study Bible,* Word).

The Jews who translated the Stone Tanach took a nonmessianic approach in translating Judges 2:1: "An emissary of HASHEM (the Name) went up from Gilgal to Bochim. He said, 'I brought you up from Egypt and I brought you to the land that I swore to your fathers.' And I said, 'I shall never annul My covenant with you.'"

From the Orthodox point of view, an emissary is either an angel or a human prophet. The Jews try to explain the use of "I," which sounds as if God were speaking, by saying the prophet was speaking as a representative of the Lord.

The term Shiloh is shrouded in mystery. Still, it is an important early announcement of the Messiah's coming.

—*James Coffey.*

Guiding the Superintendent

When the term "judge" is used in today's culture, people usually think about the judicial system. In this context, a judge is the presiding officer of the court who supervises court trials, instructs juries, and pronounces sentences.

In the Old Testament economy, a judge had other responsibilities. In order to provide His strong-willed, defiant people with consistent leadership during the time between Joshua's death and the reign of King Saul, God appointed a succession of warrior-leaders who were entrusted with their safety, welfare, and guidance.

In this week's lesson text we learn about the origin of Israel's warrior-leaders, or judges, and the cycles of blessing and cursing that dominated this historical period.

DEVOTIONAL OUTLINE

1. Judges raised up to lead Israel (Judg. 2:16-19). After God permitted Israel to occupy His Land of Promise, His people did not obey His command to completely drive out its idolatrous inhabitants. God's righteous anger was greatly kindled against His people, and He allowed them to experience great distress and a lack of leadership.

However, God did not completely dissociate Himself from His people or from the covenant promises that He had made with them. Instead, He gave His nation warrior-leaders who delivered His people out of enemy control throughout the entire time of their judgeship.

When God's appointed judge died, the people of Israel once again corrupted themselves. They stubbornly pursued the idols of the heathen nations that remained in the Land of Promise.

2. Heathen nations employed to test God's people (Judg. 2:20-23). Israel's persistent pursuit of idols greatly angered their God. Their covenant transgressions caused God to allow the heathen nations to thrive in the Land of Promise. Moreover, God promised to use these idolatrous people to torment and test Israel to see whether they would repent and serve Him or continue to serve idols.

AGE-GROUP EMPHASES

Children: As a significant part of early spiritual education, children need to be consistently taught the difference between good and bad behavior.

Have your teachers use this week's lesson text to teach the children that God is pleased with their obedience but will discipline them when they choose to disobey Him.

Youths: Young people often rebel against authority and the people God uses to exercise it.

Encourage your teachers to use this week's lesson text to help the young people embrace a different view of authority figures. Help them understand that God uses these people to get their attention and teach them to live lives of pleasing obedience.

Adults: Some adults believe that the older they get, the easier life should become—even to the point of believing that God should lightly dismiss their times of disobedience.

Help the adults celebrate God's unchanging nature, reminding them that He remains perfectly consistent in His treatment of His people. In the end (and that end may not always be in this life), He always blesses the obedient and disciplines the disobedient.

—Thomas R. Chmura.

Scripture Lesson Text

I SAM. 9:1 Now there was a man of Benjamin, whose name *was* Kish, the son of Abiel, the son of Zeror, the son of Bechorath, the son of Aphiah, a Benjamite, a mighty man of power.

2 And he had a son, whose name *was* Saul, a choice young man, and a goodly: and *there was* not among the children of Israel a goodlier person than he: from his shoulders and upward *he was* higher than any of the people.

10:17 And Samuel called the people together unto the LORD to Mizpeh;

18 And said unto the children of Israel, Thus saith the LORD God of Israel, I brought up Israel out of Egypt, and delivered you out of the hand of the Egyptians, and out of the hand of all kingdoms, *and* of them that oppressed you:

19 And ye have this day rejected your God, who himself saved you out of all your adversities and your tribulations; and ye have said unto him, *Nay,* but set a king over us. Now therefore present yourselves before the LORD by your tribes, and by your thousands.

20 And when Samuel had caused all the tribes of Israel to come near, the tribe of Benjamin was taken.

21 When he had caused the tribe of Benjamin to come near by their families, the family of Matri was taken, and Saul the son of Kish was taken: and when they sought him, he could not be found.

22 Therefore they enquired of the LORD further, if the man should yet come thither. And the LORD answered, Behold, he hath hid himself among the stuff.

23 And they ran and fetched him thence: and when he stood among the people, he was higher than any of the people from his shoulders and upward.

24 And Samuel said to all the people, See ye him whom the LORD hath chosen, that *there is* none like him among all the people? And all the people shouted, and said, God save the king.

25 Then Samuel told the people the manner of the kingdom, and wrote *it* in a book, and laid *it* up before the LORD. And Samuel sent all the people away, every man to his house.

26 And Saul also went home to Gibeah; and there went with him a band of men, whose hearts God had touched.

NOTES

Israel Rejects God as King

Lesson Text: I Samuel 9:1-2; 10:17-26

Related Scriptures: I Samuel 8:6-22; 16:1-13;
I Kings 1:32-40; Luke 4:17-32

TIME: about 1050 B.C. PLACES: Gibeah; Mizpeh

GOLDEN TEXT—"Ye have this day rejected your God, who himself saved you out of all your adversities and your tribulations; and ye have said unto him, Nay, but set a king over us" (I Samuel 10:19).

Introduction

We observed in our previous lesson that during the time of the judges, Israel faced daunting political and military problems. Its lack of unity was an invitation for neighboring peoples to invade, raid, and oppress it. To many, the solution seemed to lie in a monarchy that could unify the people.

Yet we shall see that kingship brought its own kinds of problems—loss of freedoms, arrogance of power, and trust in human instead of divine leadership.

This week's study introduces Saul, Israel's first king. Despite his ordinary family and tribal connections, his appearance won him the admiration and allegiance of his people.

LESSON OUTLINE

I. THE BACKGROUND OF THE KING—I Sam. 9:1-2

II. THE PRESENTATION OF THE KING—I Sam. 10:17-24

III. THE BEGINNING OF THE KINGDOM—I Sam. 10:25-26

Exposition: Verse by Verse

THE BACKGROUND OF THE KING

I SAM. 9:1 Now there was a man of Benjamin, whose name was Kish, the son of Abiel, the son of Zeror, the son of Bechorath, the son of Aphiah, a Benjamite, a mighty man of power.

2 And he had a son, whose name was Saul, a choice young man, and a goodly: and there was not among the children of Israel a goodlier person than he: from his shoulders and upward he was higher than any of the people.

The identity of Saul's father (I Sam. 9:1). Although Samuel was a capable and godly judge, his sons did not follow in his footsteps (8:1-3). This fact, combined with Israel's continuing weakness, led the tribal leaders to demand a king (vss. 4-5). Samuel warned them what the institution of monarchy would do to the nation, but they remained adamant. God then set about to reveal to Samuel and Israel who their king would be (vss. 10-22).

{Saul, the Lord's choice, was the son of Kish, a Benjamite. Kish was a "mighty man of power" (9:1), an expression that could have positive connotations both militarily and economically; so Saul's immediate family apparently had solid local social standing. But Kish's ancestors named in this verse were undistinguished men, and Benjamin was the smallest tribe in Israel.}[Q1]

In addition, Kish's home city of Gibeah (cf. 10:26) did not have a good name. It had become notorious through an incident of gang rape and murder (Judg. 19) and was the focal point of a civil war against Benjamin that followed (chap. 20).

The characteristics of Saul (I Sam. 9:2). {Kish's son Saul was praised for his physical qualities. This man, whose name means *asked of God,* was "choice" and "goodly." Although these terms can be used of nonphysical qualities, the rest of the verse makes it clear that here they mean impressive and handsome. His height (close to seven feet tall) also was part of his physical appeal.}[Q2]

Such characteristics were extremely desirable in kings of ancient times. The Israelites had already asked for a king so that they could be like other nations, having one to judge them and lead them in battle (I Sam. 8:20). God now provided a man who came close to fulfilling their ideal. He chose Saul, we see in retrospect, to show Israel that these externals are not what matter most (cf. 15:28; 16:6-7).

Although Saul is here called a "young man" (9:2), we learn later that he had a son of fighting age named Jonathan (13:2, 16). He might therefore have been close to forty years of age at this time. "Young" should thus be taken in a relative sense. His physical attributes may also have given him a youthful appearance.

THE PRESENTATION OF THE KING

10:17 And Samuel called the people together unto the LORD to Mizpeh;

18 And said unto the children of Israel, Thus saith the LORD God of Israel, I brought up Israel out of Egypt, and delivered you out of the hand of the Egyptians, and out of the hand of all kingdoms, and of them that oppressed you:

19 And ye have this day rejected your God, who himself saved you out of all your adversities and your tribulations; and ye have said unto him, Nay, but set a king over us. Now therefore present yourselves before the LORD by your tribes, and by your thousands.

20 And when Samuel had caused all the tribes of Israel to come near, the tribe of Benjamin was taken.

21 When he had caused the tribe of Benjamin to come near by their families, the family of Matri was taken, and Saul the son of Kish was taken: and when they sought him, he could not be found.

22 Therefore they enquired of the LORD further, if the man should yet come thither. And the LORD answered, Behold, he hath hid himself among the stuff.

23 And they ran and fetched him thence: and when he stood among the people, he was higher than any of the people from his shoulders and upward.

24 And Samuel said to all the people, See ye him whom the LORD hath chosen, that there is none like him among all the people? And all the people shouted, and said, God save the king.

Israel convened at Mizpeh (I Sam. 10:17). Through the circumstances of Saul's search for his father's lost donkeys, the Lord brought Saul and Samuel together (9:3-19). {Samuel told him the donkeys had been found, but he also revealed that he was destined to be king (vs. 20). Before Saul left Samuel's presence the next day, Samuel anointed him and gave signs by which he would have his appointment confirmed (9:25—10:8).}[Q3] These signs came to pass, and Saul returned home (vss. 9-16).

It was essential that Israel have God's choice confirmed to them as well; so Samuel called the people to Mizpeh (the name means "watch tower"), to cast lots for their king. It was assumed that the Lord would guide them in this way to the right man.

Israel rebuked by Samuel (I Sam. 10:18-19*a*). Before having the people cast lots, {Samuel again brought a divine rebuke on them for their improper motives in demanding a king.}[Q4] "Thus saith the Lord God of Israel" casts Samuel in the role of a prophet with an important message from God.

The Lord reminded Israel of all He had done for them in the past (vs. 18). He began with the redemptive acts by which He had delivered them from the Egyptians and their cruel slavery. He then spoke of His deliverance "out of the hand of all kingdoms." These included those they had encountered during their travels between Egypt and Canaan—the Amalekites, Edomites, and Moabites, as well as the Amorite kings, Sihon and Og, east of Jordan.

The "kingdoms" here also included all the tribes of Canaan, each with its petty king, who were subdued by Joshua. In addition, Israel was delivered from all those who oppressed them. This is probably a reference to those who raided their land during the time of the judges—Mesopotamians, Moabites, Philistines, Canaanites, Midianites, Ammonites, and others. All this time the Lord alone was their King, and He graciously rescued them.

But the Israelites were not satisfied with this arrangement. Rather than recognize their spiritual condition as the cause of their adversities, they blamed their problems on their political organization. Instead of thanking God for rescuing them in time of need, they lamented that they had no physical person to lead them. If only they had a *human* king!

{In wanting a king for these reasons, they had rejected their God (vs. 19). They had ceased to see life in theistic terms. They defined their problems as earthly ones and then sought a human solution to them. They deluded themselves into trying to solve national problems by political means alone. The spiritual dimension of life was lost.}[Q5]

Saul sought by lot (I Sam. 10:19*b*-21). Having rebuked the Israelites for their ingratitude, Samuel nevertheless went forward with the process of identifying their king. {He commanded them to present themselves before the Lord "by your tribes, and by your thousands (clans)."

Then, by a divinely directed process of casting lots, the choice was narrowed as most were eliminated.}[Q6] Casting lots was a common practice among ancient people in making decisions and in gambling (cf. Esth. 3:7; Jonah 1:7; Matt. 27:35). When used by Israel, it was assumed that the Lord would oversee the procedure to accomplish His will (Prov. 16:33). The actual means Israel used in casting lots is nowhere described.

As the lots were cast, "the tribe of Benjamin was taken" (I Sam. 10:20). Within the Benjamite clans "the family of Matri was taken" (vs. 21), and from them Saul was eventually taken. A problem arose, however, when Saul could not be found.

Saul brought before the people (I Sam. 10:22-23). Saul's absence necessitated a further inquiry directed to the Lord. Where was this man? Had he arrived yet? How might they find him? God's answer was "He hath hid himself among the stuff." "The stuff" refers to the baggage, or supplies, of those who had assembled there. We are not told how this answer was given, although it is possible that the high priest was present and that he consulted the Urim and Thummim in his breastplate (cf. Ex. 28:30; Lev. 8:8).

It is indeed amazing to think of this handsome, strapping man, so kingly in appearance, hiding among the baggage while the nation waited to acclaim him. How can we explain his behavior?

{It could be accounted for as an evidence of humility. At this stage of his life, Saul revealed an appealing, unassuming modesty. He was an unsophisticated man from the country who had never dreamed of being king.**}**[Q7] He had felt uncomfortable imposing on Samuel (I Sam. 9:7), and when the prophet told him of his destiny, he was astounded. He was conscious of his humble connections, and he wondered why Samuel should say such things about him (vs. 21).

Furthermore, after being anointed, Saul returned home and did not even tell his relatives what had happened (10:16). The same unassuming manner is also evident in the events following his presentation to Israel. He returned to his farm, ignoring his critics (vss. 26-27), and when the first military challenge came, he was following the cattle home from the field (11:4-5). He was a man who at this point was unspoiled by a lust for power.

Modesty may have caused Saul to shrink from any public exposure that could be interpreted as self-aggrandizement. But his hiding (10:22) may also have betrayed a weakness—the fear of taking responsibility and a tendency to be indecisive. This too was to be manifested in later actions. In the an early engagement with the Philistines, it was Jonathan, not Saul, who took the initiative (cf. 14:1-2). Moreover, when Goliath challenged Israel (chap. 17), Saul trembled with all the rest (vs. 11).

Whatever Saul's reasons for concealing himself, he was soon found and brought before his countrymen. What a magnificent sight he was, standing head and shoulders over all of them! Any weaknesses he had were, for the time, hidden under a flawless exterior. He was every inch a king.

Saul acclaimed by Israel (I Sam. 10:24). {Samuel, for all his reservations about the monarchy, presented Saul enthusiastically to the people: "See ye him whom the Lord hath chosen, that there is none like him among all the people?"**}**[Q8] He too was impressed by Saul's appearance, and knowing that God had chosen him for this office, he sincerely hoped that he would succeed.

{The people responded by shouting their enthusiastic approval.**}**[Q8] "God save the king" in verse 24 could be translated, simply, "Let the king live!" We would probably say, "Long live the king!" The same acclamation appears later in the recognition of Solomon (I Kgs. 1:34, 39) and Joash (II Chr. 23:11), as well as of Absalom (II Sam. 16:16) and Adonijah (I Kgs. 1:25), who were pretenders to the throne.

In this way, the Israelites let their monarch know that they supported him and wished him good health and long life. They saw their well-being bound up in his; through him they expected to see their national hopes fulfilled.

THE BEGINNING OF THE KINGDOM

25 Then Samuel told the people the manner of the kingdom, and wrote it in a book, and laid it up before the Lord. And Samuel sent all the

people away, every man to his house.

26 And Saul also went home to Gibeah; and there went with him a band of men, whose hearts God had touched.

The words of Samuel (I Sam. 10:25). Now that the king had been recognized, {Samuel "told the people the manner of the kingdom." "Manner" should be understood as "ordinances" or "regulations."}[Q9] These no doubt included the regulations for kings written in the Mosaic Law (Deut. 17:14-20). In the Lord's economy for Israel, kings were not to be absolute in power or originators of Israel's laws. They were to have no religious authority to challenge or usurp the place of the priests, and they were always subject to prophetic rebuke.

It is also likely that Samuel reiterated at this time the impact the monarchy would have on the people, especially in the responsibilities they would have to their king. He had already done this in I Samuel 8:10-18, but the repetition would remind them that they could never complain of despotism, for they had asked for this kind of government. Both monarch and subjects were thus given official notice of their responsibilities before God.

Samuel then "wrote it in a book, and laid it up before the Lord" (10:25). This was a scroll that was considered a binding contract for future generations. It had become common practice to put important matters in writing (cf. Ex. 17:14; Josh. 18:9; Job 19:23-24).

The importance of this scroll is evident from the fact that it was to be placed before the Lord. Most likely, it was deposited in a secure place in the tabernacle. Samuel then dismissed the congregation to return to their homes.

The followers of Saul (I Sam. 10:26). As noted before, {Saul also returned to his home in Gibeah and went back to farming.}[Q10] He apparently made no conscious effort to establish a court or raise an army. Those things would follow in due course. We should not equate Israel's monarchy at this time with the ornate setting of Solomon or of the Egyptian and Babylonian kings. It began in rustic circumstances.

{Saul did not return alone. "There went with him a band of men, whose hearts God had touched."}[Q10] These men recognized Saul as God's chosen and gave full allegiance to him. They did not at this time constitute an army, but as a royal escort they formed the nucleus of one.

Saul had his critics as well (vs. 27), but he began his rule in an atmosphere of promise.

—Robert E. Wenger.

QUESTIONS

1. From what kind of family and tribal background did Saul come?
2. What appeal did Saul have to those who wanted a king?
3. What happened between Saul and Samuel before the national convocation at Mizpeh?
4. Why did Samuel rebuke Israel before they chose their king?
5. Was monarchy wrong for Israel? Explain.
6. What method was used in identifying Israel's king?
7. What is a possible explanation for why Saul hid himself among the baggage at Mizpeh?
8. How did Samuel and the Israelites express their approval of Saul as king?
9. What did Samuel discuss with the people after Saul was chosen?
10. Where did Saul go after his recognition? Who went with him?

—Robert E. Wenger.

Preparing to Teach the Lesson

Under the judges, Israel had been a theocracy. God Himself ruled through judges He raised up. The people envied their pagan neighbors, who had kings ruling over them. They wanted their own king to rule them. In this week's lesson we see how God arranged for Israel's first king to be chosen.

TODAY'S AIM

Facts: to introduce Saul and review the circumstances that surrounded his selection as the first king of Israel.

Principle: to teach that despite the folly of men, God's sovereignty prevails.

Application: to encourage Christians to yield to God's will instead of insisting on their own way.

INTRODUCING THE LESSON

Peer pressure is a force to be reckoned with in many people's lives. Seventeen-year-old John wanted his own car, even though his father was opposed to the idea. His father thought that a car would be a distraction in his son's life. He wanted John to concentrate his energies on his studies so that he could win a college scholarship. John, however, kept insisting on having his own vehicle. "After all," he said, "all my friends have their own cars."

Finally, John's father grew tired of listening to his son's begging. He took John to a local dealership and helped him select a good car at a fair price. He even supplied the down payment for the vehicle, with the understanding that John would make his own payments.

John enjoyed driving his car, but it took a toll on his grades. He failed to win the scholarship to the school of his choice. Instead, he had to work his way through a junior college and make car payments at the same time. He got what he wanted, but he lived to regret his shortsighted decision.

Israel's request for a king was also granted, but there were lessons yet to be learned about God's way being the best way.

DEVELOPING THE LESSON

1. Saul's résumé (I Sam. 9:1-2). The only fact known about any of Saul's ancestors is that his father, Kish, was a man of power and substance. Locate the land of Benjamin on the map. The tribe occupied land north of the Dead Sea and west of the Jordan River. Study tools such as *Nelson's Illustrated Bible Dictionary* (Lockyer, ed., Nelson) give specific details. Benjamin was the tribe of Saul of Tarsus, the apostle Paul.

Note the descriptive words used of Kish's son in verse 2. He was a fine physical specimen, who stood head and shoulders above his peers. Nowadays, a politician's popularity is enhanced if he is photogenic and looks good on television. Saul too was popular for his appearance.

2. Samuel's rebuke (I Sam. 10:17-19). Summarize the events recorded in 9:3 through 10:16, to provide context for the lesson text. Shy Saul was discovered by Samuel and installed as Israel's first king. It was now time to call the people together. Locate "Mizpeh (Mizpah)" on the map. There were six different Mizpehs in ancient Israel. The Mizpeh of 10:17 was the one in Benjaminite territory, near Geba and Ramah.

Samuel spoke as the mouthpiece of God. Through Samuel, God reminded His people that it was He who had delivered them from Egypt and other enemies. He also communicated His disappointment that they had rejected

Him by demanding a king. Discuss this with the class. In what sense was the demand for a king a rejection of God? Israel was to experience a transition from a theocracy to a monarchy. This seems to have indicated a lack of faith on the part of Israel. God Himself had been sufficient for them before. Why not now?

3. Saul revealed (I Sam. 10:20-26). Help your class visualize the magnitude of this great gathering of the tribes of Israel. Apparently, lots were cast to determine first the clan and then step by step down finally to the man whom God had chosen to be king.

Samuel had already anointed Saul (cf. vs. 1). The new king was humble and shy, afraid to become the focus of attention. He hid so well that it took divine revelation to show where he was (vs. 22). As the class members focus on verse 23, remind them that this is the second time Saul's extraordinary height has been mentioned.

Discuss how people today tend to place undue emphasis on people's physical attributes. Beautiful people typically are valued over others. What a superficial criterion of worth!

Samuel declared that Saul was God's choice. Discuss this in light of Genesis 49:10, in which the tribe of Judah was singled out as the possessor of the royal scepter. Saul may have been God's short-term choice to teach Israel a lesson, but God's long-term choice would be David and his descendants.

The nature of the new monarchy was specified in writing and solemnized in a public ceremony. Refer to Deuteronomy 17:14-17, which includes Moses' regulations for kingship.

Notice that when the official installation was over, all the people went to their homes, as did Saul. Locate Gibeah on the map. There was no capital city, no palace, no government, and apparently no plan for future action. An unspecified number of men were motivated by God to attach themselves to Israel's new king.

ILLUSTRATING THE LESSON

The drawing provides a background for this week's lesson on Saul, Israel's first king.

CONCLUDING THE LESSON

God's will was to rule Israel directly in a theocracy. The people, however, wished to have a human king. God acquiesced to their demands by allowing Saul to be their first king. Saul was tall and physically impressive. God directed Samuel to present Saul to the people after warning them that He considered their demand for a king a rejection of Himself. Saul was shy and humble. He hid himself. When he was finally discovered, he was presented to Israel as God's choice to be king. When everything was over, everyone, including Saul, went home to await future developments.

ANTICIPATING THE NEXT LESSON

Read Joshua 24:1, 14-24 as you prepare for next week's lesson. We will consider Joshua's final words to Israel.

—Bruce A. Tanner.

PRACTICAL POINTS

1. Impressive physical qualities do not disqualify one from spiritual leadership, but neither do they guarantee spiritual success (I Sam. 9:1-2).
2. To reject the Lord's will is to reject the Lord Himself (10:17-19).
3. Wise is the person who is not overly eager to assume a position of power (vss. 20-22).
4. It is not a blessing but a curse when ungodly people get what they want (10:23-24; cf. 8:4-22).
5. We would have fewer regrets if we remembered that our decisions are being made "before the Lord" (10:25).
6. We should be thankful for the support of godly people, remembering that such support is a gift from God (vs. 26).

—Jarl K. Waggoner.

RESEARCH AND DISCUSSION

1. What do Samuel's words and actions in I Samuel 10 reveal about the character and ways of the Lord?
2. Why do people who should know better sometimes reject God's ways (vs. 19)?
3. Why did God use the method He did to reveal the man He had already chosen to be king (vss. 20-21; cf. vs. 1)?
4. Why do you think the people were so pleased with the selection of Saul to be king (vss. 23-24)? What warning is there for us in this?
5. What positive qualities do you see in Saul at this point in his life?

—Jarl K. Waggoner.

ILLUSTRATED HIGH POINTS

A mighty man of power (I Sam. 9:1)

A young pastor started out in the ministry with a lot of success. His neatness in dress, charming personality, and speaking ability brought people from long distances to hear him. Because of the large number of people, it was decided to have two Sunday morning services. The ministry grew to include a radio program, a youth center, a shelter for homeless people, and even a nursing home center.

As the pastor's prestige grew, the biblical standards he once had held began to fall. His compromise eventually changed his original goal for the ministry. Worldly activities became a part of the work. As the spiritual standards were lowered to accommodate people, the ministry suffered greatly. The pastor who once had been strong in his biblical convictions now became increasingly involved in unethical practices.

Hearts God had touched (10:26)

The missionaries in a central African country saw the need to establish a high school for their children. They believed that if they could provide a high school education on their field, they could keep more missionary parents on the field longer. The need for workers was made known to the missionaries' supporting churches. A number of men immediately responded and went to Africa to construct the high school building for the missionaries and their children.

When the building was completed, a dedication service was scheduled. Even though the volunteer workers were back in America and unable to attend the dedication of the building, they were recognized by the missionaries for the vital part they had in the overall ministry there in Africa.

—V. Ben Kendrick.

Golden Text Illuminated

"Ye have this day rejected your God, who himself saved you out of all your adversities and your tribulations; and ye have said unto him, Nay, but set a king over us" (I Samuel 10:19).

"How sharper than a serpent's tooth it is to have a thankless child." These are the words that Shakespeare puts into the mouth of King Lear, in the famous play of the same name, as he complained about one of his cruel daughters. Lear, of course, has some character faults of his own. How much more unjust was the ingratitude and spiritual blindness of the children of Israel toward the Lord God!

Throughout the Old Testament leading up to the Scripture passage for this week, we read of how gracious and patient God had been with His people as He delivered them from slavery in Egypt and from many other periods of oppression as well. He had brought them to the Promised Land. Time after time in the era of the judges, God had sent deliverers, only to see the people soon lapse into sin and rebellion once again.

Now the people were demanding that Samuel provide them with an earthly king. What is the explanation for this lamentable, insulting, and foolish ingratitude?

The obvious first answer, of course, is that fallen creatures are prone to sin. Because of that, we must always be on the watch for ways in which the world may be squeezing us into its mold (cf. Rom. 12:2). The world's way is often the path of least resistance—or at least the path seems easier at first. We find out later that the enemy of our souls extracts a steep price for our foolish choice to follow a worldly course.

When we probe a little deeper for the source of the people's desire for a king, we come to perhaps the foundational issue behind their action, and our spiritual failures as well—a lack of faith.

There are several layers of truth in the Bible's affirmation that the just shall live by faith (cf. Hab. 2:4; Rom. 1:17; Gal. 3:11; Heb. 10:38). At the heart of the gospel, of course, is the glorious truth that believers are justified, declared righteous, through faith in Christ. This faith is a living faith, and so it results in a new way of living as well. As the author of Hebrews says, "Without faith it is impossible to please him [God]" (11:6).

Faith is "the evidence of things not seen" (Heb. 11:1). The Israelites had experienced the goodness of God through the years, but they of course could not see Him. Lacking a robust faith, they wanted a king that they could see with their own eyes, just like the nations around them had.

To live for God in this fallen world, we must "look not at the things which are seen, but at the things which are not seen: for the things which are seen are temporal; but the things which are not seen are eternal" (II Cor. 4:18). Paul goes on to say, "For we walk by faith, not by sight" (5:7).

We should not be too quick to criticize the people of Israel for their foolish demand. We too are prone to grasp tangible worldly props to hold us up instead of depending on the presence and promises of God. Let us call to mind all the ways that He has delivered us from evil and gratefully submit to Him as the King of our lives.

The security that the world offers will prove illusory. God alone is our refuge and strength.

—Stephen H. Barnhart.

Heart of the Lesson

Warnings sometimes appear in Scripture where you least expect them. Such is the case with today's passage. You would not expect to find a warning in the account of the selection of the first king of Israel. God, however, used this occasion to give His people a warning. Ironically, God's grace is also quite evident. Not only did He guide Israel in the choice of a king; He also provided men to help and encourage him.

1. Warning from God (I Sam. 9:1-2; 10:17-19). The people of Israel had been crying out for a king. There was one major problem with this: They failed to realize that this constituted a rejection of God as their King. God gave them what they asked for, but it was not what was best for them.

Here is a problem we all face. It is easy to become all wrapped up in our circumstances and problems. As time goes on, we become so focused on ourselves that we fail to realize how self-centered we have become.

We need to heed the words of James 4:3-4: "Ye ask, and receive not, because ye ask amiss, that ye may consume it upon your lusts. Ye adulterers and adulteresses, know ye not that the friendship of the world is enmity with God? whosoever therefore will be a friend of the world is the enemy of God." When we become self-centered in our prayers, we have become friends of the world.

2. Guidance from God (I Sam. 10:20-22). The events surrounding the choice of Saul should remind us to be wary of basing our decisions on merely external matters. An ancient nation's choice of a king was often based on such issues as wealth, power, and political support. Here, however, God chose a humble individual from the smallest tribe in Israel (cf. 9:21).

It is difficult to "walk by faith and not by sight" (II Cor. 5:7). We naturally make decisions based on the facts we are aware of; what we should do, however, is ask for and rely on the guidance of God, who knows even the factors we are not aware of. Each step in the process of choosing Saul was done with complete reliance on the Lord's direction. How often are we willing to break from making "routine" decisions and instead seek God's solution to a problem?

This passage reminds us of the need to go deeper and seek God's perspective on things when we are making decisions. We must not become all wrapped up in merely surface issues.

3. Encouragement from God (I Sam. 10:23-26). The man God chose to be king over His people was physically impressive. In fact, there was no one his equal among the people. Saul nevertheless was so timid that he hid in order to avoid being brought before the people. He now received some much-needed encouragement from those gathered around him as they shouted, "God save the king!" In addition, God touched the hearts of several courageous men to accompany Saul and help him in the daunting task he had been saddled with.

This example shows us that God provides His grace in the areas we need it most. It also makes it clear that we do not have to fear failure or opposition. Our God is the sovereign Lord of hosts, and no one can hinder Him from accomplishing His purposes.

How are you doing in these areas? Are your prayers self-centered or God-centered? Are you basing your decisions on surface issues? Are you aware of God's provision of grace in your area of need? Do not despair! Call upon God now.

—James R. Gordon.

World Missions

The very reason missionaries and others are needed to share the gospel of Christ is, in essence, the same reason God gave Israel a king. That reason is people's rejection of God. That attitude is seen repeatedly throughout history as recorded in the Bible.

There was the generation that preceded the Flood and then the generation at Babel. The rise of idolatry and various false religions give evidence of a wholesale rejection of God. Even after God had chosen a people for Himself, we find they too rejected Him on a regular basis.

The casual reader of the Bible will quickly encounter more incidents of God being spurned than he would want to keep track of. No more than a casual look at the world today is needed to see that the vast majority of mankind is lost and has no use for the living God. Sadly, attendance at many Christian churches and the number of closed churches reveal a less-than-enthusiastic desire for worship and to know God's Word.

The major reason for this situation is, of course, sin and all its disastrous effects on the human soul. One of the resultant effects is that people have either forgotten or are ignorant of what God has done. In their turning away from God, they have become intellectually oblivious to the wonder and love and grace and majesty of Almighty God.

People conveniently overlook the fact that it is God who provides the seed, sends the rain, and causes the sun to shine. They need to be taught the truth about God and His deeds, as well as the truth about themselves. They need someone who cares for them even though they do not care for their own soul.

People in general also are ignorant of what God wanted to do. His plan for the ages as laid out in the Bible will come to pass, and all mankind will play a part in it. The part they play will depend on their faith and their relationship with Jesus Christ.

This is where the missionary, the pastor, the Sunday school teacher, and every believer come in. There is a message to be told to the nations, beginning with the person next door, across the street, in the same office, or sitting at the next desk in school. The message, of course, is the good news of Jesus Christ: who He is and what He has done. The message needs to be conveyed about His intercession with the Father, His future return in glory, the need for repentance and faith, and all the other wonderful truths in the Bible.

Although God graciously exhibits great patience with those who have rejected Him, the need is urgent in terms of getting the message out to as many as possible. The need has never been greater. The home, the neighborhood, the world needs more Samuels—those who are doing the will of God by boldly proclaiming to people where they have gone wrong and what God says needs to be done.

Samuel also displayed the kind of attitude today's servant needs. That is the attitude of concern that causes the messenger to uphold people in prayer (cf. I Sam. 12:23) even though they have rejected the Lord. May God call and raise up a vast army of willing servants for a great missionary advance in these last days. May there be many souls who once rejected the Lord who find salvation before the end.

—Darrell W. McKay.

The Jewish Aspect

Since Samuel's sons had failed to direct Israel in godly ways, the Israelite people requested that Samuel give them a king. The people wanted to be like other nations (I Sam. 8:1-5). The people preferred having a strong human leader to depending upon God as their Deliverer.

The Lord selected a king for Israel who would be to their liking. The Haggadah states that Saul was chosen for his military prowess, his unusual handsomeness, his modesty, his innocence, and the merits of his ancestors. Saul's grandfather Abiel was especially celebrated for lighting the streets after dark to enable people to go to special houses for study (Roth and Wigoder, eds., *Encyclopedia Judaica,* Coronet).

Choosing a king, however, was not compatible with Israel being a theocracy—a nation ruled directly by God. For this reason Samuel said, "Ye have this day rejected your God" (10:19). Up to that time, God had raised up judges and priests to lead His people according to His will. Samuel feared that a king would not seek God's will when ruling but would rely on his own wisdom and seek his own selfish desires.

When God chose Israel to be His special people (Ex. 19:4-5), it was understood they were to be governed by God. For this reason God gave Israel the commandments. The concept of Israel being a theocracy has not diminished over time in the minds of many Jews. These Jews maintain that the power of government should be "vested in the spiritual leadership wielding its authority in the name of God" (Wigoder and Werblowsky, eds., *Oxford Dictionary of the Jewish Religion,* Oxford).

From the time of the Middle Ages, Jewish life has been dominated by the rabbinate, considered God's leadership. It has "exercised legislative functions based on the halakhah" (Wigoder and Werblowsky). "Halakhah" refers to the normative practice of behavior established by the majority opinions of the rabbis during past history. Jews use the term for the standard for fulfilling the rabbinic teachings of the Torah (Law). Many in the State of Israel use the term *theocracy* to refer to subjecting all things to halakhah.

The idea that Jews are being directed by God and that other nations are not has led to some animosity. Negative feelings especially have appeared when national leaders have demonstrated grace toward Jews. When Napoleon Bonaparte emancipated Jews following the French Revolution, a forged letter was sent to him by anti-Semitic people, blaming the Jews for the revolution.

This tactic has been repeated through the years as a number of forged documents have been written by anti-Semitic groups to renew persecution against the Jews. *The Protocols of the Learned Elders of Zion* was one of these. This forged document purported "to describe a plot by International Jewry to seize control of the world" (Dudley, ed., *The Encyclopedia Americana,* Americana). Hitler seized on the propaganda in this document to severely persecute Jews.

Although some Jews believe in the coming Messiah who will reign over the earth, no Jewish group has tried to establish such a worldwide rule themselves. Many Jews realize that only Messiah can bring to the world the peace spoken of in Scripture. The same Messiah that Jewish people anticipate is the Christ whose kingdom will triumph.

—Theodore G. Smetters.

Guiding the Superintendent

Once the children of Israel arrived in the Promised Land, they were told to destroy its inhabitants. To some degree this was accomplished, but a number of nations continued to harass the Israelites. For this and other reasons, the people demanded a king, thinking that a monarchy similar to those in the surrounding nations would assure them of victory over their enemies (I Sam. 8:1-22). Even though Samuel outlined the consequences of such an arrangement, the people were determined to have a king. God granted their request.

DEVOTIONAL OUTLINE

1. Saul seen (I Sam. 9:1-2). Saul was from the tribe of Benjamin, who were descendants of one of Jacob's favorite sons. Saul's father, Kish, was "a mighty man of power."

Young Saul was tall and good-looking, natural qualities that would make him a favorite among the people he was chosen to rule. He apparently possessed leadership qualities that he might have learned from his own father, though he was reluctant to accept the crown.

2. Saul silent (I Sam. 10:17-21). As the spiritual leader of the nation, Samuel called Israel together for a solemn assembly to publicly identify the new king. Reminding them of their deliverance from Egyptian bondage, Samuel again pressed home the truth that their desire for a king was a rejection of their governance by God Himself.

Tribe by tribe and family by family, God's choice was narrowed down. In some way, perhaps through the Urim and Thummim (Ex. 28:30), God identified His choice for the new king. For whatever reason, perhaps simply out of shyness, Saul was nowhere to be found.

3. Saul selected (I Sam. 10:22-24). Again the people sought the Lord's guidance and discovered that the man they were seeking had hidden himself among the baggage. Once he was brought before the people, Saul stood out because of his height.

Because of Saul's impressive physical stature, the people were further convinced that this indeed was the man God had chosen to lead their nation. Like several other kings of Israel, however, Saul began well but ended badly (28:1-20; 31:1-6). This was a direct result of his unwillingness to fully obey the Lord (15:1-26).

4. Saul supported (I Sam. 10:25-26). Even though Saul had been identified as the new king, the formal inauguration would occur later (11:15). Certain men "whose hearts God had touched" (10:26) enthusiastically followed Saul, and most of the nation fully supported the new monarchy.

Not all, however, were eager supporters of the new king, as the reference to "children of Belial" indicates (vs. 27). "Belial" is a Hebrew word meaning "of no use" and usually denotes worthless individuals. It was used of Satan by Paul in the New Testament (II Cor. 6:15).

AGE-GROUP EMPHASES

Children: The various qualities of good leadership in church, school, family, and nation should be stressed, along with the importance of showing respect for those in authority.

Youths: Israel did not weigh all the consequences of a monarchy. Learning to anticipate consequences is part of good decision making.

Adults: Adults should consider the impact of both supporters and detractors on the success of any leader.

—John A. Owston.

Scripture Lesson Text

JOSH. 24:1 And Joshua gathered all the tribes of Israel to Shechem, and called for the elders of Israel, and for their heads, and for their judges, and for their officers; and they presented themselves before God.

14 Now therefore fear the Lord, and serve him in sincerity and in truth: and put away the gods which your fathers served on the other side of the flood, and in Egypt; and serve ye the Lord.

15 And if it seem evil unto you to serve the Lord, choose you this day whom ye will serve; whether the gods which your fathers served that *were* on the other side of the flood, or the gods of the Amorites, in whose land ye dwell: but as for me and my house, we will serve the Lord.

16 And the people answered and said, God forbid that we should forsake the Lord, to serve other gods;

17 For the Lord our God, he *it is* that brought us up and our fathers out of the land of Egypt, from the house of bondage, and which did those great signs in our sight, and preserved us in all the way wherein we went, and among all the people through whom we passed:

18 And the Lord drave out from before us all the people, even the Amorites which dwelt in the land: *therefore* will we also serve the Lord; for he *is* our God.

19 And Joshua said unto the people, Ye cannot serve the Lord: for he *is* an holy God; he *is* a jealous God; he will not forgive your transgressions nor your sins.

20 If ye forsake the Lord, and serve strange gods, then he will turn and do you hurt, and consume you, after that he hath done you good.

21 And the people said unto Joshua, Nay; but we will serve the Lord.

22 And Joshua said unto the people, Ye *are* witnesses against yourselves that ye have chosen you the Lord, to serve him. And they said, *We are* witnesses.

23 Now therefore put away, *said he,* the strange gods which *are* among you, and incline your heart unto the Lord God of Israel.

24 And the people said unto Joshua, The Lord our God will we serve, and his voice will we obey.

NOTES

Joshua's Final Exhortation

Lesson Text: Joshua 24:1, 14-24

Related Scriptures: Exodus 19:7-8; Joshua 8:30-35; 24:2-13; Luke 14:25-35

TIME: about 1390 B.C. PLACE: Shechem

GOLDEN TEXT—"If it seem evil unto you to serve the Lord, choose you this day whom ye will serve; . . . but as for me and my house, we will serve the Lord" (Joshua 24:15).

Introduction

Moses and the Israelites had left Mount Sinai after the giving of the Law by God. When they came to the border of Canaan, the majority refused to enter in and possess the land. As a result, God caused them to wander in the wilderness for forty years while the first generation that had come out of Egypt died. The new generation, led by Joshua, entered the Promised Land, conquered the heathen living there, and settled down.

As Joshua neared the end of his life, he assembled the leaders of the nation and urged them to be faithful to God and the covenant He had made with them. Pagan religious influences from Mesopotamia, Egypt, and Canaan were spiritual threats that needed to be forcefully resisted.

Joshua adamantly called upon the Israelites to make a clear choice. They could choose to serve Yahweh exclusively, or they could turn to polytheism, but they could not have it both ways. The people readily agreed to serve the Lord only.

LESSON OUTLINE

I. ASSEMBLY—Josh. 24:1

II. ADMONITION—Josh. 24:14-20

III. AGREEMENT—Josh. 24:21-24

Exposition: Verse by Verse

ASSEMBLY

JOSH. 24:1 And Joshua gathered all the tribes of Israel to Shechem, and called for the elders of Israel, and for their heads, and for their judges, and for their officers; and they presented themselves before God.

One person who is righteous can have a positive effect on a whole nation of misguided people. Joshua was such an individual, and the Israelites who had settled Canaan needed the challenge he wanted to give them as his leadership career approached its end.

Not everyone in Israel could make the trip to Shechem. {This convocation was set up for representatives of the various tribes to attend. They included elders, heads (subordinate leaders), judges, and officers (officials). They would be able to go back home and report what had happened, and they could be involved in making necessary changes.}Q1

{Note the fact that they came together not only to meet with Joshua but also to present themselves before God. Therefore this was not merely a political gathering. It was also a sacred assembly.}Q2

ADMONITION

14 Now therefore fear the LORD, and serve him in sincerity and in truth: and put away the gods which your fathers served on the other side of the flood, and in Egypt; and serve ye the LORD.

15 And if it seem evil unto you to serve the LORD, choose you this day whom ye will serve; whether the gods which your fathers served that were on the other side of the flood, or the gods of the Amorites, in whose land ye dwell: but as for me and my house, we will serve the LORD.

16 And the people answered and said, God forbid that we should forsake the LORD, to serve other gods;

17 For the LORD our God, he it is that brought us up and our fathers out of the land of Egypt, from the house of bondage, and which did those great signs in our sight, and preserved us in all the way wherein we went, and among all the people through whom we passed:

18 And the LORD drave out from before us all the people, even the Amorites which dwelt in the land: therefore will we also serve the LORD; for he is our God.

19 And Joshua said unto the people, Ye cannot serve the LORD: for he is an holy God; he is a jealous God; he will not forgive your transgressions nor your sins.

20 If ye forsake the LORD, and serve strange gods, then he will turn and do you hurt, and consume you, after that he hath done you good.

Challenge (Josh. 24:14-15). At the beginning of his speech, Joshua reviewed what God had done for Israel from the time of Abraham to the settling of Canaan (vss. 2-13). Considering all the blessings the Israelites had received from the Lord, {Joshua challenged them to fear Him, meaning they were to give Him their reverence.

In addition to fearing the Lord, the Israelites were urged to serve Him in sincerity and truth, meaning they should do it in a genuine and honest way.

In addition to fearing and serving the Lord, the Israelites were told to put away the idols representing the gods their ancestors had served on the "other side of the flood, and in Egypt" (vs. 14).}Q3 It is very doubtful that the flood mentioned here referred to the worldwide deluge in Noah's time. {It more likely referred to the Euphrates River. The land beyond it, Mesopotamia, was the original home of Abraham.}Q4

{Apparently, some of the Israelites had idols from Mesopotamia and Egypt hidden among them. They also had idols representing gods of the Amorites, among whom they dwelled in Canaan.}Q5 Unwilling to exterminate all the pagans in Canaan, some Israelites had fallen prey to their false religious beliefs and practices.

Joshua was very blunt in stating that if the Israelites found it undesirable to serve Yahweh, they should openly choose other gods, whether those of Mesopotamia, Egypt, or Canaan. {Joshua was equally frank in stating that as far as he and his household were concerned, they would serve the Lord.}[Q6]

Here was an example of national leadership we might wish we could see in world leaders today. Too many of them are self-serving or so corrupt that they care little for the welfare of their own people.

Some today might wonder how Joshua dared to speak not only for himself but also for his whole household. During that patriarchal period, it was not unusual for a man to include all of his family members and servants in statements he made. The same might be said of various cultures in our time. We know that devotion to God is an individual matter, but a united and well-led family can have a joint testimony.

Care (Josh. 24:16-17). The assembled delegates at Shechem appeared to be shaken by Joshua's remarks and might even have been somewhat resentful. {They felt that they had shown gratitude to the Lord for bringing them and their fathers out of the land of Egypt, performing miracles in their sight, and preserving them while they passed through hostile pagan people's territories. They felt they had appreciated the divine care they had received.}[Q7]

Contradiction (Josh. 24:18-19). God's care for them continued when they entered Canaan and had to fight the Amorites living there. They failed to mention that they had not fully obeyed God's command to be more thorough in ridding the land of those who had long polluted it with their evil ways.

The leaders of Israel then declared, "We [will] also serve the Lord; for he is our God" (vs. 18). Joshua's response in verse 19 raises some questions. Did he think they were too quick to make this commitment? Since they did not immediately act to rid themselves of idols, did Joshua fear they still retained the misguided notion that Yahweh was willing to be but one of a host of gods they could serve?

Such attitudes are, in essence, still present among some who like to claim the name "Christian." We are reminded of theological liberals today who consider themselves so broad-minded that they see the God of Christianity to be on only an equal footing with a host of false gods claimed by other religions. They say that it does not matter what you believe as long as you are sincere and that all faiths lead to the same end. In this way, they try to take away the unique position the true God holds in the universe.

{Joshua warned the Israelites that they would not be able to serve Yahweh, for He is holy. He is a jealous God, meaning He will not share His glory with other so-called gods.}[Q8] People who view Him in the wrong way cannot hope to find forgiveness for their sins from Him.

Biblically speaking, it is a contradiction in terms to say that anyone can serve God along with other gods (Josh. 24:14-15), mammon (earthly wealth, Matt. 6:24), or any other being or thing. He stands above all else. He is exclusive and unique. He is different not just in degree but also in kind.

Consequences (Josh. 24:20). Although the leaders of Israel had said that they would not forsake Yahweh, {Joshua said that they would be guilty of forsaking Him if they persisted in serving strange gods. If that happened, Yahweh would turn against them. He would hurt them in a disciplinary way in an effort to drive them back to Himself.}[Q9] You might want to turn your attention to Hebrews 12:1-15 for scriptural elaboration on this subject.

The next step beyond disciplinary action is severe punishment. Joshua told the leaders of Israel, "The Lord . . . will . . . consume you, after that he hath done you good" (Josh. 24:20). That "good" may have referred to God's care of Israel from Egypt to Canaan. However it should also be noted that chastisement by God, though difficult to endure, does have a kind intention. It makes people aware of their sinful condition and leads them toward repentance and forgiveness.

If this fails to produce the proper reaction, God is prepared to bring His judgment upon the unrepentant. This was something Joshua wanted his nation to avoid. Having challenged their commitment and given them due warning, Joshua now waited to see whether they were still ready to eradicate idol worship and serve Yahweh exclusively.

AGREEMENT

21 And the people said unto Joshua, Nay; but we will serve the LORD.

22 And Joshua said unto the people, Ye are witnesses against yourselves that ye have chosen you the LORD, to serve him. And they said, We are witnesses.

23 Now therefore put away, said he, the strange gods which are among you, and incline your heart unto the LORD God of Israel.

24 And the people said unto Joshua, The LORD our God will we serve, and his voice will we obey.

Choice (Josh. 24:21-22). Clearly the leaders of Israel did not want to bring God's wrath upon themselves and their people back home, and they had no intention of doing so. They repeated their determination to serve Yahweh, with the implication that He would be their sole deity. This affirmation of monotheism was rare in the ancient world, where polytheism was the norm. It set the Israelites apart from the other peoples of that time.

Joshua accepted the decision of the delegates as being sincere. In order to strengthen their resolve, he told them, "Ye are witnesses against yourselves that ye have chosen you the Lord, to serve him" (vs. 22). They responded, "We are witnesses."

What this meant was that they were pledging themselves to remember and confirm the decision taken that day if there was ever any question about it. We are not told how many attended the assembly, but there may have been several score or several hundred individuals. Any one of them might subsequently be questioned about what had happened, and thus every delegate felt compelled to tell the truth about it.

Since the biblical requirement was that any charge should be upheld by two or three individual witnesses (cf. Num. 35:30), the fact that all of the delegates to the assembly agreed to be witnesses against themselves and one another if they forsook the Lord was very impressive.

Conformity (Josh. 24:23-24). **{**Joshua took advantage of the unified opinion expressed by the leaders of Israel to strongly urge them to put away the false foreign ("strange") gods that were among them.**}**[Q10] It seems safe to assume that Joshua was referring to all the idols kept by Israelites throughout all of the tribal territories in Israel. It no doubt also applied to any idols carried by the Israelites when they traveled outside the nation's borders. This was a call for total conformity.

A spiritual vacuum would be created by getting rid of idols, and that vacuum had to be filled. **{**Joshua thus told the people to incline their hearts to the God of Israel.**}**[Q10] Students of human nature often agree that there is a need in every human heart for acceptance of and devotion to a power above and beyond what the earth has to offer. Theologians call this the quest for God, which arises naturally from the needs of the human heart. If the vacuum is not filled by God Himself, something destructive is probably going to take its place. We know that Satan stands ready to provide dangerous substitutes.

Joshua must have considered what happened that day a spiritual highlight in Israel's development. The people at the assembly spoke for themselves and the people back home whom they represented, stating for the third time their intention to serve the Lord God and obey His voice (vs. 24).

Following the Lord requires more, of course, than mere words of commitment. Joshua himself had seen how a previous generation had enthusiastically declared their allegiance to God (Ex. 24:3, 7) but then had repeatedly broken God's covenant with them (Deut. 9:6-7). He wanted to be sure his people were genuinely devoted to following the Lord, and now he was no doubt encouraged.

Going beyond the text for this lesson, we see that Joshua made a covenant with the people that day at Shechem. He wrote the words of the covenant in the book (scroll) of the law of God. He took a great stone and set it up under an oak tree located near the tabernacle, which had been temporarily set up there. He designated the pillar as a stone of witness, as if it had heard all that the Lord had said to those assembled. With this done, Joshua dismissed the delegates to go home to their tribal territories (vss. 25-28).

The enduring quality of what happened at Shechem is attested to by verse 31—"And Israel served the Lord all the days of Joshua, and all the days of the elders that overlived Joshua, and which had known all the works of the Lord, that he had done for Israel."

It did not last long after that, however. The book of Judges, which follows the book of Joshua chronologically, describes a period of backsliding, trouble, and deliverance. The various judges were actually deliverers from oppression more than officials dispensing justice when disputes occurred.

Markedly different from Joshua 24:31, Judges 21:25 declares, "In those days there was no king in Israel: every man did that which was right in his own eyes." God, who was supposed to be King over Israel, was not accepted in that role. Because they neglected the law of God, the people had no true knowledge of right and wrong.

The Israelites in the time of the judges lacked a strong leader such as Joshua to hold them to account and pull them back to the covenant made with God. We need leaders of Joshua's ability and devotion today to hold people accountable to the Word of God and to doing what is right.

—Gordon Talbot.

QUESTIONS

1. In what representative way did Joshua summon all the tribes of Israel to Shechem?
2. How do we know the assembly was both political and sacred?
3. What three things did Joshua ask Israel to do (Josh. 24:14)?
4. What did Joshua mean by "the other side of the flood"?
5. What were three sources of the idols retained by the Israelites?
6. What did Joshua declare regarding himself and his household?
7. Were the Israelites grateful for God's care for them?
8. How did Joshua respond when the leaders first declared that they would serve the Lord?
9. Why might God turn and hurt Israel after He had helped them?
10. What two things did Joshua urge the repentant Israelites to do?

—Gordon Talbot.

Preparing to Teach the Lesson

Our study this week looks at the renewal of God's covenant with the people of Israel. They were no longer in the wilderness. They had entered the Promised Land.

TODAY'S AIM

Facts: to study how the covenant was renewed under the leadership of Joshua.

Principle: to show that it is right to follow only the Lord our God and serve Him alone.

Application: to demonstrate that as Christians, we are called to follow only our God in a pluralistic society where false gods may seek to lure us away.

INTRODUCING THE LESSON

Today we live in a very pluralistic society. We have to contend with other cultures and worship of gods in our midst that challenge our faith. Our lesson this week shows us the right way to respond in such situations.

Many years had passed since the people of Israel responded with enthusiasm to follow all the instructions of the Lord under Moses. The people of Israel were now in the Promised Land of Canaan. Joshua and Caleb had led them there. Their hopes and dreams for a life in the new land had materialized, but they had to stay faithful to the Lord, who had brought them this far. The challenge before them was to make the right choice and follow the one true God despite the paganism around them.

DEVELOPING THE LESSON

1. Summons before God (Josh. 24:1). When Joshua called the leaders and all the people of Israel together to hear what God had to say, they knew that it was something crucial. It was often a time for blessing or punishment. Attempt to create in your class a sense of the awe that one feels when one comes into the holy presence of God and hears His words.

Note that this happened at a place called Shechem. Shechem was one of the assigned cities of refuge (Josh. 20:7) where those who took life unintentionally could go and receive protection, but it is most known for the decision that the Israelites made to follow God above all else.

2. The challenge (Josh. 24:14-15). Joshua challenged the people to serve the Lord with their whole hearts. The class may want to discuss the significance of this to our country today and the choices we are making along these lines. It is important to emphasize the fact that a nation that follows God will receive His blessings.

The challenge from God that Joshua gave Israel was to put away the idols of their ancestors and serve God alone. It may be profitable here to discuss the "gods which your fathers served" (vs. 14) as it applies to us today. Discuss what we need to discard and where we need to go from here. Note that in verse 15, Egypt is a symbol of the old life of bondage to sin. The new life lay ahead of them. God wants us to participate in the new life He has prepared for us, but first we have to discard the old.

It is here that we see Joshua making a public declaration of his allegiance to his God. He and his whole household would serve the Lord at all costs. Here is an example for us to follow. The challenge is for us as well. Today, in the twenty-first century and in a pluralistic society, will we take a stand as Joshua did? It is appropriate to discuss the challenges of following God today in a secular society.

3. The people's response (Josh. 24:16-18). Where there is a challenge, there is always a need for a response. Here the people responded that they were willing to follow God all the way. They recognized the acts of God in delivering them out of Egypt (where they were slaves for at least one hundred years) and in His protection over them in their wilderness years. They also acknowledged God's deliverance of them from their enemies.

The lesson for us is to remember what God has done for us and then serve Him with our total devotion.

4. Commitment to a tough road (Josh. 24:19-22). While Joshua could have been thrilled to hear that the people wanted to follow God alone, he reminded them that the road ahead was not going to be easy and that God would not tolerate sin. He would destroy them if they turned to other gods.

As believers, we often think that when we get saved, everything will be easy. The truth is that sometimes things get tougher because Satan knows he has lost yet another to God. Allow the class to share their own struggles on the rough road after they became Christians.

The people insisted that they would still follow their God and that their minds were made up. With our choice to follow God comes the responsibility of accountability. Many Christians today accept Christ as fire insurance from hell but fail to take into account the responsibility of discipleship that follows our decision. Remind the class of this crucial part of following our Lord today.

5. The decision (Josh. 24:23-24). Joshua told the people to destroy their old ways, their idols, and everything that turned them away from God. Then they were challenged to follow God together. The people accepted willingly with a determination to please God.

We are reminded here that when we choose to follow God, we cannot carry with us the old idols of the world. They have to be left behind. Discuss with the class what "idols" they have carried into the new life and how to leave them behind.

ILLUSTRATING THE LESSON

Choosing to serve God means leaving the world behind.

CONCLUDING THE LESSON

Throughout this week's lesson we have been reminded that Joshua and his people lived among many enemy nations. It was easy to pick up their cultures and the worship of their gods, but God had called the people of Israel to be set apart from that. Joshua led them in the challenge to follow God alone and set the example for them by declaring his family's full allegiance to God.

We have to choose whether we will follow God completely. Following God alone means that we have to leave the world's evil system behind.

ANTICIPATING THE NEXT LESSON

In our next lesson we will explore how Israel failed to keep their promise to worship only the Lord.

—A. Koshy Muthalaly.

PRACTICAL POINTS

1. At key times in our lives we are rightly called on to confirm our dedication to the Lord (Josh. 24:1, 14).
2. If we object to serving the Lord, we will still end up serving someone or something (vs. 15).
3. Considering all He has done for us, the Lord is certainly worthy of our unreserved loyalty (vss. 16-18).
4. A promise to serve God is not something to be taken lightly or frivolously (vss. 19-20).
5. Promises of faithfulness to God must be backed up with concrete action (vss. 21-24).

—Kenneth A. Sponsler.

RESEARCH AND DISCUSSION

1. Many Israelites were still holding on to idols in Joshua's day (Josh. 24:14). What lessons can we learn from this, and what idols might we be holding on to?
2. Was Joshua really giving people the option of serving other gods rather than the Lord (vs. 15)? Why or why not?
3. What are some of the things the Lord has done for us that place us under obligation to serve Him faithfully (vs. 17)?
4. Why did Joshua insist that the people would be unable to serve the Lord (vs. 19)? Is there any reason for such warnings today?
5. How can we hold people (including ourselves) to their commitments in our day (vss. 20-22)?

—Kenneth A. Sponsler.

ILLUSTRATED HIGH POINTS

Choose you this day whom ye will serve (Josh. 24:15)

John Amery fought for the British in World War II but was captured by German forces. While in captivity he proposed setting up a military unit made up of prisoners of war from the British Empire. It became known as the British Free Corps. Although they had uniforms with a Union Jack (British flag) patch on their sleeves, these men fought for the Germans in the battle for Berlin. After the war, Amery was tried, sentenced, and executed as a traitor (Dear and Foot, *The Oxford Companion to World War II,* Oxford).

To us, the enormity of Amery exchanging his loyalty to his homeland for service to the Nazis is jarring. Do we realize how critical it is for us to remain unflinching in our loyalty to the Lord?

Witnesses against yourselves (vs. 22)

After serving in the Nixon administration, Chuck Colson became a Christian as a result of talking with a friend and reading C. S. Lewis. Later he was indicted for having a hand in Watergate crimes. He knew he was innocent of the specific charges, but after an agonizing self-examination, he made an extraordinary move in order to remain loyal to Christ: he pleaded guilty for something he had done but was not even charged with! In so doing he became a witness against himself and went to jail.

Although Israel pledged to obey God's law, the purpose of the law was to prove their guilt (Rom. 3:20; II Cor. 3:7-9)! If the Jews in the time of Christ had become witnesses against themselves and admitted their guilt, they would have walked through the door of faith (Gal. 3:21-25).

—Todd Williams.

Golden Text Illuminated

"If it seem evil unto you to serve the Lord, choose you this day whom ye will serve; . . . but as for me and my house, we will serve the Lord" (Joshua 24:15).

It has often (and accurately) been said that God has no grandchildren. Each new generation must make its own decision about its relationship to God. The generation of Israelites that received the Law at Sinai and vowed obedience to the Lord had perished in the wilderness. Only those who were under twenty years of age at the time of the rebellion at Kadesh-barnea (cf. Num. 14:29-31) survived the wilderness wanderings and entered the Land of Promise.

This new generation had heard Moses repeat the Law just before they crossed the Jordan (Deut. 5). Now they were being challenged by Joshua, Moses' successor, to commit themselves to a life of service to the Lord.

Many young people take their salvation for granted because their parents are Christians or church members. Salvation and commitment to the Lord, however, is an individual decision. All members of each new generation need to hear the gospel and commit themselves to the Lord. No one else can do it for them.

Joshua's challenge to the Israelites demonstrates another great truth: God wants us to make a specific, wholehearted commitment to Him. Nebulous feelings of love for God are not enough; we must make a conscious decision to do what pleases Him.

Joshua reminded the people that their ancestors had served many gods and that the occupants of the land they had just conquered did the same. It was time for them to decide whether they would worship idols or destroy them. Just as the previous generation had had to decide whom they would serve (at Sinai), so their children, now grown men and women, also had to choose. God does not accept ambivalence (cf. Rev. 3:15-16).

Worship that is superficial is not real worship. Obedience that does not come from the heart is not at all what the Lord wants from His people. It must spring out of love and commitment. This is something not only we but also our children and their children must learn.

Joshua asked the people to think about it. How did they see serving the Lord? Did it seem the right thing to do, or did it not at all appeal to them? Was it evil in their sight, or was it good?

The integrity of Joshua is evident in that he had already made his choice, as had his household. Regardless of how the people decided, he would serve the Lord. That is the mark of a true and courageous leader. He knew where he was going and what he wanted to do. There was no need to take a poll to see what the people wanted to do, no need to survey them to find out which direction to go and which god to serve.

Joshua set the example for the people; he was challenging them to do likewise. He knew that God wants such decisions to spring from within, not from without. There is a lesson here for those in leadership, especially in the church. Committed leaders need to set the example and challenge the people to consider who God is and what He has done and make the logical choice when it comes to matters of worship and service.

What we need is godly men in the pulpit leading God's people.

—Darrell W. McKay.

Heart of the Lesson

It is sad when we disobey God. Not only do we miss out on blessings He wants to give us, but we also have to live with the consequences of our sin. The Israelites are a perfect example of this truth.

Because of their disobedience, the older generation was sentenced to forty years of wandering in the desert. There were only two exceptions: Caleb and Joshua, the two spies who believed God could help them gain the Promised Land of Canaan.

God rewarded Joshua by naming him successor to Moses. Those were big sandals to fill! God was faithful to Joshua, though, allowing him to successfully lead the people to take the cities of the area to become their own. It may have taken seven years to conquer the land, which was only possible by God's miraculous hand.

Joshua's career as a leader was now coming to an end. He was old and his life was nearing its end. Joshua called together all the people for his farewell address.

1. Joshua's challenge (Josh. 24:1, 14-15). Joshua assembled all the people at Shechem. This was an important place, for God had appeared to Abraham there many hundreds of years before. Shechem became a city of refuge and one of the towns given to the Levites.

The leaders presented themselves to the Lord. Joshua challenged them to present themselves to the Lord with singleness of heart. They needed to fear Him and serve Him completely.

After all He had done for Israel, God demanded complete allegiance to Himself. He commanded the people to throw away their false gods and serve Him. How it hurt Him that the people still clung to their idols!

Joshua challenged the people to make a clear-cut choice. He urged them to stop sitting on the fence of indecision. He stood up for God and made his own decision public: he and his household would serve the Lord. It was his hope that the people would make the same response.

2. Israel's response (Josh. 24:16-18). The people readily agreed with Joshua. They knew it was the correct answer to make; so they did not have to think hard about it. They knew God's miracles of the past in the wilderness and during the conquests. They agreed to serve the Lord, calling Him "our God." They said they were ready to obey Him.

3. God's covenant renewed (Josh. 24:19-24). Joshua cautioned the people not to make a hasty decision. He reminded them of God's holiness. They needed to remember how unrighteous they often were. They had to count the cost before agreeing to the covenant.

The people continued to agree. Joshua took them at their word, calling them to be witnesses. He told them they needed to show obedience by throwing away their idols as a sign of their loyalty to God. They agreed.

Joshua then recorded in the "book of the law of God" (vs. 26) all they had agreed to do. He also set a huge stone as a memorial of the covenant.

Israel had a problem with idolatry throughout their history. Too often they wanted to fit in with the pagan society around them. Do you strive to be part of the world too? Anything in our lives that we place above God in importance is sin. God needs to have first place.

—Judy Carlsen.

World Missions

My first attempt at preaching was in the Sunshine Mission in Saint Louis. We arrived early enough to look the rescue mission over closely. There was a large portrait of Edward A. "Daddy" Card, the founder. My pastor explained that Daddy Card had been saved in the Pacific Garden Mission in Chicago. He later felt led to take up the work of dealing with the broken men and women cast up on the river city.

Investing his life in the loveless, Card grew in Christlikeness. Some called him "Old Glory Face," for he closed every prayer with the words "that will be glory for me." Charles Gabriel, the great songwriter, dedicated the hymn "O That Will Be Glory" to Daddy Card.

Incidentally, though I was quaking with fear, my message in Saint Louis went well. One man, a Jew named Solomon, was saved.

After my visit to the Sunshine Mission, I could hardly wait to visit the famous Pacific Garden Mission. I arrived in Chicago and found the mission abuzz, with great numbers of people coming and going. The mission director, the late Harry Saulnier, welcomed me and invited me to stay. I dined with the mission staff that evening. The food was plain and wholesome.

The evening service was an eye-opener. The men began to file in, having been invited by mission workers on the street. Some men lurched in, under the influence of alcohol. It was necessary to attend the hour-long gospel service in order to be invited to dine afterward. The music was loud, and the preaching was sound. Some were so dissipated they could not respond to the invitation. Some found their way forward, and, as has happened continually since the day the mission opened, one or more made a profession of faith.

I spent the evening in the workers' dormitory. Spartan, army-style bunks were ranked across the large room. The curfew caused a rush on the washroom. My bunk was next to that of a well-dressed man. I tried to make conversation with him, but he was uncommunicative. He wore an expression of great heaviness.

At breakfast the next morning, a muscular man with all the marks of a hard life on his face led us in a rousing chorus of "Every Day with Jesus" (Loveless). The breakfast portions were plain but plentiful.

Carl F. H. Henry, the founder of *Christianity Today* magazine, wrote that the early years of the mission were marked by the services of Harry Monroe, Mel Trotter, and Billy Sunday (*The Pacific Garden Mission,* Zondervan).

Monroe directed the Mission for thirty years. He led Trotter and Sunday to the Lord.

Mel Trotter was a hopeless alcoholic whose wife had given up on him. On his way to the Chicago River to end an ill-spent life, Mel was saved. His wife then took him back, and Trotter proclaimed, "As for me and my house, we will serve the Lord" (Josh. 24:15). Trotter served six years as director and during his life helped to supervise sixty-seven other rescue missions.

Billy Sunday, the famous baseball player and a leading American evangelist, did not join the mission staff, but it was a lifelong love for him. In his public ministry, Sunday led multitudes to faith in Jesus Christ.

—*Lyle P. Murphy.*

The Jewish Aspect

The Hebrew name for Jesus is "Yeshua," or "Joshua." "Yeshua" means "Yahweh is salvation." Our God's very nature is to save people, and I praise Him for His grace.

In his farewell address to the Hebrew nation, Joshua set before Israel the choice that is ever before the Jewish people: they can seek and follow the God of their own inspired Scriptures, or they can follow a vain way of life without knowing God and His Word.

Dr. Arthur Kac was a Jewish man who chose to follow the Lord, just as Joshua did.

Arthur grew up in Warsaw, Poland, during the first two decades of the twentieth century. As a boy he received extensive training in the Hebrew language, the Tanakh, and the Talmud. After World War I, he became a Zionist. These zealous young men and women believed Jews could save themselves as a people only by returning to the land of Israel (Kac, "How a Jewish Radiologist Found His Redeemer," *The Happy Surfer Messianic Page*).

In 1925 Arthur met Joseph Landsman, an expert in the Hebrew Scriptures. Together they studied the Bible and the Talmud. Many Hebrew Christians study the Talmud because of its importance to Jewish thought, but they do not believe the Talmud is inspired Scripture.

Through Landsman's influence, Arthur became a believer in the Lord Jesus Christ. Even though he went to medical school and became a doctor, Arthur Kac remained a Hebrew scholar all his life. He always took the time to read the Bible, and he wrote several books about the doctrine of the Messiah and the future of the nation of Israel.

As a doctor, Arthur Kac knew how sickness and death haunt mankind. Humanity's ultimate enemies are sin and death. Dr. Kac saw Jesus the Messiah as mankind's only hope. He traced the messianic hope back to Genesis 3:15, which speaks of Him crushing Satan's head. He also traced the messianic hope to the line of men and women who would come from Shem: "Blessed be the Lord God of Shem" (9:26).

Following the apostle Paul, Dr. Kac believed the Messiah was actually the ultimate descendant of Abraham and Sarah: "Now to Abraham and his seed were the promises made. He saith not, And to seeds, as of many; but as of one, And to thy seed, which is Christ" (Gal. 3:16).

The Lord told Abraham that kings would come from him (Gen. 17:6). In this light, Dr. Kac further traced the messianic King to the tribe of Judah. He understood 49:10 as a key messianic verse: "The sceptre shall not depart from Judah, nor a lawgiver from between his feet, until Shiloh come; and unto him shall the gathering of the people be."

Dr. Kac pointed out the connection between Genesis 49:10 and Ezekiel 21:25-27: "And thou, profane wicked prince of Israel [King Zedekiah], whose day is come, when iniquity shall have an end, thus saith the Lord God; Remove the diadem, and take off the crown: this shall not be the same: exalt him that is low, and abase him that is high. I will overturn, overturn, overturn, it: and it shall be no more, until he come whose right it is; and I will give it him."

Dr. Kac noted the similarity between "until Shiloh come" (Gen. 49:10) and "until he come whose right it is" (Ezek. 21:27). He thought the verses were parallel messianic prophecies (Kac, *The Messianic Hope*, Baker).

—James Coffey.

Guiding the Superintendent

I used to possess an excellent memory. When I was in high school, my memory was almost photographic, which made it very easy for me to get excellent grades without too much study time.

Now that I am in my fifties, life has become a bit more complicated. Oh, how I long for the days of excellent memory! I am thankful for an understanding and loving wife who gently reminds me of things I have forgotten.

During a point in Israel's history, God's people needed a reminder—and not necessarily a gentle one. Israel had forgotten the demands of their covenant relationship with God. In Israel's case, memory was not the problem—the problem was with their sinful hearts.

In this week's lesson we discover how a godly man named Joshua was used by the Lord to remind His people about their accountability to their God and how God's people responded to Joshua's challenge.

DEVOTIONAL OUTLINE

1. Joshua's challenge to serve the Lord (Josh. 24:1, 14-18). Joshua gathered the leaders of the nation of Israel together at Shechem and reminded them of God's faithfulness to His covenant promises. Joshua then issued a thorough challenge, commanding them to renew their covenant relationship by respectfully serving the Lord and ridding themselves of idols.

God's people responded to Joshua's challenge by recounting God's faithfulness to His covenant and renewing their commitment to serve Him.

2. Joshua's repeated challenge to forsake idolatry and serve the Lord (Josh. 24:19-24). Joshua realized the seriousness of this significant moment in Israel's history. He made certain that Israel understood it too. Joshua basically stated that the people of Israel were incapable of forsaking their idolatrous past and fulfilling their renewed commitment to serve the Lord. Israel responded to Joshua's charge with a confident verbal commitment.

Joshua then rechallenged Israel to forsake their idolatrous ways and relate to their God with heartfelt conviction. God's people responded a third time by stating that they would serve Him with obedient hearts.

AGE-GROUP EMPHASES

Children: Have your teachers use this week's lesson text to teach the children about God's faithful love for them. Even when Israel disappointed Him by serving false gods, God gave them an opportunity to change their minds and hearts and return to Him. That is true love!

Youths: Young people especially need to know of God's faithful character. Youthful transgressions often lead to a life of despair. Remind the young people that God never gives up on His covenant promises and will always welcome His repentant children back into His presence with open arms.

Adults: Many adults look back on their family history and wish that they had done things differently, especially when it comes to parenting decisions. Age and experience confirm that serving Jesus Christ always results in God's blessings.

Encourage the adults by reminding them that it is never too late to echo Joshua's godly pronouncement: "As for me and my house, we will serve the Lord" (Josh. 24:15).

—Thomas R. Chmura.

Scripture Lesson Text

JUDG. 10:10 And the children of Israel cried unto the Lord, saying, We have sinned against thee, both because we have forsaken our God, and also served Baalim.

11 And the Lord said unto the children of Israel, *Did* not *I deliver you* from the Egyptians, and from the Amorites, from the children of Ammon, and from the Philistines?

12 The Zidonians also, and the Amalekites, and the Maonites, did oppress you; and ye cried to me, and I delivered you out of their hand.

13 Yet ye have forsaken me, and served other gods: wherefore I will deliver you no more.

14 Go and cry unto the gods which ye have chosen; let them deliver you in the time of your tribulation.

15 And the children of Israel said unto the Lord, We have sinned: do thou unto us whatsoever seemeth good unto thee; deliver us only, we pray thee, this day.

16 And they put away the strange gods from among them, and served the Lord: and his soul was grieved for the misery of Israel.

17 Then the children of Ammon were gathered together, and encamped in Gilead. And the children of Israel assembled themselves together, and encamped in Mizpeh.

18 And the people *and* princes of Gilead said one to another, What man *is he* that will begin to fight against the children of Ammon? he shall be head over all the inhabitants of Gilead.

NOTES

The Lord metaphorically or allegorically depicted as a scorned, jealous lover.

Rebuke and Repentance

Lesson Text: Judges 10:10-18

Related Scriptures: Deuteronomy 32:15-18; Judges 10:1-9; Nehemiah 1:4-10; Isaiah 63:15-19; Daniel 9:3-19

TIME: 1087 B.C. PLACE: Israel

GOLDEN TEXT—"The children of Israel said unto the Lord, We have sinned: do thou unto us whatsoever seemeth good unto thee; deliver us only, we pray thee, this day" (Judges 10:15).

Introduction

Do you ever wonder whether God gets tired of those who regularly drift off into sin and repeatedly have to confess their sin and get right with Him again? Does He ever get fed up and stop wanting to help?

We appreciate knowing of God's sovereignty, but Scripture reminds us that this does not negate our obligation to make good choices. Israel repeatedly made wrong choices.

Judges 10:6-8 is an astonishing account of how far from the Lord the people of Israel went in their pursuit of sin: "The children of Israel did evil again in the sight of the Lord, and served Baalim, and Ashtaroth, and the gods of Syria, and the gods of Zidon, and the gods of Moab, and the gods of the children of Ammon, and the gods of the Philistines, and forsook the Lord, and served not him. And the anger of the Lord was hot against Israel, and he sold them into the hands of the Philistines, and into the hands of the children of Ammon. And that year they vexed and oppressed the children of Israel."

LESSON OUTLINE

I. CONFRONTATION WITH GOD—Judg. 10:10-14

II. CONFRONTATION WITH AMMON—Judg. 10:15-18

Exposition: Verse by Verse

CONFRONTATION WITH GOD

JUDG. 10:10 And the children of Israel cried unto the LORD, saying, We have sinned against thee, both because we have forsaken our God, and also served Baalim.

11 And the LORD said unto the children of Israel, Did not I deliver you from the Egyptians, and from the Amorites, from the children of Ammon, and from the Philistines?

12 The Zidonians also, and the

Amalekites, and the Maonites, did oppress you; and ye cried to me, and I delivered you out of their hand.

13 Yet ye have forsaken me, and served other gods: wherefore I will deliver you no more.

14 Go and cry unto the gods which ye have chosen; let them deliver you in the time of your tribulation.

A confession (Judg. 10:10). "The Israelites were guilty of becoming like those whom they were supposed to drive out of the land. {"[Verse 6] catalogs the most extensive description of apostasy found in the book. There is a sevenfold litany of gods; in other words, their apostasy was complete. Not only did they serve these gods; they now ignored the one true God.}[Q1] Their actions were dangerously close to Paul's portrait of a culture of decadence (Rom. 1:21-25)" (Phillips, *Holman Old Testament Commentary: Judges, Ruth*, Broadman and Holman).

{This time when Israel cried out to the Lord, it was with words of confession and acknowledgment of their sinfulness. Every time prior to this in Judges, we read that Israel cried out to the Lord because of the enemy, but without mention of any regret for sin or repentance on their part.}[Q2]

They apparently were brought to repentance this time by the degree of suffering they were enduring from their enemies. {Two groups of people were harassing them, on opposite sides of Israel: the Philistines and the Ammonites (Judg. 10:7).}[Q3]

Before Moses died, two and one half tribes had asked permission to settle east of the Jordan River (Num. 32). Their agreement was that they would send military men across the river to help the other tribes conquer Canaan; then they would return to their own settlements. Moses agreed to this, and Joshua honored it after Israel had control of the land in its entirety. These tribes were especially affected by the dominance of the Ammonites at this time (Judg. 10:8). Soon the Ammonites extended their to areas west of the river as well (vs. 9).

{For eighteen years these groups harassed Israel and left them severely distressed.}[Q3] These were the circumstances that caused the people of Israel to cry out to God in confession of their sins. It was not common for them to recognize the cause of their suffering, but somehow this time they did. How often does God use trying circumstances to get the attention of His children and His children fail to recognize His hand in their situations? We tend to forget His constant control of our experiences.

When the people of Israel acknowledged the sinfulness, they spelled out exactly what they had been doing. {They said that they had both forsaken their own God and had served false gods.}[Q4] Is it possible that they actually realized that God had repeatedly blessed them when they were obedient and punished them when they were disobedient? Perhaps this was so, but God's response indicates their confession might not have been completely sincere.

A reminder (Judg. 10:11-12). God was not quick to grant immediate forgiveness and deliverance from their situation. Instead, {He reminded them in the form of a question about several previous deliverances from enemies. Seven different nations from which God had given them deliverance in the past are mentioned in this list; yet verse 6 names seven different groups of false gods they had turned to.}[Q5] Is it any wonder that God's wrath was upon them?

God first mentioned their deliverance from the Egyptians. His reminder took them all the way back to the Exodus, which is one of the most significant miraculous events in the entire history of Israel (Ex. 14—15). The fact that God led perhaps over two million people out of one nation and directed them for forty years until they reached their promised destination is beyond comprehension. That one event alone should have been enough evidence to Israel that God loved them and wanted nothing but the best for them.

The second deliverance God mentioned was from the Amorites. This included the two kings, Sihon and Og, that they had defeated on the east side of the Jordan River prior to entering Canaan (Num. 21). Here is what Rahab said to the two spies when they came to her place in Jericho: "For we have heard how the Lord dried up the water of the Red Sea for you, when ye came out of Egypt; and what ye did unto the two kings of the Amorites, that were on the other side Jordan, Sihon and Og, whom ye utterly destroyed" (Josh. 2:10).

Ammon had been part of the coalition that King Eglon of Moab had led in subjugating Israel (Judg. 3:12-13). We studied God's deliverance from this group earlier this quarter. Although we are not given many details about it, God also delivered Israel from the Philistines under Shamgar (vs. 31). That was also a miraculous deliverance, for Shamgar killed six hundred men with nothing more than an ox goad. The Sidonians are included in a list of enemies in 3:3, but we are not told anywhere else about the deliverance alluded to there.

The Amalekites had been enemies of Israel from as far back as the time of their travels from Egypt. In Exodus 17:8-16 we read that they attacked Israel and that Joshua defeated them while Moses was on the mountain with his hands raised. God declared at that time that He would eventually destroy them completely. They are mentioned in Judges 3:13 and 6:3 as joining with others in harming Israel. Regarding the Maonites, there is no biblical record of their being a problem prior to this, but obviously they were.

God was giving Israel time to reflect on what He had done for them in the past. This led to a challenge they needed to face.

A challenge (Judg. 10:13-14). {The statements from God in these verses are what cause us to think that maybe the Israelites were not totally sincere in their confession.}[Q6] Not only did God take time to remind them of several previous deliverances from various enemies, but He also rebuked them for abandoning Him in order to serve other gods. Furthermore, He said He was not going to deliver them anymore. It appears that God does indeed get tired of His fickle children repeatedly falling away and being unfaithful.

{The Lord then told the Israelites they should go cry out to the gods they had chosen to follow and let them deliver them this time.}[Q7] It was a logical challenge. After all, if their objects of worship were indeed gods, they should have the power to help when they were needed. It is a fact of life that many people who choose to live life the way they want, leaving God out of the picture, will cry out to Him when they get into trouble. Then, if God does not do for them what they ask, they become angry and bitter against Him.

In Proverbs 1:20-33 wisdom is personified and pictured as calling out to us through many everyday circumstances. She is trying to get our attention and get us to realize when we are living without godly wisdom in our lives. When we refuse to listen and then get into trouble, wisdom will laugh at our calamity and will not come to our aid in such situations. When we refuse to heed wisdom's ways and follow God's leadership, we end up suffering the consequences of our choices.

That was basically what God was telling Israel at this time. If they insisted on serving other gods, He was not going to respond to their desperation. They could search for help from those gods. We know, of course, that there could be no help from those false gods. That surely was exactly the message God was sending His people, forcing them to acknowledge the stupidity of their ways. No doubt His challenge caused them to accept the fact that they had no assurance that those gods could do anything.

CONFRONTATION WITH AMMON

15 And the children of Israel said unto the Lord, We have sinned: do thou unto us whatsoever seemeth good unto thee; deliver us only, we pray thee, this day.

16 And they put away the strange gods from among them, and served the Lord: and his soul was grieved for the misery of Israel.

17 Then the children of Ammon were gathered together, and encamped in Gilead. And the children of Israel assembled themselves together, and encamped in Mizpeh.

18 And the people and princes of Gilead said one to another, What man is he that will begin to fight against the children of Ammon? he shall be head over all the inhabitants of Gilead.

A response (Judg. 10:15-16). When the Midianites were oppressing Israel and Israel cried out to God, God sent a prophet with a special message (6:7-10). He reminded the people of their exodus from Egypt, how He had instructed them against fearing other gods, and how they had failed to obey Him. Repeatedly in the past, Israel's concern had been more for their deliverance than for a relationship with God. It seems that was the nature of their initial confession this time also and what prompted God to respond as He did.

A clear change of attitude is evident in Israel's response now, however, and it is obvious that their cry was now sincere. W. Gary Phillips wrote, "Israel realized the first lesson of 'Repentance 101'—God is not stupid and will not be manipulated by false sincerity." Out of desperation, Israel faced reality and came to understand that God was there and was able to help them—but only if their hearts were right and their repentance was sincere.

{The beginning of this statement was genuine confession: "We have sinned" (Judg. 10:15).}Q8 Israel recognized that only by being right with God could they expect the deliverance they desperately wanted. And the only way to be right with Him was to confess their sin and be clean in His presence. It is important for every one of us to recognize this truth. If we are going to expect God to help us in circumstances that are beyond us, we need to be in a right relationship with Him. We cannot be living in sin and still expect His assistance.

{The second part of their statement was a request that God would do whatever seemed fitting to Him if He would only deliver them from their oppressors at this time.}Q8 They were willing for God to punish them if He saw fit. They were willing to go through anything that would secure their deliverance from their enemies. Sometimes God's people continually resist the conviction He places upon them until they reach a point of desperation. God loves us so much that He cannot allow us to continue living in sin.

{After their plea came concrete evidence that their repentance was genuine. They removed the foreign gods from their midst and began to serve the Lord again.}Q8 Herbert Wolf wrote, "Israel demonstrated the genuineness of her repentance by throwing out the idols she was worshiping and by being willing to return to God on His terms" (Gaebelein, ed., *The Expositor's Bible Commentary,* Zondervan). That is a crucial truth for every believer. We cannot live our lives on our terms; we must live them on God's terms. The result will be true joy as we please Him.

{The end of Judges 10:16 is an encouraging insight into the character of our God: "His soul was grieved for the misery of Israel."}[Q9] We know that God is personal and as such possesses intellect, emotion, and will. But we probably fail to think about His emotions much. We know He loves, but here is a look at His sympathetic feelings toward those He loves. When we hurt, God hurts with us. When we cry out to Him from painful circumstances we can hardly bear, His heart grieves with ours.

A question (Judg. 10:17-18). After Israel's confession and plea (and after we read of God's sympathy toward them), the Ammonites came and encamped in Gilead. Israel encamped at Mizpeh. These Ammonites, along with the Philistines, had been causing trouble for Israel for years. It appears that Israel had determined this could go on no longer. {They had one big problem, however; they had no one to lead them into battle against these enemies!}[Q10]

The big question thus revolved around who was going to step up to lead the fight against the Ammonites. This scene portrays confusion, does it not? The enemy has gathered, and the defending nation has gathered its troops, but there is no leader! It would seem to be a little late to be forming an army and finding a leader, but perhaps because of the dominance that had been exhibited by the enemies for so many years, there had been no opportunity to fully organize an army.

Everyone seemed to be in agreement on one thing, however. If someone would step forward and successfully lead these people against the Ammonites, that one should be made the leader of all the residents of Gilead. Apparently there was no one there with the natural gift of leadership. Or perhaps the real truth is that there was no one there with the courage to take on the responsibility now facing them, that is, confronting the enemy forces of Ammon.

The next chapter of Judges tells how God raised up Jephthah to be the leader who was needed so badly. God did respond to the sincere repentance of His people. He gave them the help they needed.

—*Keith E. Eggert.*

QUESTIONS

1. What details are given in Judges 10 about Israel's departure from God that show their depravity?
2. How was the people's initial cry to God different from other times?
3. Who were the enemies, and how long had they dominated Israel?
4. What was Israel's twofold sin that they confessed to God?
5. What did God remind Israel of when they cried out to Him?
6. What makes us think that Israel was not sincere when they first approached God with their plea?
7. To whom did God say Israel should appeal for assistance?
8. How do we know Israel became sincere in their cries to God?
9. How did God respond to Israel's repentant attitude and actions?
10. What problem did Israel have when the Ammonites gathered for battle?

—*Keith E. Eggert.*

Preparing to Teach the Lesson

In our lesson this week, we will learn the results of returning to God in obedience. We learn this from the life of the people of Israel.

TODAY'S AIM

Facts: to show how God paved the way for victory when Israel returned to God in obedience.

Principle: to see that God blesses His people when they return to Him in obedience.

Application: to stress that we should be quick to confess sin and turn back to God in obedience.

INTRODUCING THE LESSON

The greatest stories of restoration begin with a confession of sin. Just look at the life of David in the Bible. When he was boldly confronted about his sin, he confessed it. Genuine confession always leads to obeying God again. Just look at the life of Jonah, with whom we are all familiar. God blessed Jonah when he made up his mind to return to God and obey Him. In our lesson this week, we learn that obedience to God brings forth blessing and always involves a change of lifestyle.

DEVELOPING THE LESSON

1. Israel's cry and confession of sin (Judg. 10:10). As just mentioned, the first step in returning to God is confession of sin. Israel had seen God work in their lives so much that they really had no excuse to turn away from Him. Sadly, when prosperity comes our way, it is easy to forget God. So it was with Israel. But after eighteen years of oppression by the Ammonites (vss. 7-8), the people finally cried out to God. They acknowledged their sin of turning away from Him.

Notice what they said in their confession. They said that they had sinned because they had forsaken the true God and worshipped the Baalim (plural of Baal), which were false gods. When we are too busy to acknowledge the true God, we have forsaken Him. Ask the students to describe the dry spells in their lives when they did not care to acknowledge God in any way. No doubt these days were marked by not reading their Bibles or praying to their God. Unconfessed sin keeps us far from Him even when He is near.

Confession, of course, must be sincere. God knows full well the difference between a heartfelt confession of sin with intent to change and an outward admission motivated solely by the desperation to have unpleasant circumstances removed. The latter must have been the case with the Israelites, as we see from God's initial response.

2. God's response to His people's cry (Judg. 10:11-14). Notice what God said to the Israelites in response. He reminded them of the many times He had saved them from their enemies. Then He listed a few to jog their memories. Let the class members read some of these out loud (vss. 11-12). This is a good time to take stock of God's goodness to us. Ask students to recount times when the Lord rescued them.

God then told the Israelites that they could cry out to the false gods they had chosen to follow and let those gods deliver them. Even though they had previously turned away from God, the Israelites knew that only the Lord could save them from this situation. After all, they had seen Him work on their behalf over and over again. Get the class to think about what "false gods" they rely on instead of turning to the Lord when they get into trouble. Then point them back to the only One we should ever trust.

God also told them that He would not be their rescuer anymore. Those were harsh words, but they were meant to challenge the genuineness of the people's confession. God does not want mere robotic obedience. The goal is for people to desire to obey. Our choice to obey must be genuine. God is only too happy to restore us when we truly return to Him and confess our sins (cf. I John 1:9).

3. A sincere confession and return to God (Judg. 10:15-18). The Israelites acknowledged their sin and let God know that they were ready for any punishment He would impose on them for their turning away from Him. They put away their false gods and began following the Lord again. God's heart was heavy when He saw the misery of His people. Emphasize to your students that our God hurts when we turn away from Him and suffer the consequences of doing so. He desires for us to return to Him.

At this point, God began to restore His people. The Ammonites were back again to oppress them. The Israelites gathered together, and they sought someone to lead them against the enemy. God was again taking back His own people and working on their behalf. Point out to the class that the people were only beginning to be restored, but there were already signs that God was pulling them together again for another victory. All this started with obedience to God.

Point out to the class that the defeated and broken Israelite people were now coming together again and were in the process of seeking a leader. Their wilted spirits were now reviving and getting ready for another big battle. New hope was alive in their hearts only because God was now back in their lives and in their camp. This came to be only because by God's grace they chose to obey and return to God.

The way to restoration and victory is to return to God. The first step is confession of our sin. Then we have to find out what we need to do and obey Him. God is willing to restore His fallen children.

ILLUSTRATING THE LESSON

Returning to God starts with genuine confession of our sin and always leads to obedience.

CONCLUDING THE LESSON

We can all remember a time when we have strayed from God and, like David after his sin with Bath-sheba (cf. Ps. 51), felt estranged from Him. This week we have seen specific steps that we can take to get back on the right track. The first of these is to acknowledge that we have sinned. This opens the door for God to take us back and restore us.

ANTICIPATING THE NEXT LESSON

Next week we will consider King David's gripping story of adultery, murder, and restoration, as well as the wondrous mercy of God.

—A. Koshy Muthalaly.

PRACTICAL POINTS

1. True repentance starts with confession of sin and a recognition that all sin is against God (Judg. 10:10; cf. Ps. 51:3-4).
2. God's past deliverances serve as reminders to obey Him in the future (Judg. 10:11-12).
3. An impotent god is not worth following (vss. 13-14).
4. True repentance seeks God's forgiveness on God's terms (vs. 15).
5. There is no genuine repentance without renouncing the false gods in our lives (vs. 16).
6. God is always compassionate; He sees our misery and answers our smallest cry of faith (vss. 17-18).

—Don Kakavecos.

RESEARCH AND DISCUSSION

1. What circumstances drove the Israelites to cry out to God in repentance (Judg. 10:6-9)? Are we in danger of serving false gods today (Ex. 20:3)?
2. Why do you think the Lord did not answer the Israelites' cry for deliverance immediately (cf. II Cor. 7:9-11)?
3. For what reasons do you think people choose to serve the gods of this world and of their own culture rather than the Creator God revealed in the Bible (cf. I Kgs. 11:4; Rom. 1:16-25)?
4. What are the components of true repentance demonstrated in today's lesson text? Can they always be verified by others?

—Don Kakavecos.

ILLUSTRATED HIGH POINTS

Served the Lord (Judg. 10:16)

During the Vietnam War, my uncle flew for the Strategic Air Command. The air force trained him, along with all the other pilots, to run from his barracks to his plane at the sound of a buzzer. He could not begin to remember how many times he had dropped knife and fork and sprinted to his bomber.

Then he came home to California and a welcome home party at a local restaurant. Everything was fine until Uncle Ray jumped up without warning and ran outside to the parking lot. Catching up with him when he finally stopped running, I asked, "Where are you going?"

"I am looking for my plane" was his bewildered reply as he looked about in vain.

"But what caused you to run out here?" I asked.

"I heard the buzzer."

Then I realized that directly over our table was a buzzer used to call waiters to pick up their orders for table service.

Humble, immediate obedience—is this not what Jesus Christ desires from His followers?

Put away the strange gods

A mother tells this story about her fifteen-year-old rebellious daughter. It started with the girl wearing dark clothes and running with a questionable crowd.

The evidence was plain. This girl, though she had grown up in the church, was involved with witchcraft and the occult. The parents acted immediately. They whisked her away to her aunt, a solid Christian. She enrolled the troubled teenager in a program called Bondage Breaker. She took her niece with her to Bible study. One day the young girl gave her life to the Lord.

—Ted Simonson.

Golden Text Illuminated

"The children of Israel said unto the Lord, We have sinned: do thou unto us whatsoever seemeth good unto thee; deliver us only, we pray thee, this day" (Judges 10:15).

We find the people of Israel here in the midst of one of their repeated cycles of life in the time of the judges. A judge provided by God delivers them, they fall into sin again, and they experience oppression again as the Lord chastens them. The people then repent and call upon God for help.

We might well ask ourselves how long we would put up with this kind of behavior from a slow-learning people. We forget, of course, that we are prone to the same type of cycle in our own lives! Thankfully, God is patient and long-suffering toward us.

The wonderful truth is that God is glorified by the display of His grace in the lives of His people. As David says in Psalm 103, "The Lord is merciful and gracious, slow to anger, and plenteous in mercy. He will not always chide: neither will he keep his anger for ever. . . . Like as a father pitieth his children, so the Lord pitieth them that fear him. For he knoweth our frame; he remembereth that we are dust" (vss. 8-9, 13-14).

The Lord Jesus told Peter to forgive seventy times seven times, meaning times beyond counting (Matt. 18:21-22). This reflects the heart of God toward His people as they turn to Him. As Psalm 50:15 says, "Call upon me in the day of trouble: I will deliver thee, and thou shalt glorify me." God is glorified as we gratefully receive His blessing of deliverance.

We might well wonder, of course, how sincere the people in this Judges passage were in their repentance. Was it an example of a "foxhole" promise to God in a desperate effort to get out of their suffering? We could almost read this sort of motivation into their words—"do anything You want, just get us out of this."

The fact is, though, that the people at least acknowledged that they had sinned. And the very purpose of God's chastening is to bring us to the point of crying out to Him. He is not fooled. He knows that our devotion is not perfect on this side of heaven (think again of the Psalm 103 passage we cited). But still He is gracious to us.

We must not think, of course, that God will just overlook our sin. The chastisements that God brought upon the people in Judges are proof of that. He would test the people to show if they really meant He could do with them what He would if only He delivered them.

One reason we must not presume upon God's mercy is that sin is the mortal enemy of our hearts. It brings guilt, of course, but it also hardens those who persist in it. The time may come, as it did for the nation of Israel, when a person will no longer turn to God in repentance. The result for Israel would be the Babylonian Exile and eventually the destruction of Jerusalem in A.D. 70.

But these sobering considerations should not keep us from rejoicing in the mercy of God toward sinners. We must not let our guilt and shame over sin keep us from the only remedy for our plight—the grace of God.

We may not understand how God can possibly forgive us again and again, but that is what makes the salvation message of Scripture such good news indeed. As we come to Him in repentance, He forgives us and grants us the blessings of a relationship with Him.

—Stephen H. Barnhart.

Heart of the Lesson

The Lord continued to send Israel judges to deliver them from their oppressors. The most recent had been Tola and Jair, judges who brought the nation relief and rest for a number of years (Judg. 10:1-5). But these two did not seem to have any lasting spiritual influence, for Israel "did evil again in the sight of the Lord" (vs. 6).

This time the apostasy involved the worship of the gods of Canaan, Syria, Sidon, Moab, Ammon, and Philistia and the total abandonment of the worship of the Lord. Interestingly, many of the gods they served were gods of nations that oppressed Israel.

As a result of the apostasy, the Lord brought Israel into subjugation to the Philistines to the southwest and the Ammonites to the east (10:7). This crushing oppression continued for eighteen years.

1. The people's confession (Judg. 10:10). As they had done so many times before, the Israelites cried out to God. This time, however, they seemed to recognize the reason for their suffering, for they confessed that they had sinned by forsaking the Lord to serve other gods.

2. The Lord's challenge (Judg. 10:11-14). Such a confession of sin was needed, but it was not enough. The Lord reminded Israel that they had repeatedly sought His help only to turn from Him again once He had delivered them from their enemies. Thus, the Lord challenged the genuineness of their confession. He told them to seek the help of the gods they had chosen to serve.

God did not (and does not) tolerate worship that is merely out of convenience. It is an affront to Him when people turn to Him for help when they have no intention of truly following Him. This had been the case in the past; so it was appropriate that God challenged Israel's confession.

3. The people's repentance (Judg. 10:15-16). The people responded to the Lord by repeating their confession of sin. They realized that the pagan gods they had served could give no help. Israel had turned wholeheartedly to those gods, but they offered no deliverance to the people. So now they turned again to the Lord, confessing their sin and humbly asking for His help.

This was not all the Israelites did, however. The people "put away the strange gods from among them, and served the Lord" (vs. 16). Genuine confession of sin is always accompanied with genuine repentance. The change in their actions confirmed the reality of their confession, and the heart of God was moved.

4. The people's commitment (Judg. 10:17-18). Once they had returned to the worship of the Lord, the people determined to fight for their freedom. They decided this even before God raised up a judge. Although they had no one among them to lead them, they were ready to go forward in faith, trusting God to deliver them. This brief account stands as a light in the dark days of the judges.

It often takes devastating events to bring people to their senses and to repentance. Our prayer should be that God would use whatever means is necessary to accomplish His work in people's lives. And we should stand ready so that when people are brought to their lowest point, we can point them to the God who forgives and delivers.

—Jarl K. Waggoner.

World Missions

The period of the judges was a sad and disappointing era in Israel's history. But although the chronic cycle of national rebellious idolatry, national defeat and oppressive servitude, national repentance and obedience, and recurring rebellious idolatry demonstrated Israel's sinful bent toward selfishness, it also highlights God's redemptive forgiveness and grace. Moreover, one must not overlook the moments when Israel chose to obey the Lord and experienced spiritual freedom and His goodness.

As I considered this week's lesson text in the light of a missions emphasis, my mind and heart were drawn to the account of Jonah, who was commanded by God to go to the city of Nineveh and "cry against it; for their wickedness is come up before me" (Jonah 1:2). Jonah sought instead to flee from God's presence by going to Joppa and sailing to Tarshish.

Through a series of powerful and miraculous events, Jonah eventually obeyed God. As a result, the city of Nineveh and its inhabitants repented and were spared God's judgment. Jonah, though, reverted to his narcissism and had to be confronted by God, who cared more for people's souls than for Jonah's comfort.

What is demanded of a missionary to be wholly obedient to God's call of actively pursuing the ongoing Christian effort of spreading the gospel? This question can be partially answered by considering the Person of Jesus Christ, God's obedient Son, and His high priestly prayer found in John 17:1-26.

First, obedience is intimately connected to God's authoritative Word. Jesus glorified His Father by being obedient to God's will for His life (see verses 1 and 5). Following His example, Jesus' disciples received God's Word and kept it, which means that they attended carefully to it and obediently observed it. Their obedient attitudes had a physical cost, of course. Jesus' disciples were constantly pursued by enemies who hated them and God's Word.

An obedient missionary who is committed to the ongoing Christian effort to spread the gospel will live according to the authoritative Word of God and willingly suffer the consequences of that obedience. The result will be sanctification (cf. vss. 17-19), a purifying and renewing not only of the soul of the missionary but also of the souls of those reached with the gospel who come to believe in the Lord Jesus Christ for eternal life.

Second, Jesus' obedience is intimately related to the spiritual principles of incarnation and sacrifice. Jesus Christ voluntarily and obediently laid aside His eternal power and glory (cf. vs. 4) and "made himself of no reputation, and took upon him the form of a servant, and was made in the likeness of men: and being found in fashion as a man, he humbled himself, and became obedient unto death, even the death of the cross" (Phil. 2:7-8).

Obedient missionaries will follow the principle of sacrificial incarnation. They will do their best to learn the language of the people group to whom they are sent and to learn and adapt to the customs of their culture. Hudson Taylor of the China Inland Mission understood this principle. When he dressed as the Chinese dressed, fellow missionaries despised him. But he made friends and eventual converts of the people he had come to reach.

—Thomas R. Chmura.

The Jewish Aspect

Chutzpah is a curious Yiddish word (by way of Aramaic) that typically means *fearless self-confidence, audacity, or cheekiness*. The Jewish humorist Leo Rosten explained it as the quality of a person who "having killed his mother and father, throws himself on the mercy of the court because he is an orphan" (*The Joys of Yiddish,* Harmony).

The term *chutzpah* is used frequently in the Talmud. It appears in many maxims and proverbs created by the rabbis. One most notable saying is "Impudence [chutzpah] succeeds even with God" (Sanh. 105*a*). After Israel had spurned God and eagerly worshipped pagan idols of metal, wood, and stone, it showed extreme chutzpah for the people to ask the Lord to rescue them from their oppressors. We see their audacity spotlighted in God's response to Israel's cries (Judg. 10:11-13). What reason did He have for helping them when they had so blatantly insulted Him? Even as He did so, He made a point of showing Israel the tragic irony of worshipping false gods and then not depending on them for help (vs. 14).

And yet, despite the ridiculous incongruities present in the situation, in one sense Israel did the right thing: they turned back to the one true God. He was the one who had made them a nation to begin with. It was He who had chosen Abraham, blessed his descendants, multiplied their numbers in Egypt, and then rescued them from cruel slavery. in addtion, the Lord had sustained the nation throughout their wanderings in the wilderness and caused them to possess the Promised Land, which was flowing with milk and honey. By crying out to the Lord in their distress, Israel was at least acknowledging His enduring love and care for them. They were admitting that deep down, they understood He was truly the only one who could rescue them.

But despite the fact that Israel was right in calling on God, there still remained the problem of their myriad and terrible offenses against Him. The Lord was truly angry with them. The oppression that was vexing them so severely had been sent by the one they were asking for help (vs. 7)! Why would Israel entertain any expectation of assistance?

Thankfully, God is abounding in mercy (Ps. 103:8). In fact, it is His great kindness that leads anyone to turn to Him for help (Rom. 2:4). Without that essential characteristic of God, no amount of chutzpah would be of any help. The knowledge that God is forgiving and compassionate is what inspires hopeless rebels to consider repenting. We can see this in Israel's response to God's challenge: they admitted their transgressions and got rid of their idols (Judg. 10:15-16). They even confessed that they were willing to undergo more punishment from God than what they had already received! They began again to worship the Lord.

It had taken real chutzpah for rebellious Israel to ask the Lord to rescue them. But the rabbinical maxim "Chutzpah succeeds even with God" is not a good precept to follow, since He opposes the proud (I Pet. 5:5). Thankfully, He also gives grace to those who humble themselves before Him (vs. 6).

Because Israel did humble themselves in repentance, we see that the Lord looked upon their misery and had pity (Judg. 10:16). Where chutzpah alone would have been disastrous, through repentance and humility Israel did succeed in securing the Lord's help.

—Todd Williams.

Guiding the Superintendent

Why do people blame God for their troubles and yet never consider that their behavior is offensive to God? There are many who have no need for God until they find life unbearable or there is some great need in their lives, and so it was with Israel in the days of the judges.

DEVOTIONAL OUTLINE

1. An admission (Judg. 10:10). Once again, like so many times before, God's chosen people awakened to the truth that they had been going down the wrong road and serving false gods. One might think it strange that they had not noticed that earlier God had used the nations around them to discipline them; yet anyone who is honest with himself knows how easy it is to rationalize one's conduct.

After years of distress at the hands of their enemies and with war staring them in the face, the Israelites sought God's mercy and protection. They not only admitted they had sinned; they also named the sin—a practice that should likewise be followed by Christians when they sin. We should name the sin for which we seek cleansing.

2. A history lesson (Judg. 10:11-12). Like a parent who has heard the same song sung by a disobedient child time and time again, God in essence asked, "How many times have I heard your cries in the past and delivered you?" Then He refreshed their memory, rehearsing the many times from Egypt onward. The list is impressive, especially in light of Israel's conduct.

God is a forgiving God, for which we can be thankful. But one should never presume upon the Lord's mercy—especially after trampling His grace under foot in a rebellious spirit.

3. A denial (Judg. 10:13-14). In what might be called an act of tough love, God told His people He was not going to deliver them this time. They had not responded faithfully to the mercy He had already shown them. They had quickly strayed back into idolatry. God told them that if they wanted to have other gods, they could go ahead and have them. But then Israel should ask *them* for deliverance from trouble. Today we might put it this way, "You have made your bed; now lie in it."

One has to wonder whether perhaps the Lord today is refusing to respond to the prayers of some people because they have forsaken Him and think of Him only when a need arises.

4. A walk to match the talk (Judg. 10:15-18). Even though the Lord had denied Israel's request for help, they decided to submit themselves to Him and put away their idols. It was a case of sensing they needed to show God that the cry of their heart was sincere and that they really wanted to reestablish a right relationship with Him. The Lord watched without responding.

The Lord would later respond, but for the time being He left them to their own devices. Perhaps they might learn the lesson better if they had to struggle a while longer.

AGE-GROUP EMPHASES

Children: Instruct children to confess an area of sin to the Lord and ask His help in not sinning again.

Youths: Lead the youth to understand that the world has many idols that seek to lure them away from God.

Adults: Show the adults that sometimes tough love may be necessary for the child who errs repeatedly.

— Darrell W. McKay.

SCRIPTURE LESSON TEXT

II SAM. 11:2 And it came to pass in an eveningtide, that David arose from off his bed, and walked upon the roof of the king's house: and from the roof he saw a woman washing herself; and the woman *was* very beautiful to look upon.

3 And David sent and enquired after the woman. And *one* said, *Is* not this Bath-sheba, the daughter of Eliam, the wife of Uriah the Hittite?

4 And David sent messengers, and took her; and she came in unto him, and he lay with her; for she was purified from her uncleanness: and she returned unto her house.

5 And the woman conceived, and sent and told David, and said, I *am* with child.

14 And it came to pass in the morning, that David wrote a letter to Joab, and sent *it* by the hand of Uriah.

15 And he wrote in the letter, saying, Set ye Uriah in the forefront of the hottest battle, and retire ye from him, that he may be smitten, and die.

16 And it came to pass, when Joab observed the city, that he assigned Uriah unto a place where he knew that valiant men *were.*

17 And the men of the city went out, and fought with Joab: and there fell *some* of the people of the servants of David; and Uriah the Hittite died also.

18 Then Joab sent and told David all the things concerning the war.

26 And when the wife of Uriah heard that Uriah her husband was dead, she mourned for her husband.

27 And when the mourning was past, David sent and fetched her to his house, and she became his wife, and bare him a son. But the thing that David had done displeased the LORD.

12:13 And David said unto Nathan, I have sinned against the LORD. And Nathan said unto David, The LORD also hath put away thy sin; thou shalt not die.

14 Howbeit, because by this deed thou hast given great occasion to the enemies of the LORD to blaspheme, the child also *that is* born unto thee shall surely die.

15 And Nathan departed unto his house. And the LORD struck the child that Uriah's wife bare unto David, and it was very sick.

NOTES

David's Sin and Punishment

Lesson Text: II Samuel 11:2-5, 14-18, 26-27; 12:13-15

Related Scriptures: Exodus 20:13, 14, 17; Leviticus 18:20; 20:10; Matthew 5:27-28; John 8:3-11

TIMES: 991 B.C.; 990 B.C. PLACE: Jerusalem

GOLDEN TEXT—"Wherefore hast thou despised the commandment of the Lord, to do evil in his sight? thou hast killed Uriah . . . and hast taken his wife to be thy wife" (II Samuel 12:9).

Introduction

There is a direct connection between pride and moral failure. "When pride cometh," wrote Solomon, "then cometh shame" (Prov. 11:2). He also warned that "pride goeth before destruction, and an haughty spirit before a fall" (16:18). Many believers can testify about how they fell into sin at the time they supposed they were invincible. Like Simon Peter, who rashly boasted that he would never forsake Christ, many of us find ourselves denying Him in words and deeds.

God called King David "a man after his own heart" (I Sam. 13:14); yet even he did not escape the arrogance of power and the moral tragedy that followed.

LESSON OUTLINE

I. **DAVID'S ADULTERY— II Sam. 11:2-5**

II. **DAVID'S CRIME— II Sam. 11:14-18**

III. **DAVID'S PRESUMPTION— II Sam. 11:26-27**

IV. **DAVID'S REPENTANCE— II Sam. 12:13-15**

Exposition: Verse by Verse

DAVID'S ADULTERY

II SAM. 11:2 And it came to pass in an eveningtide, that David arose from off his bed, and walked upon the roof of the king's house: and from the roof he saw a woman washing herself; and the woman was very beautiful to look upon.

3 And David sent and enquired after the woman. And one said, Is

not this Bath-sheba, the daughter of Eliam, the wife of Uriah the Hittite?

4 And David sent messengers, and took her; and she came in unto him, and he lay with her; for she was purified from her uncleanness: and she returned unto her house.

5 And the woman conceived, and sent and told David, and said, I am with child.

The temptation (II Sam. 11:2). The Bible is amazingly frank about the sins of human heroes. The hero in this case, though not perfect, had previously been exemplary in conduct and godly in attitude. Now, however, basking in the successes God had given him, David put himself in the way of temptation.

In the spring of the year, when kings normally accompanied their armies into battle, David remained in Jerusalem. He sent his army to fight the Ammonites and besiege their capital, Rabbah. But he sent them under Joab, his general (vs. 1). This behavior was highly unusual for a king in that day.

The account that follows reveals the extent to which {David had succumbed to the luxuries associated with power and had let down his spiritual guard.}[Q1] "In an eveningtide" he "arose from off his bed" (vs. 2). Although it was not unusual for people in a warm climate to take an afternoon nap, this ease was in stark contrast to the rigors and perils of his army at Rabbah.

Satisfied with rest and yet unfulfilled because of inactivity, David "walked upon the roof of the king's house." He cannot be blamed for enjoying the cool evening breeze there, but his eyes led him into sin. "He saw a woman washing herself; and the woman was very beautiful to look upon."

The sin (II Sam. 11:3-4). It is possible that Bath-sheba, knowing the nearness of the palace, deliberately bathed in the open courtyard in order to seduce the king. If so, she would have to share the blame for the moral failure that followed. David's actions were nevertheless inexcusable. Instead of turning from her charms, he "enquired after the woman."

She was identified as "Bath-sheba, the the daughter of Eliam, the wife of Uriah the Hittite" (vs. 3). {Her family connections were impressive. Her father was a soldier, and her grandfather quite possibly was Ahithophel, David's counselor (15:12; 23:34).}[Q2]

Bath-sheba's husband, Uriah the Hittite, was one of many mercenary soldiers of non-Israelite origin who served in David's army (cf. I Sam. 26:6). He apparently had become a worshipper of Yahweh (his name means Yahweh is my light). He was completely dedicated to his commander and the nation (II Sam. 11:11), and for his valor {he was recognized as one of thirty-seven mighty men of David (23:39).}[Q2]

Ignoring the fact that Bath-sheba belonged to another, David "sent messengers, and took her; and she came in unto him, and he lay with her" (11:4). The sinfulness of this act is increased by the fact that Uriah had dedicated himself to David's service and trusted him.

Why would a man who had been content to wait fifteen years for God to give him his kingdom now hastily take another man's wife? {The answer must lie in the arrogance that too often accompanies power. David had already violated God's pattern for marriage by practicing polygamy (2:2). In spite of His warning that a king must not multiply wives (Deut. 17:17), David did so. After he began to subdue his enemies and gain recognition, he established a harem (II Sam. 5:13).}[Q3]

Although a harem was a status symbol for an oriental king, it was wrong for David and it opened the door for his adultery. He apparently rationalized that a king was entitled to any woman he desired and that this included another man's wife. David had come to believe that being king placed him above God's law. Sadly, his arrogance has been repeated too often by other believers whom God has promoted to prominence.

The description of David's deed is ironic: "He lay with her; for she was purified from her uncleanness" (11:4). The "uncleanness" was related to Bath-sheba's menstrual cycle (cf. Lev. 15:19-24), and it was mainly ceremonial in nature. Her purification is probably mentioned here to indicate why she could lie with David; it also tells us she was not pregnant at the time. The irony is that these who were ceremonially clean became morally defiled by their sin.

The result (II Sam. 11:5). Although she "returned unto her house" (vs. 4) as if nothing had occurred, Bath-sheba conceived (vs. 5). Since she was not pregnant when she lay with David and since her husband had been away at war, it was clear to her that David was the father of her unborn child. She therefore informed him, "I am with child."

DAVID'S CRIME

14 And it came to pass in the morning, that David wrote a letter to Joab, and sent it by the hand of Uriah.

15 And he wrote in the letter, saying, Set ye Uriah in the forefront of the hottest battle, and retire ye from him, that he may be smitten, and die.

16 And it came to pass, when Joab observed the city, that he assigned Uriah unto a place where he knew that valiant men were.

17 And the men of the city went out, and fought with Joab: and there fell some of the people of the servants of David; and Uriah the Hittite died also.

18 Then Joab sent and told David all the things concerning the war.

When Bath-sheba revealed her pregnancy, David knew he was in trouble. But rather than admit his sin, he tried to cover it. **{**His plan involved bringing Uriah home from the battle so that he would have intercourse with his wife and David's paternity of the child would not be discovered.**}**[Q4] The plan failed. Uriah's loyalty to David and Israel's cause kept him from enjoying conjugal pleasures even while on furlough (vss. 6-13).

The command given (II Sam. 11:14-15). David was now desperate, and the only remaining solution he could imagine was to have Uriah killed. It is incredible that the man who for so long refused to solve his problems by killing Saul now tried to do so by killing one of his most loyal soldiers! But his earlier problems were those of a righteous man; so he could trust God to solve them. Now they came from his own sin, and he was left alone.

{David sent Uriah's death warrant to Joab by Uriah's own hand when he returned to the front (vs. 14). The letter ordered Joab to put Uriah "in the forefront of the hottest battle" and then to withdraw so "that he may be smitten, and die" (vs. 15).**}**[Q5]

The coldheartedness of this order is frightening. It brings to mind the way Jezebel later destroyed the innocent Naboth in order to obtain his vineyard for Ahab. In that case, a false charge led to the execution (I Kgs. 21:9-13), but David did not even give a reason why Uriah had to die. In his arrogance as king and his desperation as a sinner, his arbitrary command was reason enough.

The deed committed (II Sam. 11:16-17). **{**Joab was a hardened commander to whom death among his troops was no stranger. Besides, he was in no position to question David's order, for he himself had resorted to trickery to do away with

Abner, a man David greatly admired (cf. 3:26-30).}[Q6] He therefore surveyed the military situation to see how he might best dispatch Uriah to his doom.

Joab did not carry out David's orders precisely as given, that is, by withdrawing from Uriah and leaving him to his fate. {But he did assign him "unto a place where he knew that valiant men were" (vs. 16). The term "valiant men" refers to Ammonite soldiers inside the wall who were defending the city. Joab probably deliberately dispatched Uriah to a place unnecessarily close to the wall (cf. vs. 20).}[Q7]

Uriah was not the only one placed in mortal danger. Others who were loyally serving in David's army were sent in as well; so when the Ammonites attacked, these men died along with Uriah (vs. 17). Here, then, is another tragic result of David's sin: in assuring the death of one particular soldier, he occasioned the deaths of others. This is a typical pattern: sin concealed will always multiply itself.

The message sent (II Sam. 11:18). After the deed was done, "Joab sent and told David all the things concerning the war." The messenger was not sent with a bald message that Uriah had been killed. He was told to give a broad picture of what was happening, including the sending of men too near the wall. If David became angry about this, the messenger was to pacify him with the news of Uriah's death (vss. 19-21).

The messenger followed instructions, faithfully telling how some soldiers had been killed by archers from the wall. He added that Uriah was dead as well (vss. 22-24). David was satisfied, observing that "the sword devoureth one as well as another" (vs. 25). This is the answer of a man without sympathy, who had so hardened his heart that the life of one of his best soldiers meant nothing to him.

DAVID'S PRESUMPTION

26 And when the wife of Uriah heard that Uriah her husband was dead, she mourned for her husband.

27 And when the mourning was past, David sent and fetched her to his house, and she became his wife, and bare him a son. But the thing that David had done displeased the LORD.

The mourning (II Sam. 11:26). Bath-sheba received the news of her husband's death and mourned for him. This most likely lasted seven days (cf. Gen. 50:10; I Sam. 31:13).

It is interesting that throughout this chapter, Bath-sheba is mentioned by name only once; she is otherwise called "the wife of Uriah." Even when her name is given (II Sam. 11:3), she is called Uriah's wife. It is clear that God wished to emphasize that she belonged to Uriah, not David. Indeed, the verse concerning her mourning (vs. 26) states three times that she was Uriah's. Thus, the adulterous relationship with David is implicitly condemned.

The marriage (II Sam. 11:27). David wasted no time in marrying Bath-sheba. As soon as the time of mourning was past, he "sent and fetched her to his house, and she became his wife." {This unseemly haste could not fail to arouse suspicions about their relationship, but David took her quickly so that she could be married to him as long as possible before she gave birth. This was so the child might still be regarded as David's legitimate (though somewhat premature) son.}[Q8]

In due time Bath-sheba bore David a son. Throughout the narrative the son is never named, and he lived only a short time (12:18). It is probably fitting that he remained unnamed here, for "the thing that David had done displeased the Lord" (11:27). Through his wiles, David seemed to have achieved his goal. Uriah was dead, Bath-sheba was his wife, and eventually their child would be born within the bonds of marriage.

In all of this, David had tried to exclude God from consideration. But the Lord would not be denied.

DAVID'S REPENTANCE

12:13 And David said unto Nathan, I have sinned against the Lord. And Nathan said unto David, The Lord also hath put away thy sin; thou shalt not die.

14 Howbeit, because by this deed thou hast given great occasion to the enemies of the Lord to blaspheme, the child also that is born unto thee shall surely die.

15 And Nathan departed unto his house. And the Lord struck the child that Uriah's wife bare unto David, and it was very sick.

David's confession (II Sam. 12:13*a*). Prior to these final verses in our lesson text, we are told that God sent Nathan to David with a parable that would reveal the true nature of his sin (see verses 1-12).

{Faced with the heinousness of his sin, David responded, "I have sinned against the Lord" (vs. 13). Although brief, this confession was genuine. He made no excuses, and he did not try to minimize the sins.}[Q9] And even though he knew he had sinned against Uriah, Bath-sheba, and even himself, he saw his deeds as ultimately against the Lord Himself (cf. Ps. 51:4).

Nathan's pronouncement (II Sam. 12:13*b*-15). Nathan reassured David that the Lord had forgiven his sin and that he would not die for it. David deserved to die, as he himself had proclaimed in his reaction to Nathan's parable. The law provided no sacrifice for willful sins, and it prescribed the death penalty for both adultery and murder (Ex. 21:12; Lev. 20:10). But God in His grace allowed David to live.

{Tragic consequences would follow, nevertheless. As already noted, evil would plague David's family from that day on (II Sam. 12:10-12). In addition, the child whom Bath-sheba bore him would die (vs. 14).}[Q10] This was because David, through his sin, had given occasion to the Lord's enemies to blaspheme His name. As announced, then, the child became terminally ill (vs. 15) and died seven days later (vs. 18).

Our text leaves the solemn reminder that no believer, however godly, is immune to sin. It also reminds us that sin, when not confessed and forsaken, reproduces itself. Finally, we learn that sin often has consequences that continue even after God has forgiven the sinner. Let us therefore always claim God's grace to overcome temptation.

—Robert E. Wenger.

QUESTIONS

1. To what are we alerted at the beginning of this account?
2. What were Bath-sheba's family connections? What kind of soldier was Uriah?
3. How had David's situation predispose him to commit adultery?
4. How did David try to keep his paternity of Bath-sheba's child unknown?
5. What did Uriah carry back to the battle with him?
6. Why did Joab obey David's order without question?
7. What did Joab do to have Uriah killed?
8. Why did David marry Bath-sheba so hastily?
9. How did David react when faced with his guilt?
10. What were the results of David's sins?

—Robert E. Wenger.

Preparing to Teach the Lesson

David had been chosen by God and blessed by God in many wonderful ways, but he was still susceptible to temptation. In this week's lesson we examine the sad account of David's tragic sin.

TODAY'S AIM

Facts: to review the account of David's tragic sin with Bath-sheba.

Principle: to expose the dynamics of temptation and the destructive nature of sin.

Application: to warn Christians against falling into temptation and sin as David did.

INTRODUCING THE LESSON

The pastor of a large church recently shocked the members of his congregation with the announcement that he and his wife of over twenty years were getting a divorce. The reason was all too familiar. The highly successful pastor had fallen into an illicit relationship with the church organist. Two families were destroyed and great damage was done to the church as a result of the selfish sin of one man and one woman.

Regrettably, this is not an isolated example. Because of sexual sin, the Christian landscape in recent years has become littered with broken marriages, ruined ministries, and disillusioned Christians. Christian leaders and politicians make headlines, but others fall too.

David's tragic fall should serve as a grave reminder to all of us of how terrible and destructive this kind of sin can be. Pray that God will use this lesson to keep vulnerable Christians from ruining their lives and testimonies.

DEVELOPING THE LESSON

1. Sin committed (II Sam. 11:2-5). David was, by this time, middle-aged. He was staying at home in Jerusalem while his army fought.

There is no indication that David was seeking an illicit relationship. He already had multiple wives and concubines. Discuss what responsibility, if any, Bath-sheba bore in David's temptation. Why would it be incorrect to blame Bath-sheba for David's sin? Class members should remember that no matter what temptation presents itself, we are still responsible for our own behavior.

Chart David's descent into sin as revealed in verses 2-4. First he looked; then he inquired. Next, he willfully sinned by pursuing a relationship with another man's wife. Discuss again Bath-sheba's responsibility as things progressed. She seems to have been a willing participant in the sinful act. Perhaps she was flattered or was overly impressed by David's authority. Anything short of rape would leave Bath-sheba morally responsible also.

Verse 4 states that Bath-sheba "was purified from her uncleanness." Merrill wrote that David "discovered her identity at once and, assured of her ritual purity (cf. Lev. 12:2-5; 15:19-28), had intercourse with her" (Walvood and Zuck, eds., *The Bible Knowledge Commentary,* Victor). David had obviously lost his moral perspective if he was concerned about ritual purity but unconcerned about adultery! Such is the nature of sin. Imagine how David felt when he learned that Bath-sheba was pregnant.

2. Sin concealed (II Sam. 11:14-18). When David's attempt to manipulate Bath-sheba's husband failed (vss. 6-13), he resorted to more drastic measures. Notice the cruel irony of faithful

Uriah carrying his own death sentence back to Joab. Notice also how far David was willing to go to conceal his own sin. He had moved from adultery to murder. Willful sin begets more sin. Willful sin deadens the conscience, making it easier to sin in other areas.

Discuss what, if any, responsibility Joab had in this matter. Loyalty is good—but to what point?

3. Sin confirmed (II Sam. 11:26-27). Focus on Bath-sheba's mourning. Her sincerity is questionable. Her mourning may have been largely for appearance' sake. She did what custom dictated.

To conceal their sinful behavior, David moved as quickly as possible to marry Bath-sheba. There was no turning back now. David had to follow through on what he had started. It seems that his conscience was completely dead at this point; he was ready to simply get on with his life. But point the class to the last statement in verse 27: "The thing that David had done displeased the Lord." Read Galatians 6:7.

4. Sin confessed (II Sam. 12:13-15). The faithful Nathan courageously confronted his sinful king (cf. vss. 1-12). This led David to the confession we read in verse 13: "I have sinned against the Lord." Make it clear to the class that this is the only acceptable way to deal with sin in our lives (cf. Prov. 28:13; I John 1:9). No rationalizations or excuses will do. David's repentance and confession resulted in his own life being spared.

Second Samuel 12:14-15 deals with the consequences of David and Bath-sheba's sin. We cannot sin with impunity. God forgives sin, but this does not mean that He cancels out all its consequences.

Note that David's actions had "given great occasion to the enemies of the Lord to blaspheme" (vs. 14). Discuss how sin can ruin a person's testimony. God takes this very seriously!

ILLUSTRATING THE LESSON

The downward spiral illustrates how willful sin leads to greater sin and serious consequences.

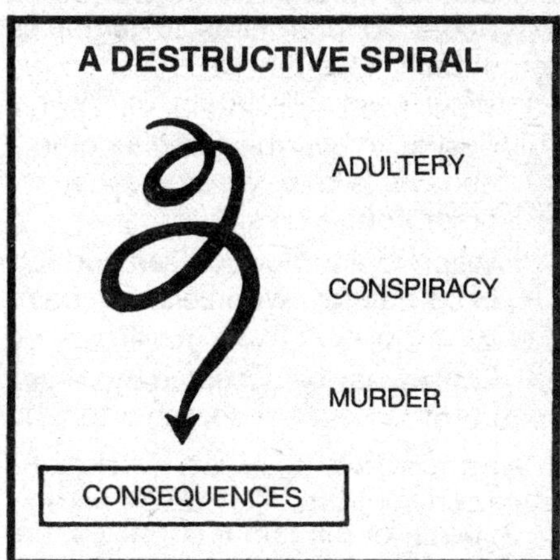

CONCLUDING THE LESSON

David had been a great man of God and a great king, but he could not coast on past victories. He was susceptible to temptation, and he fell into serious sin when he let down his guard. Adultery led to an attempted cover-up and finally to a murder conspiracy. Sin is not manageable. We deceive ourselves if we think that we can manage temptation and control the degree to which we will fall. As David learned, sin has consequences.

Encourage students to take a stand against temptation early and to think seriously about the long-term devastation that can be the result of short-term pleasure. Emphasize the need to repent and confess sin to God. Learn from David's example!

ANTICIPATING THE NEXT LESSON

Next week we will study a fiery oracle of the prophet Amos. God was disgusted with Israel's smug religiosity. Read up on the history of that time.

—*Bruce A. Tanner.*

PRACTICAL POINTS

1. Let us not forget that Satan can use the most innocent and unexpected occurrences to tempt us (II Sam. 11:2-3).
2. When we begin to allow personal desires to overrule good judgment and God's laws, we are headed for great trouble (vss. 4-5).
3. When we do not confess and forsake our sin, we inevitably compound our sin (vss. 14-18).
4. Our sin may be accepted by others, but it is never acceptable to God (vss. 26-27).
5. True confession makes no excuses for sin and recognizes that all sin is against God (12:13).
6. We should be forewarned that while the ultimate consequences of sin can be avoided through Christ's forgiveness, there may well be temporal consequences to bear (vss. 14-15).

—Jarl K. Waggoner.

RESEARCH AND DISCUSSION

1. In what sense was David's temptation and sin typical (II Sam. 11:2-5; cf. Gen. 3:6; Josh. 7:21)?
2. Do you think Bath-sheba was an innocent victim of David? Explain.
3. How did Uriah display more honorable character than David (vss. 14-18; cf. vss. 6-13)?
4. How might David have justified his actions before his contemporaries? Why did he not ultimately do that (II Sam. 11:27; 12:13; cf. Ps. 51:1-4)?

—Jarl K. Waggoner.

ILLUSTRATED HIGH POINTS

There fell some (II Sam. 11:17)

A pastor in Brazil was teaching that whatever people sow, they are sure to reap. Toward the end of his message, he told the people of an experience in his own life. He said that a boy in a village not far from where he had lived had received a new machete his parents purchased for him to use in the garden.

One day, the boy left his machete on the path while he went for a swim. Soon another boy quietly approached the machete, grabbed it, and ran off with it. He knew that if his parents saw it, they would ask where he got it; so he hid it in the grass near his house. His little sister was out playing and tripped on the machete, cutting her leg badly.

The pastor said, "The severed tendon in her leg was not repaired, and I am reminded when I see my sister walk that she will carry the scar of my sin all her life."

Displeased the Lord (vs. 27)

A group of Christian young people visited a nursing home on Sunday afternoon. Two of the boys entered a room to find an elderly man by himself. They asked whether they could visit with him. He said he would be delighted. They told him they were part of a group from a nearby church.

The elderly man began to cry. He told how he had surrendered his life to the Lord for full-time Christian service and gone to Bible college.

He said, "In my second year of college, God burdened my heart for missions. I told the Lord I did not want to be a missionary. I quit school, got married, and eventually left my wife and two children. I turned my back on God and have been unhappy since."

—V. Ben Kendrick.

Golden Text Illuminated

"Wherefore hast thou despised the commandment of the Lord, to do evil in his sight? thou hast killed Uriah . . . and hast taken his wife to be thy wife" (II Samuel 12:9).

It is hard to believe that David, a man after God's own heart, could commit such tragic sin. We should understand that it was not the first look that caused David to sin. It was letting what he saw cause him to lust after Bath-sheba. Instead of resisting temptation in the power of God, he yielded to lust and had Bath-sheba brought to him so that he could have a physical relationship with her.

This sin of adultery resulted in Bath-sheba's pregnancy. Discovering her pregnancy, David tried to get Uriah, her husband, to go home and sleep with his wife. This did not work out as David planned; so David had Uriah killed in battle. After the mourning for the death of Uriah was past, David took Bath-sheba as his wife.

James gives the commentary on David's sin: "But every man is tempted, when he is drawn away of his own lust, and enticed. Then when lust hath conceived, it bringeth forth sin: and sin, when it is finished, bringeth forth death" (1:14-15).

David knew the commandment of God. He knew that coveting or lusting after another man's wife was sin (cf. Ex. 20:17). David knew that adultery was sin (vs. 14). David knew that murder was sin (vs. 13). David was fully aware of the Ten Commandments, but he went ahead and sinned anyway and suffered the awful consequences. Why did David get caught in such a tragic situation?

In a moment of passion, David ignored or forgot the first commandment, which is to have no other gods before the true and living God (vs. 3). David replaced God with himself on the throne of his life. When he made that move, he no longer thought of doing God's will but only of what he wanted to do.

As a result, David no longer guarded his heart against sin but let sin reign over him. He yielded to sin and to being a servant of unrighteousness.

The writer of Proverbs stated God's counsel for every believer: "Enter not into the path of the wicked, and go not in the way of evil men. Avoid it, pass not by it, turn from it, and pass away. . . . Keep thy heart with all diligence; for out of it are the issues of life" (4:14-15, 23).

"Keep thy heart" (vs. 23), or guard your heart, is the challenge for each follower of Christ in our loose and immoral society today. Our politically correct society accepts every lifestyle. God accepts only the lifestyle that is presented in His Word, where He tells us that marriage is only between male and female and that there must be purity before marriage and during marriage. God's laws are for our physical and spiritual well-being. Those who live otherwise soon have to suffer the consequences of sin, as David did.

As believers in Christ, let us be quick to learn from David's tragic sin that we must keep alert all the time to the temptations of the evil one. Let us use the Word of God as Christ did—to defeat the lies of the devil and to obey the Lord (cf. Matt. 4:1-11).

—Paul R. Bawden.

Heart of the Lesson

"Sin" is not a word many people use today. This is true even though sin abounds all around us.

Our lesson reminds us that we need to beware of sin and the damage it can cause. As we examine our text, we will discover four facts about sin.

1. Sin often subtly ensnares us (II Sam. 11:2-5). As David walked around on the roof of his palace, he noticed a woman bathing. How sobering it is that such a seemingly coincidental situation would spark such tragic events?

We should never let our guard down. We must constantly be on the alert, for Satan can strike out at us at any time. As Peter warned us, "Be sober, be vigilant; because your adversary the devil, as a roaring lion, walketh about, seeking whom he may devour" (I Pet. 5:8).

We must take whatever action is necessary to remove those things from our lives that will tempt us to sin (cf. Matt. 5:27-30). If we fail to take the appropriate steps to avoid sin, it will eventually overcome us.

2. Unconfessed sin leads to greater sin (II Sam. 11:14-18). Here we see a man who is completely under the control of sin. Caught in its tangled web, he sees only one way out—he must commit another act of sin.

David failed to remember that there was another option open to him. God had made this clear to Moses when He said, "Speak unto the children of Israel, When a man or woman shall commit any sin that men commit, to do a trespass against the Lord, and that person be guilty; then they shall confess their sin which they have done" (Num. 5:6-7). A similar statement can be found in I John 1:8-9. Both passages teach us to return to God through the door of confession of sin instead of trying to cover up our sin.

3. Our sin cannot be hidden from God (II Sam. 11:26-27). All of David's planning and scheming had failed to hide his sin from God. Every detail of his sin was known to God, and God was displeased.

Here is a truth we need to remember: "[God's] eyes are upon the ways of man, and he seeth all his goings. There is no darkness, nor shadow of death, where the workers of iniquity may hide themselves. . . . Therefore he knoweth their works, and he overturneth them in the night, so that they are destroyed" (Job 34:21-22, 25).

4. We must bear the consequences of our sin (II Sam. 12:13-15). Disobedience brings along with it certain consequences. These results may be unseen for years even though they flow from the events set in motion by our disobedient act. Confession to God brings forgiveness but not necessarily freedom from the effects of our sin.

David's experience serves as a warning for us here. His family was never the same after his tragic sin. He could attest to the truth of Paul's warning, "Be not deceived; God is not mocked: for whatsoever a man soweth, that shall he also reap" (Gal. 6:7).

Are you caught in the clutches of a particular sin? Maybe you think it is a small sin. You need to remember that no matter how small a sin seems, it is still sin in God's eyes.

Go to God now and confess your sin. It is futile to attempt to hide it from Him. If you ask, He will forgive you and help you bear its consequences. Do not let sin and its tragic effects destroy your life. Call on God for mercy and grace right now.

—James R. Gordon.

World Missions

The tragic sin of King David, as heartbreaking and disgusting as it may be to many readers, presents lessons God's servants need to learn if they want to take the Great Commission seriously. These are some of those lessons.

Sin is not confined to social outcasts. While it is true that the gospel message seems especially needed by drug dealers and vandals, it is no less important for business people and IT professionals. All have broken God's law.

Some sinners are easy to spot because of their habits and manner. Others, however, because they seem outwardly moral, talk in a civil way, and do good deeds, can disguise their sin but are just as much in need of Christ as the criminals and the prostitutes. The affluent segments of society need to be targeted with the gospel and prayed for just as much as those in any other mission field.

"For all have sinned, and come short of the glory of God" (Rom. 3:23). Power, prestige, and position do not lessen the temptation to sin.

Sin is deceitful. Left unconfessed, it often leads the sinner to commit it again and even to do what is necessary to cover it up. Sin has a way of blinding people to the fact that it is wrong and can quickly become like a cancer on the soul. It can spread ever so subtly and lead us into all kinds of things that only compound the problem.

Sin displeases the Lord. For some inexplicable reason, it has a way of convincing the sinner that everything is all right, that God approves of what he has done. Sin, however, is the breaking of God's law. God is never pleased by sin, nor does He condone any sinful act. Sin committed by a king is no different in God's eyes from that committed by a thug. Sin is a burden (cf. Ps. 32).

One often does not recognize the increasing weight sin places on the heart and soul of the sinner. It can happen so gradually that the person never knows how burdensome sin is until he is totally entrapped.

Sin is forgivable. When sincere confession is made to God, He forgives. The Lord stands ready to hear the sinner's confession and to remove the burden the sinner has carried. This is the wonderful news a sinful world needs to hear, and it is what world missions is all about.

Sin may be forgiven, but its temporal consequences may still have to be dealt with. When Christ died on the cross, He paid the eternal penalty for sin. At the moment of saving faith and confession, the sinner stands before the Lord redeemed from his former condition.

There may, however, be some unpleasant and long-lasting consequences of a life of sin. The person who abused his body with sinful habits may still have to suffer physical illnesses because of his sin. Sin's results may affect the emotions or other areas of a person's being as well.

These lessons are applicable to the missionary, both personally and in terms of ministry. The missionary must never forget his own sinfulness and how alluring temptation is. The fact that he is now a missionary will in no way reduce the temptations he will face. He must be on constant watch over his own soul.

The servant of the Lord must look to himself first and then be about his ministry. The gospel must be poured from clean vessels.

—Darrell W. McKay.

The Jewish Aspect

David's adultery with Uriah's wife will forever be a blot on the life of a man whom the Lord lovingly called "my servant David" (Ezek. 34:24).

Rabbinical teaching states that adultery "is considered one of the three sins for which a Jew should be prepared to die rather than commit" (Unterman, *Dictionary of Jewish Lore and Legend,* Thames and Hudson). The seriousness of this view is understood when it is realized that the other two sins are idolatry and murder.

Stoning was the prescribed judgment for adultery during the Old Testament period. Among Orthodox Jews today, "if it is known that adultery has taken place, the husband has to divorce his unfaithful wife while she, in turn, is not allowed to marry her paramour" (Unterman).

Christians are familiar with Jesus' teaching "that whosoever looketh on a woman to lust after her hath committed adultery with her already in his heart" (Matt. 5:28). Jewish teaching, however, states that it is the deed, not the thought, that counts. That, it is argued, is why the seventh of the Ten Commandments legislates, " 'You shall not commit adultery' (Exodus 20:13)" (Telushkin, *Jewish Wisdom,* Morrow).

Although it is the deed alone that is condemned by Judaism, adultery is not treated lightly. Adultery is seen "as an act of betrayal against both one's spouse and against God" (Telushkin).

Under the teachings of the Talmud, the rabbis modified the Levitical law that made adultery a capital offense (cf. Lev. 20:10). They provided that an adulterous wife did not have to be put to death but that she was "prohibited from remaining married to her husband (even if he was willing to forgive her)" (Telushkin). We see the contemplation of this option regarding Mary when "Joseph her husband, being a just man, and not willing to make her a publick example, was minded to put her away privily" (Matt. 1:19).

In the Old Testament, a wife suspected of adultery could be tested by drinking "waters of bitterness" (cf. Num. 5:12-31). This "ordeal of jealousy" was abolished by a first-century rabbi (Wigoder and Werblowsky, eds., *Oxford Dictionary of the Jewish Religion,* Oxford).

Much of the Jewish writing about adultery deals with women who commit it. A husband suspected of adultery was not required to be put through the ordeal of drinking bitter water; nevertheless, the adultery of a husband—such as David—was not ignored.

"Adultery by a husband, . . . became grounds for divorce" (Wigoder and Werblowsky). A Jewish woman could divorce a husband convicted of being unfaithful, but she was not required to—as a man was required when his wife was convicted. This policy no doubt reflected concern for the woman, who would be unlikely to remarry even though she had not been the unfaithful one.

One reason Judaism views adultery as one of the three worst sins is that it corrupts a divine purpose of the marriage union. A major obligation of faithful Jews is "the duty of procreation" (Hertzberg, *Judaism,* Braziller). Having children—and thereby strengthening the nation—is hindered by adultery.

The New Testament teaches that adultery can be committed in the heart as well as by the body. It is unfaithfulness, and thus it serves as an appropriate picture of spiritual unfaithfulness to the Lord (cf. Jer. 3:7-9; Matt. 12:39). The church is His bride, and we must be faithful and devoted only to Him.

—Theodore G. Smetters.

Guiding the Superintendent

Surveys indicate that adultery has reached epidemic levels. Many marital breakups are the result of a spouse committing adultery. Both political and religious leaders have frequently been implicated. Considering the general disregard for marriage and biblical standards of morality today, this is no surprise. Adultery, however, is nothing new, as our text reveals.

DEVOTIONAL OUTLINE

1. Adultery committed (II Sam. 11:2-5). David was no longer the shepherd boy to whom we were introduced earlier. He was now middle-aged and had reigned as king for about twenty years. Various factors made him vulnerable to the temptation to which he was about to succumb.

One day David saw a woman from his rooftop. She was very beautiful and married to one of the soldiers in his army. Although the details are not given, David sent for her and committed adultery with her. Before long, it was discovered that Bath-sheba was carrying the child of the king.

Although some might question the wisdom of a woman bathing where she could easily be seen, nowhere does Scripture place any of the blame on Bath-sheba. As the one in authority, David was clearly in the wrong.

2. Adultery concealed (II Sam. 11:14-18, 26-27). David attempted a cover-up. He brought Uriah, the husband of Bath-sheba, home from the battlefront, hoping that he would sleep with his wife and later think that the child was his own. Uriah, however, was such a loyal soldier that he refused to go to his wife while his comrades slept in the open country (vss. 6-13).

Not wanting to be found guilty of committing a capital offense (Lev. 20:10), David devised another plan that would clear the way for him to marry Bath-sheba. David sent a letter to Joab, the commander of his army, by the hand of Uriah. The king ordered Uriah to be placed in the most dangerous position in the assault; then he was to be deserted by his fellow soldiers. Left as a sitting duck, Uriah would surely fall in battle. This, of course, is basically what happened.

David married Bath-sheba. He thought he had successfully concealed his sin, "but the thing that David had done displeased the Lord" (II Sam. 11:27).

3. Adultery confessed (II Sam. 12:13-15). There are many ways to confront sin. John the Baptist confronted Herod's adultery head-on (Matt. 14:1-12). The prophet Nathan, however, confronted David's sin through the use of a skillfully devised parable (II Sam. 12:1-7) that caused David to actually condemn himself with his own lips.

Once confronted with his sin, David confessed his transgression. With his confession of sin came forgiveness (cf. I John 1:9). But even though David's sin would be forgiven, he could not avoid the temporal consequences of his sin.

AGE-GROUP EMPHASES

Children: The importance of resisting temptation each day should be stressed to children.

Youths: Teens must learn that God is quick to forgive but that sin's devastating effects can last for years.

Adults: Adults should be challenged to deal with unconfessed sin and repent.

—John A. Owston.

SCRIPTURE LESSON TEXT

AMOS 5:14 Seek good, and not evil, that ye may live: and so the LORD, the God of hosts, shall be with you, as ye have spoken.

15 Hate the evil, and love the good, and establish judgment in the gate: it may be that the LORD God of hosts will be gracious unto the remnant of Joseph.

18 Woe unto you that desire the day of the LORD! to what end *is* it for you? the day of the LORD *is* darkness, and not light.

19 As if a man did flee from a lion, and a bear met him; or went into the house, and leaned his hand on the wall, and a serpent bit him.

20 *Shall* not the day of the LORD *be* darkness, and not light? even very dark, and no brightness in it?

21 I hate, I despise your feast days, and I will not smell in your solemn assemblies.

22 Though ye offer me burnt offerings and your meat offerings, I will not accept *them:* neither will I regard the peace offerings of your fat beasts.

23 Take thou away from me the noise of thy songs; for I will not hear the melody of thy viols.

24 But let judgment run down as waters, and righteousness as a mighty stream.

25 Have ye offered unto me sacrifices and offerings in the wilderness forty years, O house of Israel?

26 But ye have borne the tabernacle of your Moloch and Chiun your images, the star of your god, which ye made to yourselves.

27 Therefore will I cause you to go into captivity beyond Damascus, saith the LORD, whose name *is* The God of hosts.

NOTES

A Rebuke from the Lord

Lesson Text: Amos 5:14-15, 18-27

Related Scriptures: Deuteronomy 30:15-20; Amos 6:1-7; Joel 2:1-17; Matthew 23:23-28; Romans 12:9-21

TIME: about 762 B.C.

PLACE: Beth-el

GOLDEN TEXT—"Hate the evil, and love the good, and establish judgment in the gate" (Amos 5:15).

Introduction

Amos was ministering in the northern nation of Israel even though he was a resident of Judah, to the south. Although his message was first and foremost to the people of the north, those living in Judah needed to pay attention to his message too. Chapters 3, 4, and 5 of Amos begin with "Hear this word," indicating the importance of each of these messages from the Lord.

The first of the three messages was addressed to Israel. But the phrase "against the whole family which I brought up from the land of Egypt" (Amos 3:1) implies the inclusion of Judah, and they would do well to heed it also. In this message, Amos outlined some of the reasons Israel was going to face God's judgment.

The address in Amos 4 begins with an unflattering reference to the women of Israel who were living in luxury, partly by oppressing the poor and needy in the land. Judgment was on its way.

Then came His third message.

LESSON OUTLINE

I. A GODLY LIFESTYLE— Amos 5:14-15

II. A FEARFUL TIME— Amos 5:18-20

III. A REJECTED WORSHIP— Amos 5:21-24

IV. A DESERVED RECOMPENSE— Amos 5:25-27

Exposition: Verse by Verse

A GODLY LIFESTYLE

AMOS 5:14 Seek good, and not evil, that ye may live: and so the LORD, the God of hosts, shall be with you, as ye have spoken.

15 Hate the evil, and love the good, and establish judgment in the gate: it may be that the LORD God of hosts will be gracious unto the remnant of Joseph.

Seeking good (Amos 5:14). The address in this chapter began as a funeral dirge (vss. 1-3). Amos used a poetic form commonly used by prophets for songs lamenting the death of relatives, peoples, cities, and even nations. The "days of Jeroboam the son of Joash king of Israel" (1:1), during which Amos was ministering, were days of unusual prosperity. In this lament Amos mourned as if Israel's death had already occurred. He then called on her people to seek God so that they could live on and escape the judgment being announced (5:4-6).

{Another call is given in verse 14, where the prophet said the Israelites ought to seek good instead of evil.}[Q1] Notice how Micah explains this concept: "He hath shewed thee, O man, what is good; and what doth the Lord require of thee, but to do justly, and to love mercy, and to walk humbly with thy God?" (6:8). In his own explanation we see that Amos said that "the God of hosts, shall be with you" (5:14). As His people obey Him and walk with Him in His ways, the Lord, in turn, stays with them and walks with them through the challenges of life.

One of the most difficult things people face is feeling alone in life and having to face everything without companionship. This is especially true of widows, those who are divorced, and those who have never had the opportunity to get married. It can also be true of those who are in severed relationships at work or even at home. It is possible to feel alone while in a crowd. A believer, however, can know the joy of having companionship with the Father, with Jesus Christ, and with the guiding, indwelling Holy Spirit.

Israel was reminded by Amos that the assurance of God's presence comes through obedience to Him. That would give meaning to their lives. Jesus said, "He that hath my commandments, and keepeth them, he it is that loveth me: and he that loveth me shall be loved of my Father, and I will love him, and will manifest myself to him" (John 14:21).

Hating evil (Amos 5:15). Here we see Amos giving an explanation similar to that of Micah. {Three specific requirements are mentioned: hating evil, loving good, and establishing judgment.}[Q2] The prevailing attitude of this ancient Israelite culture seems to have included a hatred of those who lived righteously (vs. 10). This is not surprising since the mere presence of godly people often aggravates the wicked. They needed to reverse course by pursuing good things (vs. 14) and hating evil (vs. 15). If they did, God would spare them the awful judgment He had planned.

Do we not see a similar trend in our own society? There seems to be a growing hatred for righteousness and righteous people. The evidence of it can be seen in certain government regulations and in what the entertainment world mocks. The call is for our nation to hate that which is evil and love that which is good. Israel was not just to "seek" good, but to "love" it as well (vss. 14-15). While hatred is an intense dislike, love is a tender affection for something or someone. Love must be guided by a keen sense of right and wrong.

The Hebrew word *mishpat* in verse 15 has been translated "judgment" here. Its meaning is related to the pronouncement of a verdict. For that reason, since the rendering of a verdict is the carrying out of justice, it is sometimes translated "justice." The idea is that Israel needed to establish true justice in their land instead of allowing the lawlessness and corruption of the leaders and court system that was so prevalent. Sadly, this too seems to reflect the contemporary situation.

{The incentive accompanying these commands was that God might choose to be gracious to them.}[Q3] "Is there any hope for such a wicked society? Yes, as long as the grace of God is at work. . . . Disaster was coming to Israel, but who knew what God would do if only a godly remnant turned to Him and sought His mercy?" (Wiersbe, *The Bible Exposition Commentary,* Cook).

After Israel worshipped a golden calf, Moses said, "Ye have sinned a great sin: and now I will go up unto the Lord; peradventure I shall make an atonement for your sin" (Ex. 32:30). Maybe God would accept an atonement for them. Thankfully, the Lord did extend mercy to the people at the time of Moses, and He would do the same during Amos's time if only His people repented and turned to Him.

A FEARFUL TIME

18 Woe unto you that desire the day of the Lord! to what end is it for you? the day of the Lord is darkness, and not light.

19 As if a man did flee from a lion, and a bear met him; or went into the house, and leaned his hand on the wall, and a serpent bit him.

20 Shall not the day of the Lord be darkness, and not light? even very dark, and no brightness in it?

The Day of the Lord (Amos 5:18-19). "The popular theology of Amos's day apparently looked forward to the Day of the Lord as a time of Israel's restoration to military, political, and economic greatness; perhaps to the greatness of the reigns of David and Solomon. Amos declared such hopes futile, even pitiable. What the people looked forward to as a day of light and triumph would rise upon them instead as a day of darkness and ruin" (Radmacher, ed., *The Nelson Study Bible,* Nelson).

Amos began with the word "woe," an exclamation similar to "alas." {The people were looking to imagined blessings of the Day of the Lord without realizing that the judgments they longed for would not fall upon only their enemies as they expected. They assumed that because they were God's chosen people, they would be showered with blessings while other nations would suffer great loss. But actually, justice would fall on the rebellious people in Israel who were living according to their own ways and ignoring God and His ways.}[Q4]

{The difficulties of that day are pictured as Israel fleeing from one terrifying danger only to find themselves facing another one. It is likened to someone fleeing from a lion and suddenly encountering a bear and to someone fleeing into a house for safety and being bitten by a serpent as he rested against the wall, panting to catch his breath.}[Q5] Those who were ungodly would find no relief upon the arrival of the Day of the Lord. They would find instead the judgment of God pursuing them and sending great danger.

A day of darkness (Amos 5:20). {As if to emphasize the surety of this truth, Amos summarized by repeating his message about the darkness. He asked rhetorically whether that day will not be darkness instead of light—in fact, whether it will not be "very dark, and no brightness in it." We understand his emphasis, for he had just pointed out that if a person escaped one form of judgment, he would immediately face another one. There would be no escape for anyone living an ungodly life.}[Q6]

"The meaning is both clear and powerful. The Israelites saw the Day of the Lord as a comforting concept. It was to them their ultimate salvation. But like the false security of the one who thinks he has escaped the lion and the one who is falsely secure in his house, the faithless Israelites will find that day to be a time of judgment for them. As a matter of fact, there is no hope for them in that day, for the Day of the Lord will bring not one ray of light" (Gaebelein, ed., *The Expositor's Bible Commentary,* Zondervan).

Zephaniah wrote, "The great day of the Lord is near, it is near, and hasteth greatly, even the voice of the day of the Lord: the mighty man shall cry there bitterly. That day is a day of wrath, a day of trouble and distress, a day of wasteness and desolation, a day of darkness and gloominess, a day of clouds and thick darkness" (Zeph. 1:14-15). Amos's message to Israel carried both a near fulfillment in the coming captivity in Assyria and a distant fulfillment for the future world that is still to come.

A REJECTED WORSHIP

21 I hate, I despise your feast days, and I will not smell in your solemn assemblies.

22 Though ye offer me burnt offerings and your meat offerings, I will not accept them: neither will I regard the peace offerings of your fat beasts.

23 Take thou away from me the noise of thy songs; for I will not hear the melody of thy viols.

24 But let judgment run down as waters, and righteousness as a mighty stream.

God's disdain for false religion (Amos 5:21-22). Amos had been quoting God (vs. 16). **{**Note the terms God used to describe His rejection of Israel's worship: "I hate," "I despise," "I will not smell," "I will not accept," and "neither will I regard" (vss. 21-22). These are extremely emphatic expressions of His total rejection of what the Israelites were doing in their ritualistic practices.**}**[Q7] Even though they were complying with the Mosaic Law in many ways, God was not the least bit pleased with them.

"Why would God do this to his people? Did they not go to worship every time they were supposed to? Did they not fulfill all God's worship requirements as set forth in Exodus, Leviticus, and Numbers? What had gone wrong? . . . Worship and ritual must be more than going through the motions, checking the inspired manual to be sure you did not miss anything. Worship can be carried out to the letter of the law and still not be worship." (Anders, ed., *Holman Old Testament Commentary,* B&H).

The people were doing the various things they thought would please God and bring His blessings to them. But God said He would not accept or even pay attention to those things! What a shock this must have been to those who had been meticulous in their offerings! What a source of anger it must have been to those who did not care about God's requirements and resented being reminded of them! It is amazing how often people become resentful upon hearing truth.

God's desire for justice (Amos 5:23-24). Even the musical praise offered by the people of Israel was disgusting to God! Their songs and the playing of their instruments had neither meaning nor pleasure for Him. **{**Their songs were nothing more than noise to Him, and He refused to listen to the accompaniments at all.**}**[Q8]

"They had both vocal and instrumental music in those sacrificial festivals; and God hated the noise of the one and shut his ears against the melody of the other. In the first there was nothing but noise, because their hearts were not right with God; and in the latter there could be nothing but (*zimrath*) cutting and scraping, because there was no heart—no religious sense in the thing, and nearly as little in them that used it" (Clarke, *A Commentary and Critical Notes,* Abingdon Press).

{As we have already noted, God is far more interested in the condition of our hearts than He is in wonderful worship performances. Amos had already described the worldly condition of the hearts of the people of Israel, so he is again emphasizing the reason for God's rejection of their worship. God really wanted worship and godly living that went together.}Q9

"Instead of feasts and fasts, instead of offerings and sacrifices, instead of singing and playing musical instruments, the Lord said He wanted justice and righteousness (cf. v. 7). Instead of a constant stream of blood flowing from sacrifices, and an endless torrent of verbal and ritual praise from His people, He wanted these ethical qualities to flow without ceasing from them. The Israelites were inundating Him with rivers of religiosity, but He wanted rivers of righteousness" (Constable, *Dr. Constable's Expository Notes,* soniclight.com).

A DESERVED RECOMPENSE

25 Have ye offered unto me sacrifices and offerings in the wilderness forty years, O house of Israel?

26 But ye have borne the tabernacle of your Moloch and Chiun your images, the star of your god, which ye made to yourselves.

27 Therefore will I cause you to go into captivity beyond Damascus, saith the Lord, whose name is The God of hosts.

An indictment (Amos 5:25-26). Amos now summarized with a question, a further explanation, and a pronouncement of judgment. God was still speaking, and He now asked Israel whether they had offered sacrifices and offerings during the forty years of wilderness wandering. The answer was affirmative, for they had done that after receiving their instructions at Mount Sinai. However, they had also practiced idolatry during those years, worshipping gods they had made for themselves (the golden calf of Exodus 32) as well as those of pagan peoples.

The people to whom Amos ministered were doing exactly what their ancestors had done—a mixture of following the ritual of the Mosaic Law and worshipping idols.

A just punishment (Amos 5:27). {God would judge Israel by sending them into captivity "beyond Damascus."}Q10 Damascus was the capital city of Syria, but their captivity would come from beyond there—namely, the nation of Assyria. When that event occurred, Israel was removed from the land and taken far away. Their pretense of worship never fooled God, and when the time came for Him to deal with them for their wickedness, He moved decisively, thus fulfilling His warning.

—Keith E. Eggert.

QUESTIONS

1. According to Amos, if Israel wanted to avoid God's punishment, what should she have sought?
2. What three things did Amos emphasize in explaining where Israel's thoughts should be?
3. What was was the incentive accompanying the command requiring these three things?
4. What wrong idea did Israel have regarding the Day of the Lord?
5. How did Amos describe what was coming in the Day of the Lord, and how did he emphasize that truth?
6. How did Amos describe the terror that would occur at that time?
7. How did God describe how He felt about the Israelites' worship practices?
8. What did He say about their music?
9. What was the reason for God's negative reaction to the worship?
10. What did God say about the coming judgment upon Israel?

—Keith E. Eggert.

Preparing to Teach the Lesson

We have heard the claims of critics that the God of the Old Testament personifies vengeance and severity. In reality, God's love and grace can be seen throughout the Old Testament. He was consistently merciful and kind to rebellious Israel. However, He loved them enough to administer discipline in different forms when it was necessary. His goal for us is that we live as He intended, echoing His ways and attributes. Joyful, spiritually abundant life is to be the result.

TODAY'S AIM

Facts: to see how God detailed for Israel the desirability and necessity of righteous living.

Principle: to show that although we are not to keep the ceremonial law, we are nevertheless called to righteous living.

Application: to live a consistent Christian life daily to honor the Lord and not incur His discipline.

INTRODUCING THE LESSON

Although they had been instructed by God in every detail of life, Israel continually turned aside to the ways of the nations around them. They added their mores and bad ethics, as well as the worship of their false gods, to the plan God had for them. When the evil therefore reached its limit, God sent discipline in the form of persecution by other nations. He also sent drought, crop failure, disease, and bad weather. Sometimes His people sought Him, repented, and once again followed His ways. Amos pointed out that their current behavior would soon result in divine correction again.

DEVELOPING THE LESSON

1. Call to godliness (Amos 5:14-15). Through His prophet Amos, God spelled it out very clearly: Seek good, not evil, and you will be the recipient of God's favor. Human beings are always seeking something, and it would make sense to seek something that would prove to be positive, not negative. This situation seems to be similar to that of Adam and Eve. They already knew good as a result of the Lord's instructions; so why would it be advantageous to know about evil? Were they going to consider doing it?

God knows what is best for His creation, including mankind. Why should we ever consider doing anything that would at best be second-rate and at worst destructive to our lives and spiritual health? The very fact that we would consider doing that which is not God's best for us would be a sinful thought and the carrying out of that thought an act of rebellion against the One who loves us.

God does not need anything, so the fulfilling of His directives does not add to His strength or well-being in any way. Actually, all of God's commands to His people are for our benefit. Even our worship of God does not enhance Him in any way, but it does benefit us. Worship puts our minds in a correct and proper framework and reminds us of our place in His grand design. By an immutable law of the soul, we tend to be drawn to the object of our worship and to become more like it. If we worship a false god and do that which is evil, we will become more like that false god and be more evil than we were.

2. Coming judgment (Amos 5:18-20). When people say, "Why doesn't God do something?" they are asking for the intervention of God in human affairs. Amos spoke of this as "the day of the Lord." He said that it was coming. If we are concerned that God do something about the evil that impinges on us, we should be obeying and honoring Him; otherwise, we must suffer the consequences of our sin. Amos mentioned disasters coming from nature, a bear or a snake inflicting harm on a person when he was already fleeing disaster.

Scripture is plain that God will one day have a time of reckoning for mankind—whether of believers at the judgment seat of Christ or of unbelievers at the Great White Throne judgment. Peter tells us, "For the time is come that judgment must begin at the house of God: and if it first begin at us, what shall the end be of them that obey not the gospel of God?" (I Pet. 4:17).

3. False worship (Amos 5:21-24). In the worship of God, as in business or sports, activity is not necessarily success. When our hearts are not in it, it is odious to God! The sacrifices given to Israel to perform were to be a sweet smell to God, but God hated them when they were offered with a divided heart. God told them to take away their meaningless ceremonial activity. He called their songs of devotion "noise." What they thought was instrumental worship, God despised. He did not want to hear it.

We can do the same thing today. We offer to God worship teams and special music that may be little more than entertainment for the congregation. "Leading in prayer" can be little more than self-aggrandizement. Our giving may be done with the intent to have God bless us with more or to get a tax deduction. We must allow the Spirit of God to examine our hearts in the light of His Word.

4. Empty offering (Amos 5:25-27). Israel had picked up on all the pagan practices the people around them were doing. They had brought into their worship—or at least into their thinking—other gods and symbols. As a result, God promised to send them into exile.

ILLUSTRATING THE LESSON

Man is to honor the Lord and reject the ways of the world around him.

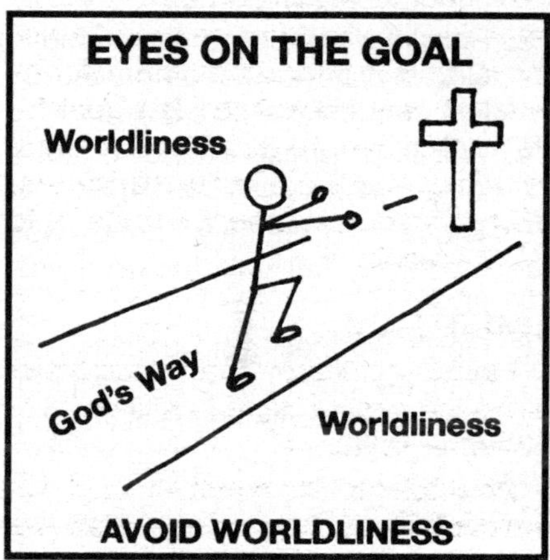

CONCLUDING THE LESSON

This lesson is far from an academic exercise or a history lesson. It is a call to us to make sure that as far as we can have any effect, we are going to have "judgment run down as waters, and righteousness as a mighty stream" (Amos 5:24). We can do this only as our hearts are cleansed from the defilements of the world by the Holy Spirit. We must confess and forsake sin in all its forms. We must insist that our churches honor the Lord without the addition of worldly elements. Simplicity and honesty in worship must prevail.

ANTICIPATING THE NEXT LESSON

The final lesson of the quarter emphasizes the tragic judgment God sent against Judah. God refused to abide their persistent rebellion.

—Brian D. Doud.

PRACTICAL POINTS

1. Our sins bring God's wrath; those who hope to escape His punishment must repent and seek to do good (Amos 5:14-15).
2. To presume upon God's mercy is to guarantee sorrow in the Day of Judgment (vss. 18-20).
3. Religious practice is detestable to God if it is not accompanied by just conduct (vss. 21-22).
4. Words of praise cannot offset a lack of justice (vss. 23-24).
5. Those who refuse to honor God inevitably fall into idolatry (vss. 25-26).
6. God's kindness and patience toward us does not preclude judgment if we continue in sin (vs. 27).

—Jarl K. Waggoner

RESEARCH AND DISCUSSION

1. Is it possible to hate the evil and not love the good (Amos 5:14-15)? Explain.
2. What evils had the Israelites "loved" (cf. 2:6—5:13)?
3. What attributes, or qualities, of God's character are at the root of His words in Amos 5:18-27?
4. What misperception did the Israelites have regarding "the day of the Lord"? Is this a danger for God's people today?
5. What do verses 21-23 tell us about worship rituals?
6. Does God hold modern nations accountable for injustices?
7. What forms does modern-day idolatry take?

—Jarl K. Waggoner

ILLUSTRATED HIGH POINTS

Seek good, . . . live (Amos 5:14)

I have a close relative who is a very gifted individual. As a young person, he would regularly play instruments and sing in church. When he went to Bible college, he was chosen to sing in one of the school's traveling music groups. Following this, he married and started a Christian home. Sadly, work and pleasure soon took control of his life, dragging him into immoral actions. Nevertheless, there is hope he will return to God and experience true life.

It may be (vs. 15)

Abraham Lincoln wanted Americans to pray, fast, and humble themselves before God. "We have forgotten God . . . and we have vainly imagined, in the deceitfulness of our hearts, that all these blessings were produced by some superior wisdom and virtue of our own. . . . It behooves us then, to humble ourselves before the offended Power, to confess our national sins and to pray for clemency and forgiveness" (Presidential Proclamation on March 30, 1863).

Presidents have issued similar decrees reminding us of our condition. If each home would gather, pray, and repent, the Lord may still "be gracious" (Amos 5:15).

A mighty stream (vs. 24)

William Booth, founder of the Salvation Army, dared to dream big dreams. As a young Christian, he brought many unbelievers to church, even though some in the church did not appreciate his efforts. He finally ventured out on his own, seeing many come to Christ through his witness. These converts soon became a mighty stream of righteousness and, in turn, began reaching others around the world.

—James O. Baker.

Golden Text Illuminated

"Hate the evil, and love the good, and establish judgment in the gate" (Amos 5:15).

Amos is someone we might call a straight shooter. His audience certainly was not left wondering what he meant to say!

The instructions in this week's golden text are easy to understand, but that does not mean they are always easy to follow. They go beyond simply following the rules. They speak to our heart attitude. We are not just to *do* good and *not do* evil, although these things are certainly required, but we are to *love* what is good and *hate* what is evil. We are to feel this way because we love God, and God is good and loves what is good. And God hates evil too (cf. Prov. 6:16-19).

What Amos says about love and hate in this verse finds an echo in the New Testament. The apostle Paul declares, "Abhor that which is evil; cleave to that which is good" (Rom. 12:9).

Our culture is not friendly to the idea of abhorring evil. But in reality, such a stance is simply the natural accompaniment of love. In Psalm 119 the writer declares his appreciation for the value of God's law and follows that by saying, "Therefore I hate every false way" (vs. 104). And Psalm 97:10 urges, "Ye that love the Lord, hate evil."

Amos was particularly concerned with social right and wrong within the nation of Israel. He sharply criticized the self-indulgent spirit and oppression he saw all around him. In the golden text, he makes special mention of fairness in the courts ("establish judgment in the gate"). The rich were taking advantage of the poor. Judges were taking bribes and not ruling justly.

We can rightly apply the denunciation of social evils in ancient Israel to the injustices we see in modern society. As good citizens, we should be very concerned about such things. That is part of being a good witness for the Lord.

But we must also remember that the new covenant counterpart to old covenant Israel is the church. So we need to take even greater care to make sure that our churches set high standards of fairness and impartiality and thus shine brightly as lights before a dark world (cf. Matt. 5:13-16).

In this regard, the epistle of James is a telling New Testament complement to the book of Amos. James reminds us of the prophet in the way that he criticizes the wealthy for their oppression and unfair judgments against the poor. He declares, "Go to now, ye rich men, weep and howl for your miseries that shall come upon you" (5:1). He describes how the rich were discriminating against poor Christians and persecuting them (vss. 1-6).

But James also warns the churches about acting in a similar manner, about doing such things like showing favoritism to the wealthy who show up at their gatherings (2:1-9). In doing this they are not being faithful witnesses to God's love.

The point here is that we must not dismiss Amos's admonitions as applying only to the distant past.

God has not changed. He still calls His people to reflect His character by loving and hating the same things that He does.

Take some time to meditate on this verse. Are your loves and hates in their proper order? Ask God to mold your heart to be more like His.

—Stephen H. Barnhart.

Heart of the Lesson

When I read the Scripture describing justice running "down as waters, and righteousness as a mighty stream" (Amos 5:24), my mind swirled as I remembered a time when my car stalled in a whirlpool of rushing, muddy water, while lightning flashed and thunder rolled and roared.

As I had headed for work, my husband shouted from the porch, "Don't take the shortcut! You might get washed off the road and into a ditch."

Already running late, however, I plopped my purse and books in the car, gunned the motor, and sped off (for the shortcut). A few minutes later, I sat, crying for God to rescue me and wondering why I had not paid attention to my husband's warning.

1. Seek good, not evil (Amos 5:14-15). These verses are filled with good advice and backed with a precious promise. Sadly, too often we ignore the promise because our wants and desires push God to the side. When those desires become our way of life, when we take advantage of others, when all we want is more money, and when we let our appetites be our guide, we are asking for trouble. God's Word declares over and over again that all this will bring His discipline upon us. Instead of His loving arms, we will feel His heavy hand.

2. The Day of the Lord is darkness (Amos 5:18-20). Even though we say we believe in God, when we live selfishly, our practices will bring upon us a time of darkness. If we do not repent, that darkness offers no hope but brings fear and creates apprehension.

We are told that the Day of the Lord is twofold, for that day of darkness is the day of God's judgment of the wicked and blessing on the good. We need to ask ourselves, "On which side am I standing?" Malachi warns us that "the day cometh, that shall burn as an oven; and all the proud, yea, and all that do wickedly, shall be stubble" (4:1). But then comes the promise "Unto you that fear my name shall the Sun of righteousness arise with healing in his wings" (vs. 2).

3. What is to come (Amos 5:21-27). Many church members have a mistaken idea of what constitutes worship. For example, they profess to believe in the Lord; however, their "belief" is confined to Sunday morning worship—unless, of course, they attended a late-night Saturday evening sporting event or party. Too many believe that because they have "accepted" God, He loves them so much they can do anything they want. Another problem is that too many "believers" do not know the definition of offerings to the Lord.

Sadly, too many do not believe God's warning that if we are hypocritical worshippers, He will cause us to "go into captivity" (vs. 27). If we seek and follow Him, we have nothing to fear about tomorrow, for God is already there.

Oh, and about my experience in the raging, swirling, muddy water—my husband had followed me. He said that because I had not told him good-bye, he knew where I was going. He waded out as far as he could, threw a rope, and pulled me out of the mire to safety.

In that same way, God cannot be fooled. He knows our hearts, our minds, and the decisions we will make. Thankfully, He is there all the time, watching for us to seek His will and turn to Him for leadership and guidance.

—Donna Smith.

World Missions

Reach and Rescue Ministries provides chapel services for women and children in homeless shelters in our city and surrounding counties. Patti, one of our dedicated children's workers, takes a group of six-to-twelve-year-olds out of the adult service and teaches them Bible lessons. Her creativity shows in the crafts and projects the children complete in their classes.

Patti is a gifted teacher whom the ministry is grateful to have. She generally reports success stories as her young students learn and respond to the gospel. Occasionally, however, there is a snag—a class clown, mass inattentiveness, or even a physical fight or two.

When a disruption occurs, Patti is quick to use the occasion as a life lesson. She teaches about wise and foolish decisions, consequences and rewards, and how God feels about the choices we make. The children leave her class knowing that God loves them and wants them to conduct themselves in a way that gives them each a blessed life. Her message is that God sees all we do and is pleased when we choose to be good.

In our lesson text, God described the abominable behavior He saw among His people. He explained throughout the fifth chapter of Amos how much Israel was sinning against Him and each other. But also evident in these passages was the call to return to God, to repent, and to accept the mercy He offered. Woven among the indictments are pleas to come back to the blessed life God intended for them.

"Let judgment run down as waters, and righteousness as a mighty stream" (Amos 5:24). In the middle of woes and punishments, God extends His mercy and offers His people a way out. He shows them how to correct their dilemma and walk in the holiness and purity He desires for them. He is teaching them how to please Him.

Our children's missionary uses this pattern as she teaches her students the kinds of choices that make God happy. Though she must correct improper behavior, she is always careful to teach the appropriate conduct to help the children learn what is expected of them and improve.

God often uses our times of disobedience as teachable moments for righteousness. He shows us that His pleasure comes when we turn away from the sins we are doing. Missionaries, especially those working with children, can use teachable moments as well. Lessons conveyed at such times often have more impact than those taught during planned sessions. The students, whether in Patti's class or in Judah and Israel, are primed to hear instruction when they have felt the reality of the consequences.

The indictments and warnings we see in our lesson are opportunities God gives us to correct our attitudes and actions. God is clear, though, in directing us to choose to repent and to lessen or avoid serious consequences.

"Be not deceived; God is not mocked: for whatsoever a man soweth, that shall he also reap" (Gal. 6:7). This truth is evident throughout our lesson. The earlier we learn this, the more likely we are to reap blessings and avoid negative results. Pray for missionaries who teach these lessons to the youngest of students.

—Beverly Jones.

The Jewish Aspect

Amos called Israel to return to the Lord (Amos 4:6, 8-11) to prepare to meet Him (vs. 12). The Hebrew verb translated "return" is the key word for "repentance." Other phrases have the idea of repentance, such as "incline your heart unto the Lord" (Josh. 24:23), "make you a new heart and a new spirit" (Ezek. 18:31), and "circumcise yourselves to the Lord, and take away the foreskins of your heart" (Jer. 4:4). Jews commonly consider all such phrases as serving to illustrate what it means to "return."

Two required elements of repentance are further detailed in this week's text: "Seek good, and not evil. . . . Hate the evil, and love the good" (Amos 5:14-15). Jews have consistently emphasized that repentance always combines these two elements: "to turn from the evil and to turn to the good. The motion of turning implies that sin is not an ineradicable stain but a straying from the right path, and that by the effort of turning, a power God has given to all men, the sinner can redirect his destiny" ("Repentance," *Encyclopaedia Judaica,* Macmillan).

Jews believe repentance is a central part of obtaining God's forgiveness of sin. God never forgives sin unconditionally but always on the basis of repentance. Many Jewish teachers agree that the "essential constituents of repentance are regret and remorse for the sin committed, renunciation of the sin, confession and a request for forgiveness, and a pledge not to repeat the offense" ("Repentance," *Encyclopaedia Judaica*). In biblical times, the appropriate sacrifices were then offered. After the temple's destruction, rabbis taught that "sincere repentance is equivalent to the rebuilding of the Temple, the restoration of the altar, and the offering of all the sacrifices" ("Repentance," www.jewishencyclopedia.com).

If an offense involves another person, then forgiveness must also be sought from the offended person. Jews will first seek to obtain that forgiveness on an individual basis. If that fails, they will take three others with them a maximum of three times to seek forgiveness. Maimonides wrote that if the offended person "still persists in his attitude he should be left alone and the victim is then sinful in refusing his pardon" ("Repentance," www.myjewishlearning.com).

Jews believed that repentance was so important to God's plan for humanity that it was created prior to the creation of the earth. "Seven things were created before the world was created, and these are they: The Torah, repentance, the Garden of Eden, Gehenna, the Throne of Glory, the Temple, and the name of the Messiah. . . . Repentance, for it is written, Before the mountains were brought forth, and it is written, Thou turnest man to contrition, and sayest, Repent, ye children of men" (*Babylonian Talmud,* Pesachim 1:5).

Repentance is critical for today's observant Jews. The month of Elul (beginning at sunset on August 16, 2023) is dedicated to seeking repentance to prepare for the coming holy days of Rosh Hashanah (Jewish New Year, beginning at sunset, September 15, 2023) and Yom Kippur (Day of Atonement, beginning at sunset, September 24, 2023). The ten days between Rosh Hashanah and Yom Kippur are specifically set aside as days of repentance. Jews believe that repentance earns them "self-redemption from the thraldom [bondage] of sin" ("Repentance," www.jewishencyclopedia.com). Salvation through Christ is not seen as necessary.

—R. Larry Overstreet.

Guiding the Superintendent

The Bible is very clear—God is all-seeing and all-knowing. Nothing will get by Him. Regrettably, in spite of this fact, many people think they can fool God by their empty and hypocritical religious activity. When a person worships God, the thing that He looks at is that person's heart. The prophets (especially Amos) tell us that God is looking for a heart committed to justice and righteousness.

In our lesson this week, we will learn from Amos what God is looking for in our worship and that mere religious activity really does not fool God.

DEVOTIONAL OUTLINE

1. What God is looking for from His people (Amos 5:14-15). God's promise is very clear. He will be gracious when His people seek to do good and be just.

As a nation, Israel had turned away from God. In Amos, this attitude was generally manifested by wholesale injustice to the poor of society. Divine judgment would come shortly upon the nation (cf. vss. 20, 27). Yet there was still hope for the righteous. God called on them, even if just a remnant, to seek that which was good and to hate evil.

2. What God despises in His people (Amos 5:18-27). Sadly, the people of Israel thought they had escaped and would escape all of God's judgment. The prophet Amos told them differently. Israel was longing for God to come and severely judge their neighbors. This divine intervention into history is known as the Day of the Lord.

Amos warned them not to long for this day, as it would bring judgment on them also. It would be a day of great "darkness" (vs. 18).

This led to a detailed description of what God hates. Amos wrote that God absolutely loathed all their religious activity—feast days, solemn assemblies, offerings, and singing.

Instead of all this religious activity and noise, what God was really looking for was justice—but not just occasional justice. God wants justice and righteousness to flow like a mighty river. "But let judgment run down as waters, and righteousness as a mighty stream" (vs. 24).

Things had not changed much in Israel since the day they had traveled the sands of Sinai, hundreds of years before. Amos reminded them that all this religious activity had been offensive to God for many years. They had offered sacrifices to God but in the same breath had worshipped the idols around them. In the end, God has only wanted a heart that is committed to justice. One can see that this is just an extension of the idea that God's people are to love others and love God with all their hearts (Lev. 19:18; Deut. 6:5).

The result of all this was simple: Israel would experience a full measure of divine judgment—destruction and deportation.

AGE-GROUP EMPHASES

Children: The overall theme of people trying to fool God willl resonate with children. Have them explore the idea of how people try to fool God and how it never works.

Youths: "Let judgment (justice) run down as waters" (Amos 5:24) is a phrase that many teens have heard many times. Ask them what that means today in light of Amos's thoughts.

Adults: What does God really expect from His followers? This passage will help adults address the issue of religious hypocrisy.

—Martin R. Dahlquist.

SCRIPTURE LESSON TEXT

II CHR. 36:15 And the LORD God of their fathers sent to them by his messengers, rising up betimes, and sending; because he had compassion on his people, and on his dwelling place:

16 But they mocked the messengers of God, and despised his words, and misused his prophets, until the wrath of the LORD arose against his people, till *there was* no remedy.

17 Therefore he brought upon them the king of the Chaldees, who slew their young men with the sword in the house of their sanctuary, and had no compassion upon young man or maiden, old man, or him that stooped for age: he gave *them* all into his hand.

18 And all the vessels of the house of God, great and small, and the treasures of the house of the LORD, and the treasures of the king, and of his princes; all *these* he brought to Babylon.

19 And they burnt the house of God, and brake down the wall of Jerusalem, and burnt all the palaces thereof with fire, and destroyed all the goodly vessels thereof.

20 And them that had escaped from the sword carried he away to Babylon; where they were servants to him and his sons until the reign of the kingdom of Persia:

21 To fulfil the word of the LORD by the mouth of Jeremiah, until the land had enjoyed her sabbaths: *for* as long as she lay desolate she kept sabbath, to fulfil threescore and ten years.

PS. 137:1 By the rivers of Babylon, there we sat down, yea, we wept, when we remembered Zion.

2 We hanged our harps upon the willows in the midst thereof.

3 For there they that carried us away captive required of us a song; and they that wasted us *required of us* mirth, *saying,* Sing us *one* of the songs of Zion.

4 How shall we sing the LORD'S song in a strange land?

5 If I forget thee, O Jerusalem, let my right hand forget *her cunning.*

6 If I do not remember thee, let my tongue cleave to the roof of my mouth; if I prefer not Jerusalem above my chief joy.

NOTES

Judgment and Exile

Lesson Text: II Chronicles 36:15-21; Psalm 137:1-6

Related Scriptures: II Kings 24:10-16; Jeremiah 25:8-11; Leviticus 26:40-45; Psalms 48:1-14; 126:1-6

TIMES: 586 B.C.; sometime after 586 B.C. PLACES: Jerusalem; Babylon

---

GOLDEN TEXT—"By the rivers of Babylon, there we sat down, yea, we wept, when we remembered Zion" (Psalm 137:1).

Introduction

In King Josiah's time, Huldah the prophetess foretold the trouble waiting for Judah. God was going to allow righteous Josiah to reign in peace, but when he was gone, divine judgment would fall on Judah.

Huldah's warning was very clear: "Thus saith the Lord, Behold, I will bring evil upon this place, and upon the inhabitants thereof, even all the words of the book which the king of Judah hath read: because they have forsaken me, and have burned incense unto other gods, that they might provoke me to anger with all the works of their hands; therefore my wrath shall be kindled against this place, and shall not be quenched" (II Kgs. 22:16-17).

There was a persistent tendency for the Israelites to divide their allegiance between Yahweh and a host of false gods. The idolatry this spawned was an abomination to the Lord and could not be allowed to continue. The time of reckoning had come.

LESSON OUTLINE

I. COMPASSION—II Chr. 36:15-16

II. CONQUEST—II Chr. 36:17-21

III. COMPLAINT—Ps. 137:1-6

Exposition: Verse by Verse

COMPASSION

II CHR. 36:15 And the LORD God of their fathers sent to them by his messengers, rising up betimes, and sending; because he had compassion on his people, and on his dwelling place:

16 But they mocked the messengers of God, and despised his words, and misused his prophets, until the wrath of the LORD arose against his people, till there was no remedy.

Message (II Chr. 36:15). Zedekiah was twenty-one years old when he began his eleven-year reign in Jerusalem. He did "that which was evil in the sight of the Lord" (vs. 12). He refused to humble himself before the prophet Jeremiah, who was God's spokesman. King Zedekiah rebelled against Nebuchadnezzar, the Babylonian king to whom he had sworn allegiance. All of his chief priests and the people in general became involved in pagan abominations and polluted the hallowed house of God in Jerusalem (vss. 13-14). God's cup of wrath was filling up and ready to boil over.

{The people of Judah may not have deserved it, but God sent them messengers from time to time to warn them to give up their evil ways and turn back to Him. He did this because He had compassion on His chosen people and on His dwelling place among them, the temple in Jerusalem. These messengers were God's prophets.}[Q1]

Mocking (II Chr. 36:16). {Sadly, the people "mocked" (ridiculed, derided, or treated with contempt) God's messengers. They "despised" the words of God and "misused," or scoffed at, His prophets.}[Q2] This continued for such a long time that the Lord's wrath was poured out on His people. There was no "remedy" to stop it, no healing to cure it, and no way to escape it.

Today we live in a world that is very similar. God sends His words out to warn people to abandon their sins. He uses personal exhortation by true believers. He uses churches, parachurch organizations, schools, literature, radio and television broadcasts, and various other means. Yet often the same thing happens as took place in ancient Israel. The people mock His messages and make themselves ripe for divine judgment. Satan is still hard at work.

CONQUEST

17 Therefore he brought upon them the king of the Chaldees, who slew their young men with the sword in the house of their sanctuary, and had no compassion upon young man or maiden, old man, or him that stooped for age: he gave them all into his hand.

18 And all the vessels of the house of God, great and small, and the treasures of the house of the LORD, and the treasures of the king, and of his princes; all these he brought to Babylon.

19 And they burnt the house of God, and brake down the wall of Jerusalem, and burnt all the palaces thereof with fire, and destroyed all the goodly vessels thereof.

20 And them that had escaped from the sword carried he away to Babylon; where they were servants to him and his sons until the reign of the kingdom of Persia:

21 To fulfil the word of the LORD by the mouth of Jeremiah, until the land had enjoyed her sabbaths: for as long as she lay desolate she kept sabbath, to fulfil threescore and ten years.

Slaying (II Chr. 36:17). {God used the Chaldeans (Babylonians), led by King Nebuchadnezzar, to chastise His people.}[Q3] The Lord had led Abraham out of the paganism in "Ur of the Chaldees" (Gen. 11:31) to go to the Promised Land of Canaan. After his descendants settled in Canaan, after they went to Egypt in Jacob's time, after they made the exodus from bondage there, and after they took Canaan back from the heathen, they were now at the mercy of Babylon and headed back to the land of the Chaldees as captives.

Nebuchadnezzar was intent on destroying what the Jews had built up in Judah. He sent his soldiers to slay young men, even in the sanctuary of the sacred temple. {No compassion was shown to men or women, young or old. It was a violent conquest and a bloody massacre.}[Q4]

The Babylonians had held the city of Jerusalem under siege for a long time. The book of Lamentations, written by Jeremiah, describes the horror of that period. When the enemies finally broke through the city's defenses, they were in no mood to be merciful. What made it even more painful was that the Lord sanctioned it as a means of divine discipline. "It is a fearful thing to fall into the hands of the living God" (Heb. 10:31).

Spoiling (II Chr. 36:18). During the reign of King Hezekiah, Merodach-baladan, king of Babylon, sent envoys to visit Hezekiah in Jerusalem. Hezekiah was so proud of his treasures that he showed them to these men. The prophet Isaiah rebuked him for doing this and prophesied that the Babylonians would eventually return and carry Judah's people and treasures away (Isa. 39:1-8). This now came to pass with the fall of Jerusalem.

In ancient times, conquering armies made a habit of ransacking the vanquished. In later times, defeated nations were forced to make reparations to their conquerors.

{Nebuchadnezzar saw to it that the precious vessels of the house of God and its treasures, along with those of the king and his princes, were carted off to Babylon.}[Q5] This was not just robbery; it was humiliating and sacrilegious to the Jews.

Sacking (II Chr. 36:19). It was common practice for a conquering army to sack a community, plundering, looting, and destroying buildings, walls, and equipment. Jerusalem was subjected to this horrifying action. {The beautiful temple was burned, the stones in the city's walls were thrown down, and the palatial homes of the nobles were set afire.}[Q6]

Jeremiah described Judah's utter defeat, a judgment he had spent his life warning Judah about. King Zedekiah and his army were captured when they tried to escape from besieged Jerusalem (Jer. 52:7-8). Nebuchadnezzar slaughtered Zedekiah's sons in front of him, put out his eyes, and imprisoned him (vss. 10-11). The other royal officials were rounded up and executed (vss. 25-27).

Serving (II Chr. 36:20-21). In cases where individuals or groups were able to escape the carnage brought on Jerusalem and the outlying area of Judah, the Babylonians rounded many of them up and led them away to Babylon, where they became servants. They remained there until Persia superseded Babylonia.

It is true that the Jews serving in Babylon were not treated as harshly as the Israelites had been treated by their Egyptian taskmasters. Through the prophet Jeremiah, the Lord told the exiles to settle down and live at peace in Babylon (Jer. 29:4-9). In fact, many remained there after the captivity was lifted seventy years later, while others returned to rebuild Judah.

Leviticus 25:1-7 shows that God's law required the land to lie fallow every seventh year as a Sabbath rest. {Jeremiah 25:11 and 29:10 state that the Holy Land would remain desolate during the seventy years of the Babylonian Captivity.}[Q7] The sense of II Chronicles 36:21 seems to be that the land had to rest for seventy years to make up for the five centuries the Sabbath rests had not been observed every seven years.

COMPLAINT

PS. 137:1 By the rivers of Babylon, there we sat down, yea, we wept, when we remembered Zion.

2 We hanged our harps upon the

willows in the midst thereof.

3 For there they that carried us away captive required of us a song; and they that wasted us required of us mirth, saying, Sing us one of the songs of Zion.

4 How shall we sing the LORD's song in a strange land?

5 If I forget thee, O Jerusalem, let my right hand forget her cunning.

6 If I do not remember thee, let my tongue cleave to the roof of my mouth; if I prefer not Jerusalem above my chief joy.

Rivers (Ps. 137:1-2). Note that this psalm has no composer ascribed to it. It has been called the Song of the Exiles. The grief expressed may be somewhat tied to how the Jews were treated in Babylon, but it is primarily concerned with what they had been forced to leave behind when they were taken out of their beloved land and taken to the east.

{It was by the rivers of Babylon that they sat down and wept as they remembered Zion.**}**[Q8] Zion was originally a hill held by the Jebusites until David took it from them. It became the temple area and eventually a synonym for the city of Jerusalem itself. It was the core location in Jewish life, and to lose it was very difficult indeed.

Verse 2 says that the captives hung their harps on the willows. The harps mentioned here were the Hebrew *kinnorot,* stringed instruments played by plucking. A more common name is "lyre," for this instrument did not resonate like a big harp. The Jews evidently kept them up off the ground when not in use by hanging them on tree branches. The sadness of the exiles is reflected in the fact that their musical instruments were not in use.

Requirement (Ps. 137:3-4). {The psalm now explains that their captors required the Jews to sing and to at least pretend that they were happy to do this. They would say, "Sing us one of the songs of Zion."**}**[Q9]

We are not told whether the Babylonians did this to taunt their captives or whether they had another motive. It may have been that they wanted to rub salt in the wounds of these unhappy exiles, considering this a source of entertainment. On the other hand, the Babylonians may have felt sympathetic toward the Jews and perhaps were trying to snap them out of their mournful attitude. Another possibility is that they were genuinely curious to learn about Jerusalem by listening to the lyrics of their songs.

We may not know just what the Babylonians were thinking, but the Jews made it clear that they found it too difficult to "sing the Lord's song in a strange land" (vs. 4). Their grief overpowered their desire to enjoy the pleasure of singing.

This incident raises two questions we might consider. First, what should we do if we are ever under the domination of enemies who demand that we do something we do not want to do? Should we try to accommodate them and gain their favor and the good treatment it may provide? Perhaps. But if anything requires us to go against God and His Word, we must refuse and be ready to accept the consequences. We must act on the principle that "we ought to obey God rather than men" (Acts 5:29). Then we must trust God to give us sustaining grace and eventual deliverance.

The second question we might consider is, How can we use our enemies' demand as an opportunity to witness to them? When Paul and

Silas were jailed in Philippi, they prayed and sang praises to God at midnight, and all the other prisoners heard them. A divinely sent earthquake freed Paul and Silas, and as a result of their testimony, the jailer and his household became converts (16:25-34). We should never place limits on where or how we can make our testimonies effective.

Remembrance (Ps. 137:5-6). It appears that the Jewish exiles in Babylon were not about to be cajoled or forced into singing for their captors. Perhaps they decided this would be sacrilegious because it would have been equivalent to desecrating the city that was associated with the only true God.

{The psalmist declared that if he ever forgot Jerusalem, his right hand should lose its cunning, or skill.**}**[Q10] That would make it impossible to play the lyre. This was the instrumental component in the ability to make music.

He also said that if he ever failed to remember Jerusalem, his tongue should stick to the roof of his mouth. He wanted this to happen if at any time he did not find the thought of Jerusalem superior to the most joyful thing that could be imagined. Such an impediment would make it impossible to sing, which is the vocal component in the ability to make music.

Music has long been an integral part of Jewish and Christian worship, whether personal or corporate. Job 35:10 refers to "God my maker, who giveth songs in the night." In Ephesians 5:19, Paul urges "speaking to yourselves in psalms and hymns and spiritual songs, singing and making melody in your heart to the Lord."

Psalm 137 ends on a very dark note, revealing the abiding hatred for Babylon then existing in the hearts of Jewish exiles. Not only did they refuse to play their lyres and sing for their captors, but the psalmist also had harsh things to say about Edom and Babylon.

Verse 7 calls on God to remember the Edomites who, on the day Jerusalem was attacked by the Babylonians, called for the city to be razed (torn down to the ground). Verse 8 addresses Babylon as a nation to be destroyed. Happiness is ascribed to whoever does to it what it had done to Judah.

—Gordon Talbot.

QUESTIONS

1. What messengers did God send to warn His people?
2. How did the Jews treat the messengers God sent to them?
3. What pagans did God use to chastise His people?
4. How would you describe the attack on Jerusalem?
5. What did the Babylonians carry away from the temple in Jerusalem?
6. What happened to the temple, city wall, and important buildings in Jerusalem?
7. How long were the Jewish captives made to serve in Babylon?
8. What did the Jewish exiles do when they remembered Zion?
9. What did the Babylonians ask the Jewish captives to do while they were in Exile?
10. How strongly did the Jewish exiles feel about Jerusalem?

—Gordon Talbot.

Preparing to Teach the Lesson

It is amazing what we miss when we suddenly do not have things we always enjoyed and took for granted. Americans have typically taken for granted their freedom to worship, their right to travel, and their right to free speech. But when we go through something like the COVID-19 lockdowns, many things in life feel very uncertain. What was once routine all at once becomes unrealistic. We may suddenly realize what is truly dear to us and what is really important in life.

TODAY'S AIM

Facts: to examine the plight of God's people in exile in Babylon.

Principle: to show that God punishes us as His children when we forget our blessings from Him and His call for our obedience.

Application: to demonstrate that we dare not forget how much God has blessed us, for doing so can lead to chastisement.

INTRODUCING THE LESSON

Oftentimes we fail to realize how much we are blessed every day. God has truly been good to us. We have the freedom to worship, to do the things we want, and to advance in life; however, it is so easy to forget the Giver of all our blessings as we enjoy them.

In our lesson text we see that God was angry with His people for failing to heed His words of instruction and admonition so that they could grow closer to Him. To enjoy His blessings without enjoying Him does not make sense. In this lesson we will see how God punished His people for their disregard of Him. We have a lesson to learn here, for we could easily fall into the same trap today.

DEVELOPING THE LESSON

1. God's anger with His people (II Chr. 36:15-16). We often think of God as purely benevolent. He has given all good things. It is hard to comprehend Him as the One who can punish and discipline us. A closer examination of Scripture, however, reveals that God does both because He loves His children.

In this section we see how God sent His prophets to instruct His people because He loved them and His temple in Jerusalem. The temple was the dwelling place of His presence. The people were so complacent and arrogant, however, that they turned a deaf ear to the prophets. In doing so, they did not just reject the servants of God; they rejected God Himself. God certainly was not going to put up with that! He does not today, either. There is a time when God's patience runs out.

Our text tells us that the people scoffed at the prophets of God and that this made Him very angry. Discuss with the class what happens when we disregard God in our society. What dire consequences might we face in doing so? Are we as a nation in danger of God's wrath today?

2. God's punishment (II Chr. 36:17-20). We read in Scripture that the Lord very often used His enemies to punish and discipline His people. This tells us two things. First, God will punish His people. Second, God is in control of even His enemies. He is absolutely sovereign.

The Chaldean people were those who resided in Babylon. Nebuchadnezzar was their king. His armies raided the land of Judah, even going into the holy temple at Jerusalem and destroying everything in their path.

The description in the Scripture text is

vivid. Both the healthy and the sick were killed. The temple utensils that were used for worship rituals were carried away, and the temple was pillaged. The temple walls were broken down, and the people were carried away as slaves to pagan lands. The people remained in exile until 539 B.C., when Cyrus, king of Persia, came to power over Babylon.

Get the class to put themselves in the shoes of God's people. Help them imagine that they have been carried away as slaves to a foreign, hostile land. This will help them feel the consequences of God's wrath upon His people as described in our text this week.

3. Desolation of the land (II Chr. 36:21). After Nebuchadnezzar's destruction, all that was left behind was a trail of smoking debris and absolute destruction. Judah had been a prosperous land. God had blessed His people. Now everything was gone in an instant. The cause was simply that hey had scorned the God who had blessed them.

In our society today we are in danger of losing everything when we forget our God. The lessons are already there for us in Scripture, and we are to heed the words of God for our day.

Ask the class whether they think that there is a possibility that we can lose everything when we turn away from God. What steps can we take to prevent that from happening?

4. Sad memories of the homeland (Ps. 137:1-6). When we have lost everything, there is plenty of time to think. That is exactly what the people of God did. They ruminated about the land that they had left behind.

The picture in these verses is a dreary one. The sounds of music and dancing were no longer heard. The people of Babylon asked them to sing some of their native songs, but the people of Judah had hung up their harps. They had no reason to sing in a land that was not their own.

What they missed the most was being home in Jerusalem. Anyone who has been abroad for any length of time will be able to identify with this. Jerusalem was home for them. The familiar sights and sounds of their culture were the things they longed for. The temple at Jerusalem and their worship were an important part of that, and they truly missed them. That was their source of joy, and with the loss of them they had no desire to play any music. It was all gone now because they had rejected the prophets of God and, thus, God Himself.

ILLUSTRATING THE LESSON

God punishes His children when they stop listening to Him.

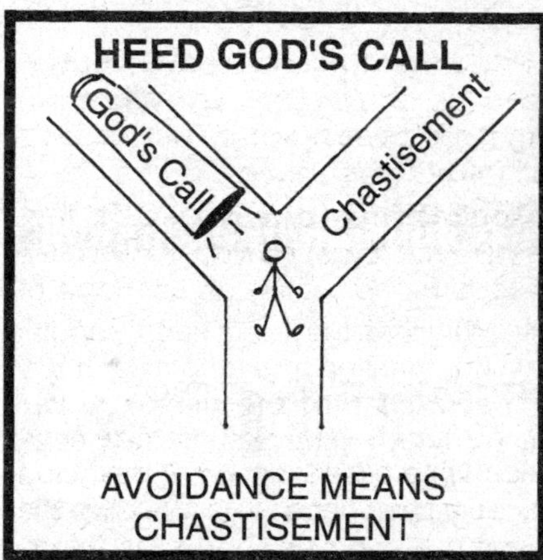

CONCLUDING THE LESSON

We have seen in our lesson this week how important it is for us to listen to the words of God daily in every area of our lives. Doing so will lead to His blessing and keep us from His punishment.

ANTICIPATING THE NEXT LESSON

Next quarter's focus is on living in Christ. The first lesson is titled "To Live Is Christ" and is based on Philippians 1:12-26.

—A. Koshy Muthalaly.

PRACTICAL POINTS

1. Continually ignoring God's warnings is a recipe for having to learn things the hard way (II Chr. 36:15-17).
2. God's judgment on a people is commensurate with their pervasive sin (vss. 18-21).
3. The scorn of the godless is especially painful when we are being disciplined by God for sin (Ps. 137:1-3).
4. It is difficult to witness for the Lord when we have strayed out of His revealed will (vs. 4).
5. Remembering one's godly heritage may be the first step back for someone who has fallen away from the Lord (vss. 5-6).

—Kenneth A. Sponsler.

RESEARCH AND DISCUSSION

1. Why did the Lord keep sending the messengers long after it was evident that the message was not getting through to the people (II Chr. 36:15-16)?
2. How would you answer objections that being conquered by slaughtering enemies was too severe a punishment for the people's sins (vss. 17-20)?
3. Why was it important for the land to receive its full number of Sabbaths (vs. 21)?
4. Why did the Babylonian captors want to hear "one of the songs of Zion" (Ps. 137:3)?
5. How can we keep our minds focused on the Lord's grace to us in times of distress and trouble (vss. 5-6)?

—Kenneth A. Sponsler.

ILLUSTRATED HIGH POINTS

He had compassion (II Chr. 36:15)

Justice was swift and often brutal in the mining camps during the California gold rush, but pity was not completely unknown. In one instance, a man was caught stealing a tiny amount of gold dust. He was given ten lashes. After dark that same day, he was caught stealing again. This time he received twenty lashes and was forced to leave the camp.

Although his back was covered with painful lacerations, the man straightaway was found in a nearby camp trying to steal a mule. He was tried at once, and the judgment against him this time was fifty lashes. When the jury of miners who made the decision saw the condition of the man's back, however, they took a second vote and extended forgiveness for the offense. The owner of the mule, filled with compassion, took the rogue to his tent and tended to his injuries.

Kept sabbath (vs. 21)

Keeping Sunday as the Sabbath was a serious issue in early New England. In the Old Cemetery in Framingham, Massachusetts, two men share a common headstone. They died on the same day—a Sunday.

The event that sent the men to their Maker unfolded like this: Abraham Rice got together with his neighbor, John Cloyes, to discuss the possibility of striking a bargain for a horse. Since everyone believed that doing business on Sunday was a violation of the Sabbath, what happened next had a great impact on the minds of all who heard about it. A surprise thunderstorm moved in. As the men shook hands on the deal, a dazzling bolt of lightning flashed from the sky and ended the lives of the two men as well as the horse.

—Todd Williams.

Golden Text Illuminated

"By the rivers of Babylon, there we sat down, yea, we wept, when we remembered Zion" (Psalm 137:1).

We have a saying: "You do not miss the water until the well runs dry." That was certainly true of the Jewish people when they went into exile. Prior to their removal to Babylon, they showed little respect for God and the things of the Lord (cf. Lev. 26:33-35; II Chr. 36:14-16, 21). Once deprived of their homeland and place of worship, however, some changed their tune.

God had warned them what would happen if they disobeyed His commands, but over time the threat lost its place in their national consciousness. Once the fear of the Lord is negated in the mind, the sinful heart takes the lead. So it was with Israel.

For many Jews who were taken captive to Babylon, life was good. Not everyone mourned the loss of homeland, for they became, if not prosperous, at least quite satisfied. We know also that when the Captivity was over, many stayed there. Only a remnant of God's people went back to rebuild Jerusalem and the temple.

For others, however, being awakened to their loss with no immediate hope of return brought great sadness. So it was with the psalmist, and he put into verse the emotions he shared with his fellow exiles who felt the same way.

"Rivers of Babylon" refers not only to actual rivers but also to the canal and irrigation system. It seems the homesick Jews would gather by themselves near some waterway to commiserate with each other and find the strength needed to endure their circumstances. They were so sorry for their plight and so emotionally beaten down by their captors that they sat and cried together.

As a pastor, I have been in homes where death has visited and friends drop by to be with the family. In those times tears often flow freely as everyone senses the loss. I have also seen how hurt young people can be when picked on by their peers at school, and again the tears cannot be contained. When you put those two scenarios together, you get something of what it must have been like for the godly Jews in Babylon. Being separated from home and persecuted by their captors was too much to accept without expressing emotion.

The people wept and were distressed because they remembered Zion. They remembered what they had once had and now were deprived of. Perhaps even the memory of the sins that had caused their loss overwhelmed them.

Memory can be both a boon and a curse. Many a person looks back over a lifetime and remembers with joy the good times, the blessings, the fun, and all the positive events of the past. Others look back and never quite get over the memory of negative things that happened to them or of some gross sin they committed.

The exiles must also have wept because they sensed just how much they had dishonored God in all this. When a repentant teenager comes to his senses and realizes how deeply he has hurt his parents by his conduct, the memory of his actions will bother him. The beautiful thing to recall, though, is how forgiving and merciful God is toward His wayward children. He may discipline them, but He does not cast them off. He especially rejoices when He sees them repent with godly sorrow.

—Darrell W. McKay.

Heart of the Lesson

God is so patient with us. He knows we are sinful; yet He loves us too much to allow us to wallow in our sin forever. God was patient with His people Israel.

1. Exile (II Chr. 36:15-21). Time was up for Judah. God had given every opportunity to the Israelites to learn the path of obedience to Him. His prophets, however, were mocked and despised and even killed.

Finally, God allowed King Nebuchadnezzar of Babylon to do his worst to Judah. His army killed many of the people by the sword. He plundered the temple of all its sacred gold and silver items. Then he burned the temple and broke down Jerusalem's city walls. He burned the palaces and took everything of value.

The Babylonians then took the remnant, those who were left, into exile. They served Babylon until the Persians came into power. God told them through His prophets that this exile would last seventy years.

2. Mourning (Ps. 137:1-6). This psalm, written about the Exile in Babylonia, is a powerful poem about the thoughts and feelings of the exiled Israelites. Imagine how you would feel after everything you held dear was taken away from you and you were forced to live in an enemy land. The people felt great sadness because of their city's devastation.

This psalm implies that their captors mocked and made fun of them, requiring them to sing happy songs for their entertainment while the exiled slaves' hearts were so heavy. All they felt capable of singing were sad songs of mourning.

This remnant of Israel living in a strange, foreign land never wanted to forget what had happened to them and their beloved land. They showed a burning loyalty and love for Jerusalem. As all humans do, they may have taken for granted what they had in the past. It took losing everything to realize how important their city and country were to them after all.

Now it was too late—or was it? God had promised this exile would last seventy years. There actually was an end in sight to their slavery and exile.

When heavy blows come, we need a time for sadness. We mourn our loss and experience sorrow because of the consequences of our sin.

Evil dominated God's people when they were captives of Babylon. Certainly, this empire was no God-loving place. The remnant were slaves to people who opposed everything good and right.

The Exile gives a clear picture of the human dilemma. Without God, we live lives as captives to Satan's power. We live in a land far away from God. It is only through Jesus Christ's sacrificial death and resurrection that we can live free from sin's chains.

Even after we trust in Jesus as our Saviour, we can sometimes drift away from Him. We may not be keeping our daily time with Him, or we may allow unconfessed sin to block our fellowship with Him. When we do that, we cannot wholeheartedly sing the Lord's song. We may try, but the words will just fall flat. We need to confess our sin, breaking down our wall of alienation from the Lord.

Sometimes God allows an unbeliever to remind us of our backslidden state. Just as He used Babylon, so too He can use sinners around us to wake us up to our need for confession of sin.

—Judy Carlsen.

World Missions

Treating the Babylonian Captivity, this week's lesson, "Judgment and Exile," evokes some understanding of the heartbreak felt by the vanquished outcasts of Judah. The distressed people of China no doubt felt the same after the Communist revolution.

In 1951, Mary Wang, a young Christian from Shansi Province, was accepted at the First Medical College in Shanghai (*With God in Red China,* Dimension Books). Accepted at first only for a short course in pediatrics, Mary was later granted permission to take the longer course, which opened up more specialties to her. Doctors were needed, for after the Communists came to power in 1949, all foreign missionary doctors were forced out of China. Since seven of the twelve medical schools in the country were missionary institutions, China was left with only 12,000 doctors for the entire country.

Medical students thus enjoyed a privileged position. The education, food, and housing were free, though the government made very spartan provisions. Would it be possible to have an open spiritual life while under an oppressive regime?

Mary bowed to pray over her food. Two hundred students stepped forward and identified themselves as believers. Mary was thrilled to pray with them, sing with them, and share spiritual confidences with them.

At first it seemed possible to combine their spiritual commitment with the hard line of the Communist regime. Mao Tse-tung championed medical training. At the same time, the government was upgrading the literacy rate from 5 percent to a higher level.

Mary was a good student. She and a male student, Chieh, were assigned to the children's hospital staff. Mary there met Faith, another Christian staff member. Mary had to be careful around Chieh, for he was a dedicated Communist. Since they studied together, he had been assigned to report on her activities.

Later, in a relaxed moment, Chieh revealed that he loathed himself. Speaking of his comrades he said, "We do not love each other." It was Mary's opening. She led Chieh to faith in Christ. He later married Faith.

There was grim news from other parts of the country. Mary's father, a pastor, was forced to flee. Four thousand believers were arrested in one part of the country. An imprisoned missionary had seen sixty-eight believers massacred.

Life grew more difficult for Mary. She was subjected to severe interrogation. She refused to renounce her father, and she could not renounce Christ. A labor camp was certainly in her future.

Mary's situation worsened. She was scheduled for sentencing when she fell ill with appendicitis. They never got around to sending her away.

In the face of oppression, evangelicals of Shanghai led a crusade in which hundreds were saved. Permitted to visit her family in Hong Kong, Mary was besieged with pleas to defect. She refused, determined to practice medicine in China; but the Lord had other plans. Mary became a worldwide representative of the imperiled Chinese people. The book she wrote electrified the Christian world and mobilized a prayer movement for the suffering church.

—*Lyle P. Murphy.*

The Jewish Aspect

"If I forget thee, O Jerusalem, let my right hand forget her cunning. If I do not remember thee, let my tongue cleave to the roof of my mouth; if I prefer not Jerusalem above my chief joy" (Ps. 137:5-6).

Hadassah Limpel was a young Israeli soldier whose life epitomized these words. Hadassah was born in Poland. She lost her family in 1939 when Hitler invaded Poland. As a ten-year-old orphan, she had to flee across the border into the Soviet Union. She walked across the Soviet Union to Iran. From Iran she journeyed to India. Hadassah then sailed from India up the Suez Canal to British mandate Palestine (Collins and Lapierre, *O Jerusalem,* Simon & Schuster).

The Jewish Agency placed Hadassah in a kibbutz. There she finally found a place of rest as a Jew among Jews. She learned Hebrew, went to school, and trained for combat. She also learned to love Jerusalem, which she hoped would become the capital of the state of Israel. Most, if not all, of her classmates had their parents, but Hadassah was alone. In all this training and activity, she was probably never exposed to any gospel truth.

To understand the battle Hadassah would participate in, you have to understand the strategic circumstances of the winter and spring of 1948. The United Nations had voted to divide Palestine into a Jewish state and an Arab state, but the Arabs of Palestine, Lebanon, Syria, Transjordan (later called Jordan), Iraq, Saudi Arabia, and Egypt said no to the U.N. partition. This is when Arab leaders began to use the statement, "We will drive the Jews into the sea."

The leaders of Israel agreed to the U.N. partition plan, but neither the Israelis nor the Arabs wanted Jerusalem to become a "U.N." city. They both wanted it for themselves.

In the opening round of the ensuing war, the Jews were gaining the upper hand in the battle for Jerusalem. Hadassah Limpel was part of the armed convoys that traveled from Tel Aviv up to Jerusalem, resupplying the 100,000 Jews who were in that city. At first the Arabs could not stop the convoys, but then they sent in the Arab Legion.

The Arab Legion was the army of Transjordan. It was founded during the British colonial period. It was equipped and supplied by Great Britain, and its officer corps was made up primarily of British officers. It was by far the best Arab army in the Middle East. The Jews could not stop them. The Arab Legion surrounded Jerusalem and blocked the road running from Tel Aviv to Jerusalem. Now the Jewish dream of making Jerusalem the undivided capital of Israel was vanishing. The Israelis had to open the road to Jerusalem or lose the city. The center of the blockade was at Latrun. The Israelis hit the Legion's defenses with everything they had, but they were quickly repulsed by the Legion's artillery.

The second Israeli attack on Latrun occurred at night. The Israelis did not have tanks. They had only armored cars and half-tracks. Hadassah Limpel was in one of the half-tracks. The attack was going well, and the Israelis were breaking through, but they made a tactical mistake. They used flamethrowers, which caused such a large fire that the armored vehicles became silhouetted against the flames. One legion officer said he distinctly saw an Israeli girl operating a radio right before an antitank round hit her half-track. Hadassah gave her life for the sake of Jerusalem.

—James Coffey.

Guiding the Superintendent

I enjoy taking vacations. My wife and I have become enamored of the historic city of Charleston, South Carolina, and have visited there at least once a year for the past several years. We look forward to staying in the historic district and enjoying the historic buildings, the homes and gardens, and the superb restaurants. When it is time to leave, though, our hearts are ready to return to our home in Ohio.

I have never known what it is like not to be able to return to my place of residence. I have never experienced a personal exile. Therefore, I can only imagine what that reality must have been like for God's people, whose rebellious, disobedient disregard for God, His words, and His messengers had caused them to be evicted from the Land of Promise.

DEVOTIONAL OUTLINE

1. The massacre and the Babylonian Exile (II Chr. 36:15-21). God's people were involved in a lifestyle of blatant, wicked idolatry. God had compassion on His people and on His place of worship. He sent prophetic messengers to the nation, calling for their repentance.

God's people mockingly disregarded His efforts to win them back, deepening the breach beyond resolution. In His wrath, God allowed the brutal Babylonians to violently attack and abuse His people, His place of worship, and the city of Jerusalem. In the end, many who had "escaped from the sword" (vs. 20) were driven into Babylon, where they were forcibly made to serve their enemies. This fulfilled the prophecy of Jeremiah 25:11.

2. An emotional song of banished people (Ps. 137:1-6). During the Captivity in Babylon, God's people lamented their chastised existence. When their captors mockingly demanded that they sing of their treasured city of Jerusalem, they responded emotionally. God's people could not envision singing of holy Jerusalem in a godless, foreign land.

In a God-ordained twist of irony, their captors' request enabled the Israelites to remember their cherished homeland. In fact, they basically committed themselves to an unswerving loyalty, uttering a curse upon themselves if they chose to disregard their holy city.

AGE-GROUP EMPHASES

Children: It is not reasonable to expect that children will understand the heartache of exiles whose homeland has been destroyed. But they should understand the pain of being punished for wrongdoing. Make sure they know that God will chastise them if they rebel against Him. Help them see that this is because of His love.

Youths: Young people tend to take many things for granted. For many, the wrenching, painful ache of loss has not deeply pierced their young hearts. As a result, many young people have difficulty appreciating what they have.

Use this week's lesson text to encourage the young people to develop an appreciation for the blessings God has allowed them to experience, especially their home.

Adults: Many adults live with hurting hearts. Many have suffered the dreadful ache of losing something or someone they deeply cherished and loved.

Remind the adults that God delights in offering His healing presence. Only He can give them peace.

—*Thomas R. Chmura.*

EDITORIALS

(Continued from page 3)

the battle plan given by God, and the Israelites followed it rigorously. The result was a miraculous collapse of the imposing city wall and complete victory for God's people. The lesson: success comes from obeying God's commands even when we cannot see the sense in them.

That lesson is greatly intensified in the study on Gideon that closes unit I. While the instructions to Joshua had no humanly discernible military impact, God's directive to Gideon ran directly contrary to universal military practice. Already vastly outnumbered by the swarming Midianite enemy, he was instructed to cut his own forces down to almost nothing! Most commanders would have rejected such an order as preposterous and suicidal, but Gideon obeyed without protest. The result was an astounding victory over an overwhelmingly superior force.

What is common to all these episodes is simple obedience to God's direction—an obedience that flows out of and expresses faith in Him. It is not always a great, heroic faith either. Gideon was still at the beginning of his faith journey and needed much bolstering and reinforcement along the way (Judg. 6:36-40; 7:9-15). He illustrates Jesus' teaching on what God can accomplish with faith as small as a mustard seed (Matt. 17:20).

Rahab also demonstrated that kind of faith when she hid the two Israelite spies and helped them escape (lesson 2). That action put her at odds with her own people and potentially in substantial danger, but she did it because she recognized the great power and purpose of God. She saw that her only hope was His mercy and favor (Josh. 2:9-12). Rahab would not be touted as a shining example of success in the world's literature, but her faith is celebrated forever in God's book (cf. Heb. 11:31).

Faith in God and obedience to Him will never make it into the world's recipe for success, but a look at the state of the world today is enough to show just how inadequate that recipe is. Believers who pursue faith and obedience may not achieve the wealth and status the world prizes (in fact, they are more likely to invite trouble and hardship), but they will find true success in what really counts, and it will be a success that never wears out or spoils. Small acts of faith now are rewarded with an eternal joy in Christ.

Learning from Failure

Kenneth Sponsler

The success stories in the Bible are inspiring and enjoyable to read. Many of us would prefer to spend all our time on them alone. We wonder why Scripture seems to devote more space to the grim side of life, especially the failures of God's people, and (if we are honest) wish it would not do so. Why not keep things positive?

Let us rather be thankful that God does not give us an unbalanced diet of sugary sweetness. The Bible stands out as the most realistic book in all the world's literature in providing a true picture of life on earth and especially of the flaws and failings of its people. In its pages we get an unvarnished portrait of our fallen nature as human beings, one that we need to face up to openly if we are to receive genuine hope for this life and the life to come. Only when we confront our sin and shortcomings can we turn to God for grace and deliverance.

The many accounts of disobedience and failure in Scripture can be grim reading at times, but their inclusion in God's Word is not intended to bring us to discouragement and despair. Nor are we meant to feel good about ourselves by taking perverse delight in the failures of others. The true purpose is stated succinctly by the apostle Paul: "They are written for our admonition" (I Cor. 10:11). The fact is, God knows we learn as much (or more) from failure than from success. So while the stories can be unpleasant, they are there for our profit and ultimate encouragement.

In light of the above, there is a lot to be gleaned from the studies this quarter. With one exception, the lessons from units II and III all focus in some way on failure or disobedience. That one exception, Joshua's final exhortation to the Israelites in lesson 9, nevertheless contains a potent warning: if we assume that we are up to the task of staying faithful to God on our own, we are setting ourselves up for failure (cf. Josh. 24:19-20). This soberness of warning finds its echo in Jesus' warning about counting the cost of discipleship (Luke 14:26-33).

Lesson 6 reveals that even the tremendous victory at Jericho was marred by failure. One Israelite, Achan, brazenly disobeyed the Lord's explicit instructions and brought trouble on the entire nation at the next battle, one that was supposed to be easy. He paid for that sin with his life and the lives of his family. The judgment may seem harsh to us, but a lighter one would not have impressed the seriousness of the sin on a nation that already had only a tenuous understanding of God's holiness.

The failure of one man expands to the entire nation in the next lesson, which recounts Israel's repeated falling into idolatry and punishment by way of oppression from enemies (Judg. 2:16-23). Nevertheless, God's continuing compassion is seen in the raising up of judges to deliver them, even though they went right back to their sin after the death of each judge.

Israel's rejection of the Lord's rule culminated in the demand for a human king to lead them (lesson 8). Remarkably, God granted their desire—not because it was rightly motivated, but because it fit into His ultimate plans for an eternal kingdom. He chose a king that fit the people's misguided inclination. As such, he would end in failure, and his dynasty would die with him.

But even David, Saul's anointed replacement and the man after God's own heart (Acts 13:22), was not immune to disobedience and disgrace (lesson 11). His brazen sin with Bath-sheba should warn all of us of the corruption in our flesh. Yet God's mercy shines through in Nathan's declaration that the Lord had put away David's sin and reprieved the sentence of death (II Sam. 12:13).

The next study (lesson 12) takes us to Amos 5:14-15, 18-27, one of the strongest rebukes by God of His people in all the Prophets. Some of the imagery is downright terrifying (see especially verses 18-20), but God did not say these things just to scare people. The passage opens with His true goal: "Seek good, and not evil, that ye may live" (vs. 14).

Our final lesson ends on a sad note, as the people of Israel find themselves in foreign exile because of their repeated and persistent sin. But just as our study of God's Word never ends with a quarter's last week, so things did not end for His people in Babylon. He was with them in their grief and sorrow, teaching them the lessons they needed to learn, and at the prophesied time, He brought them back and restored them to Him.

Failure is not an easy subject to read about, and it is even harder to go through ourselves. Yet as we see even in this quarter's lessons, God's grace is greater than our failure, and His power is not thwarted by our sin and disobedience. It is for us to respond rightly to His grace.

Three truths stand out from the lessons this quarter. First, if we find ourselves in the midst of failure due to our disobedience, we must repent. When we own up to our sin and seek God's grace, He will forgive and restore. Second, if we have been restored to fellowship and come through the failure, we should gladly thank Him and not remain mired in guilt or discouragement.

Finally, if we are doing well and enjoying the Lord's goodness, we need to remain vigilant. We need not fear failure, but we can never assume we are immune to it. Keep praying as Jesus directed, "Lead us not into temptation" (Matt. 6:13). Let us never sit in judgment on others for their failure, but rather take heed to ourselves. God can graciously preserve us both through and from failure; let us remember always to turn to Him in faith.

TOPICS FOR NEXT QUARTER

December 3
To Live Is Christ
Philippians 1:12-26

December 10
Counting All Things Loss
Philippians 3:7-21

December 17
Learning Contentment
Philippians 4:4-18

December 24
The Light of Christmas
John 1:1-5; Ephesians 5:1-2, 6-14

December 31
Chosen in Christ
Ephesians 1:3-14

January 7
God's Workmanship
Ephesians 2:1-10

January 14
The Household of God
Ephesians 2:11-22

January 21
A High Calling
Ephesians 4:1-16

January 28
God-Honoring Families
Ephesians 5:21—6:4

February 4
Spiritual Armor
Colossians 1:15-28

February 11
The Supremacy of Christ
Ephesians 6:10-24

February 18
Complete in Christ
Colossians 2:6-19

February 25
A Plea for Christlike Forgiveness
Philemon 1:4-21

PARAGRAPHS ON PLACES AND PEOPLE

LEBANON

A term describing an important geographical feature in Israel's history, the Lebanon refers to two parallel chains of mountains (called individually the Lebanon and anti-Lebanon) running south to north in the area above Israel, roughly covering the area of the modern country of Lebanon.

The name Lebanon is derived from the Hebrew root meaning "white," perhaps referring to the snow that rested on the mountains. On these majestic peaks grew the famed cedars of Lebanon, which were greatly coveted for the construction of ships and buildings. Kings David and Solomon used lumber from Lebanon to build the temple and palaces in Jerusalem.

MOUNT HERMON

This most prominent mountain of the anti-Lebanon range marked the northern boundary of ancient Israel. Its snow-capped majesty (it rises to a height of over nine thousand feet) made it a well-known landmark of the region. It was referred to by various names among Near Eastern peoples.

Although not mentioned an abundance of times in Scripture, Hermon played a significant role in the life of Israel. The snow-melt from Hermon fed the waters of the Sea of Galilee and the Jordan River, the scenes of so many important episodes in Israel's history. Its impact is seen in its use in Hebrew poetry. The lover in Song of Solomon speaks of the wildlife and beauty of Hermon to his beloved (4:8), and the psalmist compares the joy of unity to "the dew of Hermon" (Ps. 133:3).

HITTITES

The term "Hittite" is a prominent one in the ancient world; the most well-known reference is to the Hittite Empire, which was centered in the land that is now modern-day Turkey and flourished from around 1650 to 1250 B.C. In Joshua 1:4, much of Israel's inheritance, to the north and northeast (with mention made of the Euphrates River), is called "all the land of the Hittites."

By the time of David and Solomon, the power of the Hittites in the region had largely disappeared, and this was a factor in the expansion and the peace Israel enjoyed at that time. There remained Hittite people in the region, most notably the noble and victimized warrior Uriah, the husband of Bath-sheba.

ANAKIMS

The Anakim were a fearsome people, descendants of a man named Anak. They were people of giant stature who terrified the Israelite spies (with the exception of Caleb and Joshua) when they were sent by Moses into Canaan. The spies' report about these giants convinced the people they could not conquer the land. Making a spiritual application, we might think of the Anakim as representing the giant obstacles that mark our spiritual lives and tempt us to despair.

By the time the conquering Israelites were done with them, the only remaining Anakim were located in what eventually became Philistine cities, including Gath (Josh. 11:22). It seems possible that the giant Goliath, who lived centuries later, may have been a descendant of the Anakim. Goliath was from the city of Gath (I Sam. 17:4).

—Stephen H. Barnhart.

Daily Bible Readings for Home Study and Worship

(Readings are for the week previous to the lesson topics.)

1. September 3. Be Strong and Courageous

M—Joshua's Victory. Ex. 17:8-16.
T—Moses' Servant. Ex. 24:12-13; 32:15-18; 33:9-11.
W—Joshua's Faith. Num. 14:6-10, 35-39.
T—Moses' Successor. Num. 27:18-23.
F—Joshua Commissioned. Deut. 31:7-15, 22-23.
S—A New Leader. Deut. 34:1-9.
S—Divine Encouragement. Josh. 1:1-6; 11:16-19, 21-23.

2. September 10. Rahab and the Spies

M—Fear of Israel's God. Ex. 15:13-18.
T—Victory over Sihon. Num. 21:21-30.
W—Victory over Og. Num. 21:31-35; Deut. 3:1-7.
T—God Will Lead. Deut. 31:1-6.
F—Promise of Victory. Deut. 11:22-25.
S—Jericho in Fear. Josh. 2:10-14, 17-21.
S—An Unlikely Ally. Josh. 2:3-9, 15-16, 22-24.

3. September 17. The Fall of Jericho

M—Land of Promise. Gen. 15:13-21.
T—Spiritual Preparation. Josh. 5:2-12.
W—Assurance from God. Josh. 5:13—6:1.
T—Command for Destruction. Deut. 20:16-18.
F—Israel's Obedience During the Siege. Josh. 6:6-11.
S—Oath Fulfilled. Josh. 6:22-25.
S—A Miraculous Victory. Josh. 6:2-4, 12-20*a*.

4. September 24. Ehud Frees Israel

M—Cry for Deliverance. Ex. 2:23-25.
T—The God Who Sees. Ex. 3:7-10.
W—Righteousness Rewarded. Ps. 18:20-30.
T—Assurance that God Hears. Ps. 34:15-22.
F—Annihilation of Amalek. Deut. 25:17-19.
S—Subjection to Moab. Judg. 3:12-14.
S—Ehud's Triumph. Judg. 3:15-25, 29-30.

5. October 1. Gideon Conquers the Midianites

M—Midianite Oppression. Judg. 6:1-6.
T—The Lord's Rebuke. Judg. 6:7-10.
W—Double Confirmation. Judg. 6:36-40.
T—Gideon's Army Reduced. Judg. 7:5-12.
F—Gideon's Army Attacks. Judg. 7:19-23.
S—The Kings of Midian. Judg. 8:10-12, 18-21.
S—Victory for Gideon. Judg. 7:2-4,13-15; 8:22-25.

6. October 8. The Sin of Achan

M—Warning from God. Deut. 7:23-26.
T—Devoted to the Lord or to Destruction. Lev. 27:28-29.
W—True Riches. Prov. 13:7; 15:16; 16:8; 30:8.
T—Snare of Covetousness. I Tim. 6:6-10.
F—Steps Toward Sin. Gen. 3:1-7.
S—The Sinner Revealed. Josh. 7:13-19.
S—Sin Rooted Out. Josh. 7:1, 10-12, 20-26.

7. October 15. A Backsliding People

M—A Prior Warning. Deut. 12:1-9.
T—Israel's Sin. Ps. 106:34-39.
W—God's Anger. Ps. 106:40-43.
T—God's Mercy. Ps. 106:44-48.
F—Testing Israel. Judg. 3:1-7.
S—Saved from God's Wrath. Rom. 5:6-10.
S—A Downward Spiral. Judg. 2:16-23.

8. October 22. Israel Rejects God as King

M—The Burdens of a Human King. I Sam. 8:9-18.
T—A King to Lead Us! I Sam. 8:19-22.
W—Saul the Benjamite. I Sam. 9:15-21.
T—Three Signs to Prove God's Word. I Sam. 10:1-8.
F—God's Word Confirmed. I Sam. 10:9-16.
S—Samuel Instructs Israel. I Sam. 12:19-25.
S—"God Save the King!" I Sam. 9:1-2; 10:17-26.

9. October 29. Joshua's Final Exhortation

M—A Commitment Made. Ex. 19:3-9.
T—Fear the Lord. Deut. 10:12-15.
W—Counting the Cost. Luke 14:25-35.
T—A Heart for God's Will. Ps. 119:33-40.
F—Straight Talk about God. Josh. 23:14-16.
S—A Faithful God. Josh. 24:2-7.
S—Joshua's Last Words. Josh. 24:1, 14-24.

10. November 5. Rebuke and Repentance

M—God's Compassion. Ps. 103:8-13.
T—Faithful Father. Isa. 63:15-16.
W—Pay Careful Attention. II Chr. 7:11-22.
T—Righteous Judge. Rom. 2:1-11.
F—Gracious Lord. Isa. 30:18-22.
S—Disobedience Brings Oppression. Judg. 10:6-9.
S—A Cry for Deliverance. Judg. 10:10-18.

11. November 12. David's Sin and Punishment

M—Guard Your Heart. Prov. 4:20-27.
T—Destruction to the Proud. Prov. 16:17-20.
W—"Thou Shalt Not—". Ex. 20:13-14, 17; Lev. 18:20; 20:10.
T—Lustful Looks Equal Adultery. Matt. 5:27-30.
F—Faithful Uriah. II Sam. 11:6-13.
S—Nathan's Rebuke. II Sam. 12:1-12.
S—Judgment for Sin. II Sam. 11:2-5, 14-18, 26-27; 12:13-15.

12. November 19. A Rebuke from the Lord

M—A Matter of Life and Death. Deut. 30:15-20.
T—Living a Godly Life. Rom. 12:9-21.
W—Attacking Hypocrisy. Matt. 23:23-28.
T—A Path of Foolishness. Ps. 14:1-7.
F—The Day of the Lord. Joel 2:1-3, 12-17.
S—Condemning Sinful Self-indulgence. Amos 6:1-7.
S—Amos Rebukes the People. Amos 5:14-15, 18-27.

13. November 26. Judgment and Exile

M—The Joy of God's Presence. Ps. 84:1-4, 10.
T—The Joy of Worshipping God Together. Ps. 122:1-9.
W—The Glory of God's Kingdom. Ps. 48:1-14.
T—The Painful Consequences of Sin. Jer. 25:8-11.
F—Nebuchadnezzar Captures Jerusalem. II Kgs. 24:10-16.
S—Taking Comfort in Past Deliverances. Ps. 126:1-6.
S—Judah Is Exiled. II Chr. 36:15-21; Ps. 137:1-6.

REVIEW

What have you learned this quarter?

Can you answer these questions?

Success and Failure

UNIT I: Obedience and Success

September 3

Be Strong and Courageous

1. What title used of Moses was later used also of Joshua?
2. What promise did God give Joshua prior to his entering Canaan?
3. About how long did it take for Israel to capture Canaan, and how do we know that?
4. What one city was not conquered, and why was it left alone?
5. Why was it so important to know that Joshua conquered the Anakim?

September 10

Rahab and the Spies

1. What did Rahab tell the king's messengers, and how much of it was the truth?
2. What did Rahab tell the spies that she personally believed?
3. How did Rahab describe the attitudes present throughout Jericho?
4. When the spies returned, what did they first tell Joshua?
5. What conclusions about moving ahead did they share with Joshua?

September 17

The Fall of Jericho

1. What was the Lord's unusual military approach to Jericho?
2. What would this battle strategy ultimately teach Israel?
3. What was significant about the positioning of the priests and the ark in the march?
4. What did God say Israel was to do with the things and people of Jericho? What was the exception?
5. What would happen if God's orders were disobeyed?

September 24

Ehud Frees Israel

1. Which nation and king did God turn Israel over to when she sinned this time?
2. What physical trait did Ehud have that was prevalent in his native tribe?
3. How did Ehud get everyone but the king out of the room?
4. How did Ehud escape?
5. How did Ehud bring about a great victory over Moab for Israel?

October 1

God Confirms Gideon's Mission

1. Why did God decide to accomplish the delivery under Gideon in such an unusual way?
2. What was the first test God used to reduce the number of Gideon's army?
3. What did Gideon hear when he went to the Midianite camp?
4. What was Gideon's initial response after getting this message of reassurance from God?
5. What request from the Israelites did Gideon refuse?

UNIT II: Disobedience and Failure

October 8

The Sin of Achan

1. What had happened following the fall of Jericho that Joshua was not aware of?
2. What was tragically different about Israel because of what occurred during Jericho's fall?
3. What were the three steps Achan took in committing his sin?

4. What punishment did God prescribe for Achan, and who was involved in carrying it out?
5. What were the two results of Israel's punishment of Achan?

October 15

A Backsliding People

1. In what surprising way did God use the pagan nations in Canaan?
2. How did judges differ from kings?
3. Since God is unchanging, what does Judges 2:18 mean when it says that God repented?
4. What did Israel suffer as a result of not driving all the pagan people out of Canaan?
5. How did God display the true state of Israel's character?

October 22

Israel Rejects God as King

1. What appeal did Saul have to those who wanted a king?
2. Why did Samuel rebuke Israel before they chose their king?
3. What method was used in identifying Israel's king?
4. What did Samuel discuss with the people after Saul was chosen?
5. Where did Saul go after his recognition? Who went with him?

UNIT III: Lessons and Warnings

October 29

Joshua's Final Exhortation

1. What three things did Joshua ask Israel to do (Josh 24:14)?
2. What were three sources of the idols retained by the Israelites?
3. What did Joshua declare regarding himself and his household?
4. How did Joshua respond when the leaders first declared that they would serve the Lord?
5. What two things did Joshua urge the repentant Israelites to do?

November 5

Rebuke and Repentance

1. What details are given in Judges 10 about Israel's departure from God that show their depravity?
2. What did God remind Israel of when they cried out to Him?
3. To whom did God say Israel should appeal for assistance?
4. How do we know Israel became sincere in their cries to God?

November 12

David's Sin and Punishment

1. Why was David relaxing on his housetop and thus exposed to temptation?
2. How had David's situation predisposed him to commit adultery?
3. What did Joab do to have Uriah killed?
4. How did David react when faced with his guilt?

November 19

A Rebuke from the Lord

1. According to Amos, if Israel wanted to avoid God's punishment, what should she have sought?
2. What wrong idea did Israel have regarding the Day of the Lord?
3. How did Amos describe the terror that would occur at that time?
4. How did God describe how He felt about the Israelites' worship practices?

November 26

Judgment and Exile

1. How did the Jews treat the messengers God sent to them?

3. What did the Babylonians carry away from the temple in Jerusalem?
3. How long were the Jewish captives made to serve in Babylon?
5. How strongly did the Jewish exiles feel about Jerusalem?